D0926474

Sherwood Anderson's
Secret Love Letters

Sherwood Anderson's Secret Love Letters

For Eleanor, a Letter a Day

Edited with an Introduction by
Ray Lewis White

Louisiana State University Press

Baton Rouge and London

Manufactured in the United States of America
First printing
00   99   98   97   96   95   94   93   92   91   5   4   3   2   1

Designer: Amanda McDonald Key
Typeface: Primer
Typesetter: G&S Typesetters, Inc.
Printer and binder: Thomson-Shore, Inc.

Library of Congress Cataloging-in-Publication Data

Anderson, Sherwood, 1876–1941.
    [Correspondence. Selections]
    Sherwood Anderson's secret love letters : for Eleanor, a letter a day / edited
by Ray Lewis White.
        p.   cm.
    Includes bibliographical references (p.
    Includes index.
    ISBN 0-8071-1610-6 (alk. paper)
    1. Anderson, Sherwood, 1876–1941—Correspondence.   2. Anderson,
Eleanor Copenhaver, d. 1985—Correspondence.   3. Authors, American—
20th century—Correspondence.   4. Love-letters.   I. Anderson, Eleanor
Copenhaver, d. 1985.   II. White, Ray Lewis.   III. Title.
PS3501.N4Z4897   1991
813'.52–dc20   90-13331
[B]   CIP

In memoriam
Eleanor Copenhaver Anderson
June 15, 1896–September 12, 1985

Contents

Illustrations

Preface

In the autumn of 1985, in the midafternoon of the thirteenth of September, Diana called me to say that Eleanor had died. The death of Eleanor, in Smyth County Community Hospital, in her hometown of Marion, in Virginia, was not unexpected, as Eleanor had lived for eighty-nine years and for considerable time been in failing health, her condition worsening so steadily that I had for almost eight years avoided visiting her or even writing to her; and this unfortunate failure on my part toward Eleanor remains distressing as yet another of my lamented and regretted mistakes.

For this woman named Eleanor who had died the day before the telephone call came to me was Eleanor Copenhaver Anderson, the fourth wife and the longtime widow of Sherwood Anderson, the American author about whose life and writings I had come to be, for good or ill, somewhat knowledgeable. And the Diana who called me about Eleanor's death that September afternoon was Diana Haskell, respected archivist, Lloyd Lewis Curator of Midwestern Manuscripts at the Newberry Library in Chicago, and my longtime friend.

Diana's call about Eleanor's death in 1985 brought to me thoughts of my earliest meetings with that petite, gracious, and then sprightly lady who survived Sherwood Anderson after his unexpected and untoward death in 1941 and who for more than four decades thereafter acted as his heir, his executor, and his literary caretaker—this Eleanor Anderson who herself never published or tried to publish a word about her husband, instead faithfully encouraging those of us who would strive to be scholars to do the writing about Sherwood Anderson from resources made available to us through her wise trusteeship.

I recalled my first meeting with Eleanor Anderson, in 1963, when she graciously received me, then a graduate student native to the county next to her own in the Virginia Highlands but in

those early 1960s revisiting Southwest Virginia from distant resi-
dence at the University of Arkansas. Having decided somehow,
early on in graduate studies, to write my dissertation about this
Sherwood Anderson and thus seeking access to his survivors'
memories and to his preserved papers, I could not have asked for
a friend innately kinder and more eagerly useful than Eleanor
Anderson, this woman who preferred never to talk to me of herself but who talked always, openly, and energetically about her
husband's life and writings.

When I accepted Eleanor's generous and repeated invitations
to return to visit her in Smyth County, Virginia, each time that I
visited my own relatives and friends in Washington County, I
came to enjoy the warm personality, the colorful whimsies, and
the endearing quirks of this retired social worker, a woman who
was to me even then quite aged—whimsies ranging from her
complaints about the difficulties of overseeing the family farm to
her hushed request that I bring her for a secret Bloody Mary
party five fifths of vodka but that I keep this arriving alcohol a
secret from Eleanor's own Aunt May Scherer, this aged Aunt
May who lived with Eleanor and who must herself then have
been nearly ninety years old and who yet would try to guide her
seventy-year-old niece sternly toward temperance if not indeed
to complete abstinence.

So Eleanor Anderson and I became and remained friends for
many years, I approaching her often for rights to study and to
publish materials about and from her husband's life and writings
and she trusting me to dig, to plant, and to harvest in the fertile
Sherwood Anderson literary garden, always with ambition and
usually with, I hope, proper care and respect. With Eleanor's help
and encouragement, I published during the next quarter century
editions of such Anderson works as his three autobiographies, his
correspondence with Gertrude Stein, his country newspaper columns, and his earliest writings; bibliographies of Anderson studies completed by hundreds of critics and scholars throughout the
world; essays on various aspects of Anderson's life and writings
(over forty of these, all told)—work that has given me both pleasure and profession and around which my life has most happily
centered since 1963.

And I recalled, that day in 1985 when I learned that Eleanor
Anderson had died, my last visit with her, in the spring of 1977,
when I took Diana, curator of the Anderson Papers, from the
Newberry Library in Chicago far southeast to Marion, Virginia,

for her to see at home Anderson's last and best lover and in person his last and best country and to discover, we hoped, more papers and photographs for the library's already imposing archive of Anderson materials. Eleanor then, nearly eighty, was at her charming best, sharing with us materials from her husband's life and proudly showing us (Diana seeing for the first time) Sherwood's mountain home called Ripshin, the stone house sited in Grayson County, away from Marion, over toward North Carolina in those old and worn Appalachian Mountains.

From our fine April day at Ripshin in 1977, there are impromptu photographs of Eleanor Anderson happily scurrying about the summer home that she had enjoyed those long years ago with Sherwood; and one photograph of Eleanor from that day do we especially enjoy, for she is therein caught standing before a fireplace in the old stone house, in front of the cupboard that I had come very much to fancy.

For, back in the 1960s, Eleanor Anderson had, at an early meeting, unexpectedly given to this much-astounded, then-young would-be scholar some tattered old carbon-copy transcriptions made in the early 1940s—transcriptions of pages from an unpublished manuscript, a series of letters that Sherwood had secretly written for Eleanor before the two were married in 1933, letters for which I had not then come across rivals, letters personally revealing and literarily fine, letters that I, of course, immediately and desperately wanted to publish to start smartly my scholarly adventure with Sherwood Anderson and with American literature. And these letters, I came to know, had been found by Eleanor Anderson soon after her husband's death at sixty-four early in 1941 in that cupboard before which she is standing in our quite special 1977 photograph.

Thus I had by 1977 long known the secret of Sherwood Anderson's cupboard, with its hoard of extraordinary documents; and there is this, among the most uncanny of my scholarly experiences: when I learned by telephone from Diana of Eleanor's death that September afternoon in 1985, I was actually engaged in deciphering and transcribing fully for the first time these remarkable manuscripts that had been hidden in that cupboard in the stone house in the Virginia mountains decades before.

For I never lost my youthful enthusiasm for publishing an edition of the hidden Anderson letters that I learned of fortuitously in 1963. I discussed often with Eleanor the possibility of publishing an edition in her lifetime, for, no matter how personal to

Eleanor might be the material in these letters about courtship, love, family, politics, and marriage, I continued to find them quite special in origin, utterly beautiful in execution, and wholly worthy of interesting a great number of readers if edited by me. Several publishers to whom I described the project were interested in making a handsome volume of the love letters, and I surely would have enjoyed being their editor, but Eleanor—reluctantly yet probably wisely—decided that such private material should not appear in her lifetime.

Thus, with Eleanor Copenhaver Anderson now dead, I am likely the only person who is privileged to know the full contents and the striking beauty of Sherwood Anderson's secret manuscripts—these revealing letters of love and hope written in 1932 by a man struggling against many difficulties to win and to marry his beloved—and I would share finally through this edition the immense pleasure that I have taken from the letters once hidden in Sherwood Anderson's cupboard.

I am grateful to all past and present scholars and critics of the work of Sherwood Anderson, for I have depended upon their writings for both ideas and information in my preparation of this volume. The books published by Hilbert H. Campbell, Charles E. Modlin, Walter B. Rideout, James Schevill, William A. Sutton, Welford Dunaway Taylor, and Kim Townsend have been especially useful and are listed in the Selected Bibliography.

Charles E. Modlin and Hilbert H. Campbell, literary executors of the estate of Sherwood Anderson, have been instrumental in forwarding the publication of this book; and Walter B. Rideout and Charles E. Modlin have been cooperative in answering my many questions about Sherwood Anderson.

Three members of the Anderson family have been generous with their time in answering my questions—John Anderson, Chicago, Illinois; Marion "Mimi" Anderson Spear, Madison, North Carolina; and the late Mrs. Robert Lane Anderson, Pittsboro, North Carolina.

The staff of the Newberry Library, Chicago, Illinois, home of the Sherwood Anderson Papers, have been kind and helpful in aiding my research; I am especially grateful for the friendship and the encouragement of Diana Haskell, Lloyd Lewis Curator of Midwestern Manuscripts at the Newberry Library.

The staff of Milner Library at Illinois State University have been helpful over my years of Anderson study; I appreciate especially the work of Helga Whitcomb and Joan Winters.

Charles B. Harris, chair of the Department of English, and William C. Woodson, director of graduate studies in English, at Illinois State University, have provided me with support and encouragement in my research during the many years that we have worked together. Laura Gibson McGowan proved herself a patient and helpful graduate assistant.

Additionally, the following people have been informative and amicable toward my work on this book: David D. Anderson, Michigan State University; Rebecca Campbell Cape, Lilly Library, Bloomington, Indiana; James H. Clark, director, University of California Press; Mrs. Robert M. Copenhaver, Joppa, Maryland; James C. Cowan, Chapel Hill, North Carolina; Martin Davis, Alderman Library, University of Virginia; Robert Denham, Roanoke College; Mrs. H. B. Eller, Marion, Virginia; Don Francis, Marion, Virginia; James D. Hart, director, Bancroft Library, University of California, Berkeley; William Issel, San Francisco State University; Mrs. Louis I. Jaffé, Norfolk, Virginia; Paul Mariani, University of Massachusetts; Mrs. Earl L. Meyers, Arlington, Virginia; Edward R. Mulvihill, University of Wisconsin–Madison; Elizabeth Norris, librarian and historian of the National Board of the Young Women's Christian Association; Edmund Olson, Macon, Georgia; George Riser, Alderman Library, University of Virginia; Mrs. Erwin Roeser, Virginia Beach, Virginia; Yae Shinomiya, librarian, Oakland, California, *Tribune;* Michael Spear, chair of the Sherwood Anderson Foundation, Richmond, Virginia; Anne Steinfeldt, Chicago Historical Society; Teresa Taylor, University Archive, New York University; William Weber, Eastern Illinois University; Robert Williams, Richmond, Virginia; and Ruth Yeaman, Special Collections, University of Utah Libraries.

Note on Editing

Considering Sherwood Anderson's casual living and nearly constant traveling, I am amazed that he so well executed his New Year's resolution for 1932: to write one letter daily for Eleanor Copenhaver to find, enjoy, and cherish whenever he might die, for as long as the accumulated letters might last. Anderson so faithfully kept writing his daily letters and sealing them for deposit in his cache at Ripshin that the completed series through November 25, 1932, should total 330 letters. Only five letters from the series are missing—those for June 14, July 13, September 22, October 9, and November 6. As there is no reason to suppose that Eleanor Anderson, after finding the letters in the early 1940s, destroyed any of them, these five letters were probably never written. Further, on six days—January 9, February 11, 17, 18, May 21, and June 22—Anderson wrote and hid away two letters for Eleanor to find. And, although the series of letters ends soon after Thanksgiving in November, Anderson used his secret depository for a few more letters written in December, 1932, letters that I include here as a Coda. The present edition is, therefore, complete, containing every word written by Anderson with these exceptions: the name of one individual whose family might be troubled by Anderson's recollections is herein replaced by initials, and one sentence about an Anderson family member has been omitted to avoid possible embarrassment.

The goal in creating this edition of Sherwood Anderson's secret letters of 1932 for Eleanor Copenhaver has been to create a volume that is easily readable and fully informative: readable for the fine story of love and longing that the letters themselves so eloquently tell when read through from January through December; informative for illuminating the persons, organizations, books, and events that Anderson referred to in his daily letters.

Transcribing these letters from manuscript was pleasant work, for I have known and loved the materials for a quarter century; yet occasionally I found myself becoming modest about my ability unerringly to read Sherwood Anderson's handwriting. On occasion I sought the opinions of other Anderson devotees on just what the man's scribbles might mean, and the helpful suggestions of these experts have been incorporated in my text; any remaining mistakes of decipherment are solely mine and are regretted. Occasionally I have provided in brackets the word or words that Anderson clearly meant to write but that in his daily haste and fatigue neglected to indite. Some of Anderson's pet spellings (*e.g.*, "grey," "nowdays") are maintained; his misspellings are corrected; his punctuation is regularized only to accord with the system of dashes, ellipses, and subordinate phrases and clauses that he favored.

Annotation was less a problem than I had anticipated, for although I expected to identify the public figures and close friends to whom Anderson alluded, I feared inability to annotate the truly personal events and obscure individuals that he so often mentioned. Yet, given the pioneering editions of Anderson letters, diaries, and newspaper columns that came before my work and the cooperation of some Anderson family members and other individuals, I have been able to provide at least basic identification and clarification for most of the references. To avoid excessive repetition of identifications, I have provided a list entitled "Recurring Names" that will, with a little practice in use, make clear to whom Anderson referred most often. For example, when Anderson wrote of "Mary" in Virginia, he was referring to Mary Chryst Anderson, wife of his son Bob; when he wrote of "Mary" in New York City, he was referring to Mary Emmett, wife of his rich friend and patron Burt Emmett. Other matters of reference become clear when the letters are read carefully through.

Chronology

1876   Sherwood Berton Anderson born September 13 in Camden, Ohio, third of seven children of an improvident harness-maker and a hard-working homemaker

1884   Anderson family moved to Clyde, Ohio, the town where Sherwood grew up, attended school, and kept many part-time jobs and, after elementary school, full-time jobs to support the family—the town that became a kind of model for *Winesburg, Ohio*

1895   At the mother's death the family broke up, and Sherwood planned travel to Chicago, where he found work as an unskilled laborer in such businesses as cold-storage warehouses and where he might have tried to complete night classes in business subjects

1898   Anderson left Chicago to serve in Cuba (after combat had ended) in the Spanish-American War

1899   Moved to Springfield, Ohio, to complete a high-school education at the academy of Wittenberg College, where he made helpful contacts in business and advertising

1900   Returned to Chicago to work as an advertising writer and solicitor and began writing, for an advertising journal, essays about business and, later, for another magazine, essays about literature

1904   Married Cornelia Lane, well-educated daughter of an Ohio manufacturer, and continued in Chicago working in and writing about the advertising profession

1906   Moved to Cleveland, Ohio, to operate a goods-distribution company and to make his way successfully as an entrepreneur aimed at financial greatness

1907   Moved to Elyria, Ohio, to operate another goods-distribution company and to continue an upwardly mobile life; in Elyria, the first of his three children was born

1909   Started writing fiction (long unpublished) about unhappy manufacturers and financial moguls who need personal and sexual liberation

1912   Disillusioned with business and under psychological pressure, late in November underwent aphasia, amnesia, or "fugue state" that hospitalized him and ended his Ohio business career and his traditional family affiliation

1913   Returned to Chicago to live by writing advertising and for writing fiction as part of the city's artistic group; became acquainted with Carl Sandburg, Edgar Lee Masters, Harriet Monroe, Margaret Anderson, Francis Hackett, Ben Hecht, Floyd Dell, and other Chicago Renaissance figures

1914   Discovered the stylistically avant-garde writings of Gertrude Stein; published "The Rabbit-Pen," a traditional story, in *Harper's* and, in various "little magazines," less traditional stories and essays about writing

1915   In the winter, unhappy with writing derivative fiction, suddenly inspired to write "Hands," the first *Winesburg, Ohio* story, with successive stories about Winesburg coming into being over many successive months

1916   Became divorced from Cornelia Lane Anderson, married Tennessee Mitchell, and continued writing advertising copy and *Winesburg, Ohio* stories; published his first novel, *Windy McPherson's Son*, about an industrialist who has wealth but not happiness

1917   Published his second novel, *Marching Men*, about the hero's finding meaning through organizing laborers into potentially effective unions

1918   Published *Mid-American Chants*, free-verse regional poetry reminiscent of Whitman and Sandburg; lived in New York City, writing movie publicity; and sought publication of the Winesburg, Ohio, stories as a book

1919   Published *Winesburg, Ohio*, on May 8, to mixed reviews and scant sales

1920   Lived briefly in Alabama and then in Palos Park, Illinois, and published *Poor White*, a novel about the industrialization of the Midwest

1921   Visited Europe and met Gertrude Stein and other writers; published new stories as *The Triumph of the Egg*; won the *Dial* prize of one thousand dollars for his stories; by mail introduced young Ernest Hemingway to Gertrude Stein and other authors in Europe

1922   Finally abandoned his work as an advertising writer, left his second wife and Chicago for life in New York City, where he met Elizabeth Prall, bookstore manager and daughter of a successful merchant

1923   Published *Many Marriages*, a novel about sexual liberation, and *Horses and Men*, a new collection of stories; and lived in Reno, Nevada, to obtain a divorce from Tennessee Mitchell Anderson

1924   Married Elizabeth Prall; moved to New Orleans, where he advised young William Faulkner; and published *A Story Teller's Story*, his first autobiography

1925   Published a financially successful novel, *Dark Laughter*, about psychological freedom; and visited the mountains of Southwest Virginia, where he bought a small farm

1926   Published *Tar: A Midwest Childhood,* an autobio-
       graphical novel, and *Sherwood Anderson's Notebook,* a
       collection of essays; settled on his farm near Troutdale,
       Virginia, where he built Ripshin, his only permanent
       house; and then very briefly visited Europe, where he
       was depressed, uncomfortable with Hemingway, and
       uncommunicative with Stein

1927   Became owner, reporter, writer, and publisher of the
       two small Smyth County, Virginia, town newspapers,
       the Marion *Democrat* and the *Smyth County News;*
       and published *A New Testament,* prose poetry

1928   Met and fell in love with Eleanor Copenhaver, daughter
       of a prominent family in Marion, Virginia, a career so-
       cial worker with the National Young Women's Chris-
       tian Association

1929   Published *Hello Towns!* an anthology of small-town
       newspaper writings; and separated, despondent and
       perhaps suicidal, from Elizabeth Prall Anderson

1930   Began traveling secretly with Eleanor Copenhaver to
       observe and write about labor conditions in southern
       manufacturing towns

1931   Published *Perhaps Women,* a treatise on women's po-
       tential to redeem men facing the difficulties of modern
       life

1932   Became divorced from Elizabeth Prall Anderson and
       continued courting Eleanor Copenhaver; traveled to a
       radical labor conference in Europe; and published *Be-
       yond Desire,* a political novel about southern labor
       organizing

1933   Traveled across America to observe and write of
       Depression-era social conditions for *Today* magazine;
       married Eleanor Copenhaver; published his last collec-
       tion of stories, *Death in the Woods and Other Stories;*
       and began writing his final memoirs

1934   Published *No Swank*, appreciative essays about his literary friends and their books; and continued writing social essays

1935   Published *Puzzled America*, collected from his *Today* magazine social essays

1936   Published his last novel, *Kit Brandon*, about mountain moonshiners; and continued writing his memoirs

1937   Published *Plays: Winesburg and Others*; and continued writing autobiography

1938   Visited and wrote about Mexico and continued his memoirs

1940   Published *Home Town*, an illustrated treatise on the vanishing American small town and the best traditional American values once found there

1941   Died March 8, in Colón, Panama, while traveling with his wife Eleanor to visit and write about life in South America, leaving his memoirs unfinished

1942   Eleanor Anderson published the heavily edited and often rewritten *Sherwood Anderson's Memoirs* and began her duties as her husband's heir and literary executor, work that she continued (while employed in the labor movement until her retirement in 1961) until her death in 1985

Recurring Names

B. E. Copenhaver, father of Eleanor Copenhaver, educator in Marion, Virginia

Bob Anderson, Sherwood Anderson's older son

Burt Dickinson, attorney and judge in Marion, Virginia

Burt Emmett, retired advertising executive of New York City

Channing Wilson, husband of Eleanor Copenhaver's sister Mazie

Eleanor Copenhaver, Sherwood's beloved, an official with the YWCA

Elizabeth Prall Anderson, Sherwood's third wife, divorced in 1932

Frank Copenhaver, businessman in Marion, Virginia; distant relation of Eleanor Copenhaver

Funk, Charles "Andy," attorney in Marion, Virginia

Helen Anderson, wife of Sherwood's brother Karl

Henry Van Meier, husband of Eleanor Copenhaver's sister Katharine

Horace Liveright, publisher of Anderson's books

Jay Scherer, Lutheran minister, uncle of Eleanor Copenhaver

John Anderson, Sherwood's younger son

Karl Anderson, Sherwood's brother, a painter

Katharine Van Meier, sister of Eleanor Copenhaver, married to Henry Van Meier

Laura Lu Copenhaver, mother of Eleanor Copenhaver, wife of B. E. Copenhaver

Lois MacDonald, Eleanor Copenhaver's apartment mate in New York City

Mary Chryst Anderson, of Marion, Virginia, wife of Sherwood's son Bob

Mary Emmett, of New York City, wife of advertising executive Burt Emmett

Maurice Hanline, editor with Horace Liveright, Anderson's publisher

Maurice Long, deceased businessman of Washington, D.C.

Mazie Wilson, sister of Eleanor Copenhaver, married to Channing Wilson

Mimi Anderson Spear, Sherwood's daughter and youngest child

Miss May Scherer, Eleanor Copenhaver's aunt, sister of Laura Lu Copenhaver

Randolph Copenhaver, Eleanor Copenhaver's brother, a medical student

Roger Sergel, drama publisher in Chicago

Ruth Copenhaver, of Marion, Virginia, wife of Frank Copenhaver

Ruth Sergel, of Chicago, wife of Roger Sergel

Tom Smith, executive editor for Horace Liveright, Anderson's publisher

Sherwood Anderson's
Secret Love Letters

Introduction

Thursday, December 31, 1931, New Year's Eve in Marion, Virginia: a time of annual assessment and resolution, and now, for the American writer Sherwood Anderson (1876–1941), facing his fifty-fifth new year, an opportunity (welcomed or not) to survey the years past that had brought the crises and the cruxes in his personal and professional life, the events that had brought him to live in a rented room in a small town in the southern mountains.

The year 1912 had been the most important in Anderson's life, for at the end of that year he had taken the step from business to literature that had made him legendary among Americans of his generation: Anderson had, he claimed, walked deliberately away from a thriving manufacturing business in northern Ohio in order to move to Chicago, where he could become an author, an artist in storytelling. Although the degree of deliberation involved in Anderson's 1912 break with the world of business administration is debatable, the effect of that action is clear, for in only seven years this former businessman from Ohio had made himself the famous and influential author of *Winesburg, Ohio* (1919).

Anderson's presentation of himself as a man who had suddenly and dramatically changed his way of life from pursuit of wealth to pursuit of art was indeed valid, for in the first thirty-five years of his life Anderson had, through hard work and good fortune, managed to secure a respectable social position and the assurance that he knew how to thrive in a commercial civilization. After an impoverished boyhood in a large family in small Ohio towns in the late nineteenth century, Anderson had come to Chicago to work for the wealth that the American Dream promised to such eager and decent American young men; there he had found only exhausting and poorly paid labor in a cold-storage warehouse. Then, after noncombat service in Cuba in the Spanish-American War, Anderson had found a new, more direct route to success: he would further his scarcely begun high-school education through attendance at the academy of Wittenberg College in Ohio, where in one year he achieved high-school-graduate status and where he made the social contacts that allowed him in 1900 to move, a second time, to Chicago, this time to work not in a depressing cold-storage warehouse but in the comfortable modern offices of an advertising agency, one of the burgeoning new American businesses of the early twentieth century.

Thus it could never have been literally true that Sherwood Anderson left business in 1912 in order to become a writer, for Anderson had all the time since 1900 been earning his living—and usually a very good living—through writing. From 1900 to 1906 Anderson worked with various Chicago advertising agencies that specialized in soliciting and placing advertisements in the scores of periodicals that then appealed to millions of farmers and their needs. He traveled to visit clients who manufactured or distributed agricultural implements and products; he found clever ways to write advertisements to offer these manufacturers' goods to the public; and he thrived in the aggressive, expanding commercial world of the great city on Lake Michigan. Then, having moved already far beyond his boyhood poverty, Anderson took the next steps requisite to fulfilling the American Dream: he found and married a beautiful, well-educated woman and planned with her the rearing of several fine children; and, tired of receiving only a percentage of the total monies that he earned for his advertising-agency employers, he acted to found and run his own business concern—to become a major figure in the world of commerce.

From 1907 through 1912, Anderson served as chief executive officer for his own goods-distribution companies in northern Ohio—companies that manufactured little but that bought and distributed by mail and rail the products of other companies. Anderson came to understand the realm of capital and management, the value of country-club contacts and public image, and the talk of investments and speculations that made up the world that he had sought and in which he had made steady progress. Yet somehow this business world became for the mature Anderson less and less the happy kingdom that he had led himself to expect, for he was becoming more and more wretched with the way that he lived and the way that he had to make his living; and he took up devices common to such unhappy people: dissipation away from his hometown and family, neglect of his social and business duties, and (strangest of all) attempts in a locked room in the attic of his home to write fiction—novels about repression and release, about business and social reform, about midlife crises resolved through escape from onerous business and family duties.

And late in November, 1912, Anderson inevitably underwent in his own life the crisis that the heroes of his unpublishable novels were suffering—a nervous breakdown. He mumbled to his secretary words about wading too long in the bed of a stream, he wrote to his wife words about too much American striving, and he wandered four days about the wintry Ohio countryside, totally lost in amnesia or "fugue state." Recovered in a Cleveland hospital, Anderson spent little if any time in trying to recoup his social and business losses, for early in 1913 he left, alone, for Chicago—this third move to the great city would become his famed escape from business into literature. Yet Anderson would not for nine more years free himself totally from business concerns, for in 1913 the former manufacturer reentered the world of advertising writing in Chicago, a world for which he now had no respect whatever but in which he would carelessly and grudgingly have to earn his living until 1922.

Thus from New Year's Eve of 1932 could Sherwood Anderson recall 1912, the most crucial year of his existence—the year of finding for himself a new way of life, a hard life devoted to becoming somehow a writer of significant fiction and poetry and essays. And he could recall the next landmark year in his existence: 1919, the year when he published as a book the stories about northern Ohio life in the 1890s that were called *Winesburg, Ohio*—the first truly modern short stories written in America.

Creating such innovative and important short stories had not been Anderson's goal as an author, for in Chicago in 1913, encouraged by his new liberated, artistic friends, he had tried long and hard to rewrite those novels brought from the attic in Ohio— novels of heavy, burdensome plot and prose, novels of good intent but poor execution. Then, frustrated in trying to write his traditional novels, in the winter of 1915–1916 Sherwood Anderson quite miraculously and perhaps spontaneously just sat down in his rented room in Chicago and wrote simply and feelingly some very short stories about an imaginary young man, George Willard, living in the imaginary northern Ohio town of Winesburg in the late 1890s and meeting there the disreputable, neurotic, un-happy, defeated, and sorrowful characters of his town—characters hitherto neglected in mainstream American fiction for their unsavoriness and their assumed unimportance. In simple, untaught prose and with touching insight Anderson created in *Winesburg, Ohio* a fictional method in which not plot or clever-ness but, instead and above all, psychological insight became the artistic goal. Thereby he transformed the American short story from a thing of formula, complete with set plot and surprise end-ing, into an object of vital, organic art—a literary demonstration that would come in time to bring fame to Anderson and to bring example to Ernest Hemingway, William Faulkner, Thomas Wolfe, John Steinbeck, Flannery O'Connor, Eudora Welty, William Sa-royan, and all their fellows and followers: in short, in 1919, with *Winesburg, Ohio*, Anderson invented the modern American short story, the one literary genre in which twentieth-century Ameri-can writers have led the world. He was thus, by the early 1920s, because of *Winesburg, Ohio* and other stories and, finally, some successful novels, one of the most important writers in his na-tion, a man from whom even greater fiction could firmly be expected.

Along with his 1912 escape from business and his 1919 pub-lication of *Winesburg, Ohio*, Anderson could from New Year's Eve at the end of 1931 look back to another year of primacy in his life: 1927, the year when he gave up the literary life of Chi-cago, New York, San Francisco, and New Orleans in order to become a resident of the small town of Marion, in Southwest Virginia. Anderson had first visited the Virginia Highlands in the summer of 1925, when a friend had advised him that the cool and lovely Appalachian Mountains were ideal as a place of escape from the torrid heat of New Orleans. Anderson lived that pleasant summer with a mountain family near Troutdale, in Grayson County, Virginia, near the North Carolina border; and he became so enchanted with the simplicity of mountain life and the beauty of mountain scenery that he bought in Grayson County thirty acres of land with the idea of building there in 1926 a home in which to live for the rest of his life. To finance the venture, An-derson had promised his New York City publisher one book per year, an arrangement that the writer soon found that he could not honorably fulfill, for he had by contract to produce on sched-ule, a stricture resulting often in material about which he could not feel total pride, and he had to travel more extensively than he had come to like. Thus, needing income but tired of wandering over America to write and to lecture, Anderson in the autumn of 1927, when visiting the town of Marion, seat of Smyth County, in Southwest Virginia, suddenly bought, for himself to operate, the two small newspapers published in Marion—the *Smyth County News* and the Marion *Democrat*.

Knowing about newspaper work only what he had learned from delivering papers as a boy in Ohio and from writing advertisements as a younger man in Chicago, Anderson for two years in the late 1920s had great fun as he published, wrote, edited, and sold the weekly issues of the Democratic and Republican newspapers of Smyth County. Quickly becoming a celebrity in his adopted small town, he demonstrated his fairness as editor by farming out to party leaders of the town the political editorials of his two papers; he attended court sessions and club meetings; he listened to gossip and news of ordinary life in the town and the mountain communities; and he wrote columns for his newspapers as a literary artist might write literature, not as a trained journalist would report news. To entertain himself and his readers, he even invented an alter ego, a naive mountain youth named Buck Fever, who would write comical versions of stories that might appear side by side with Anderson's more serious reportage of the same events. Anderson's editorship of the *Smyth County News* and the Marion *Democrat* brought national publicity to the town of Marion, a town that slowly accepted the assertive presence of this flamboyant and sometimes provocative famous outsider.

Smyth County, founded in 1832 and still predominantly rural, with huge tracts of forested mountain slopes, had in the late 1920s no more than twenty-five thousand citizens, and Marion, grown where the Holston River and two railroads crossed, had no more than four thousand residents, people who were the mostly white Protestant descendants of Scots-Irish and German pioneers. The town and county were heavily involved in the business of agriculture, but other industries had existed in the area: grist mills; iron foundries; charcoal kilns; lead, iron, manganese, limestone, salt, and gypsum mines; woolen mills; and furniture factories. By the late 1920s the county's leading industries, besides agriculture, were furniture making, chemical refining, and one other business—the Southwestern State Hospital, a state agency opened in Marion in 1887 as the Southwestern Lunatic Asylum. The housing of hundreds of state mental patients and their nurses and doctors brought steady employment to Smyth County, and in 1921 the hospital facility had been expanded to include a treatment center for the mentally deranged soldiers of World War I.

As the county seat, Marion had developed its own set of southern gentry—the lawyers, judges, shopkeepers, physicians, factory and hospital administrators, court clerks, and bankers who oversaw the operation of the town and county and who formed the local society into which Sherwood Anderson had settled comfortably. For Anderson, though still proprietor of Ripshin in Grayson County, now lived in Marion, in an apartment near his work as editor of the *Smyth County News* and the Marion *Democrat*. He socialized with the prominent families of the town and county—the Sheffeys, the Stalcys, the Scherers, the Buchanans, the Lincolns, the Peerys, the Funks, the Dickinsons, the Porterfields, and the Copenhavers; and it was one proud local family, the Bascom Copenhaver family, that most interested Anderson, national celebrity and local newspaper editor.

Bascom Copenhaver, since 1901 superintendent of schools for Smyth County, had descended from immigrant Scandinavian farming pioneers to become through Democratic party politics one of the powerful men of his area, for he had early in life allied himself with the Scherer family, descended from immigrants from Alsace-Lorraine, who controlled the one educational and cultural institution of note in the county: Marion College, founded in 1873 as Marion Female College. The Reverend John Jacob Scherer, founder and first president of the college, which had been established for the daughters of prominent gentlemen in Southwest Virginia, was a devout Lutheran; and three of his children continued his tradition of combining religious training with proper female education: John Jacob Scherer, Jr., the only son, became pastor of a large church in Richmond, Virginia; May Scherer, the second daughter, all her life taught Bible and was dean of Marion College; and Laura Lu Scherer, the older Scherer daughter, taught English at the college, married Bascom Copenhaver, then a young teacher at her father's college, and established the family that Sherwood Anderson became most interested in.

Bascom Copenhaver and his wife Laura Lu by the 1920s lived in the oldest house in Marion, Rosemont, built years before Smyth County had been officially formed. They had energetically and traditionally reared a large family of daughters and one son. Through Bascom's employment in public education and his income from his family land and through Laura Lu's teaching at Marion College, the Copenhavers had been able to provide for their several children the great advantages of education and culture. The children were generally grown up and thriving on their own when Anderson arrived in town: Mazie Copenhaver had married Channing Wilson, Ph.D., of Baltimore, Maryland; Katharine Copenhaver had married Henry Van Meier, M.D., of Stillwater, Minnesota; Randolph Copenhaver, in college to become a medical doctor, was interested in a career with the military; and Eleanor Copenhaver had become an official of the national Young Women's Christian Association. (One unfortunate Copenhaver child was never mentioned by the proud family, for this daughter, Laura Eugenia ["Jean"], had become insane and was confined all her remaining life in an institution.) As the new newspaper editor in Marion, Anderson came to admire first the lovely Copenhaver house, Rosemont. He met then and admired the lively and intelligent mother of the family, Laura Lu Copenhaver, and he met finally and fell in love with the most interesting Copenhaver of all: Eleanor.

Eleanor Gladys Copenhaver, first child of Bascom and Laura Lu Copenhaver, was born in 1896. She had become the spinster daughter of her family, devoting herself to public service in the tradition of her religious ancestors, both the Copenhavers and the Scherers. Eleanor had by 1931 worked for years with the Young Women's Christian Association—that organization founded in the nineteenth century to provide wholesome living and sound doctrine to the hundreds of thousands of young American women who had just begun to earn their living working in the factories and offices where their labor was suddenly needed. Supposedly a nonpolitical organization, the YWCA had become, by the early twentieth century, through spread of the social gospel (the idea that the teachings of Christianity were to be worked out in human society through human energy), a reformist entity, interested in educating and organizing workingwomen into labor unions and activist groups; and Eleanor found herself, bearing her ancestors' religious conscience but without their burning theology, perfectly in accord with the association's liberal social goals.

Educated in the public schools of Marion, where her father was school superintendent, Eleanor Copenhaver then attended for two years, as would have been expected, Marion College (next door to Rosemont), the institution where her relatives taught and administered, until she transferred in 1914 for her junior and senior years of study to Westhampton College in Richmond. From 1914 through 1917, Eleanor studied a broad range of liberal arts subjects at Westhampton, where she majored in English but where her grades were only average, even in her major field (she excelled, however, in Bible study). Then, awarded the bachelor of arts degree but untrained in teaching (formal teachers' training was rare in those days), the young woman returned to Marion to live with her parents and to teach for one year high-school courses in the educational system of Smyth County.

But high-school teaching, especially of science, could never have been the career aimed at by Eleanor Copenhaver; and in 1918 she undertook further professional study at Bryn Mawr College, in Pennsylvania, where she completed a two-year program in social work—specifically in community organization—a period of study interrupted in the summer of 1919 for work as director at a settlement camp for New York City women. Thus Eleanor found her profession for life, for, beginning in 1920, she worked full-time in education and organization for the YWCA; by the early 1930s she had risen to influence in the industrial division of that institution. Given the devastation of the Great Depression of 1929 and after, which had depleted the organization's treasury of voluntary donations and greatly disadvantaged the already precarious status of American workingwomen, Eleanor found reason to become radical in her political beliefs and her professional activities. Because her work involved much travel to factory sites for counseling and organizing her workingwomen clients, she was able frequently to visit with her family in Marion. It was on one of her visits home to Rosemont that Eleanor met Sherwood Anderson.

Sherwood and Eleanor met sometime in 1928, and their intellectual and physical attraction must have come upon them suddenly and surely; but there were problems that caused the couple to keep secret their activities. First, Sherwood was considerably older than Eleanor (he was almost the age of her parents); second, he was still married to his third wife, Elizabeth, who lived with him in an apartment in Marion and who was only beginning to think of leaving her increasingly strange husband for a better life without him; third, Eleanor's YWCA work required her to maintain at least the appearance of devotion to Christianity, a faith that discouraged both adultery and unlicensed love; and fourth, Eleanor's parents (especially her father) would have been hurt that this newspaper editor from elsewhere, this man who had been made welcome in their gracious family home, had fallen in love with their eldest daughter, a woman who had so far pleased her parents by her exemplary work for a religious organization. Yet love between Sherwood and Eleanor had come in 1928, and by the end of 1931 their once-secret affair was known to every member and friend of the Copenhaver family and to every interested citizen of Marion.

By the end of 1931, Sherwood Anderson and Eleanor Copen-haver had been lovers for quite a while, traveling quietly together as Eleanor went about her YWCA work and waiting until circumstances might allow them to marry. For Sherwood, who had turned over operation of his newspapers to his older son Robert, wanted to marry Eleanor but had yet to become divorced from his wife Elizabeth; and while Laura Lu Copenhaver, a benign and generous woman, had come to accept and enjoy Sherwood's courtship of her daughter Eleanor, Bascom Copenhaver had never forgiven Anderson for selfishly and permanently ruining Eleanor's reputation. (Bascom actually cared most about damage to his own reputation as church official, school superintendent, and county politician.)

By the end of 1931, Eleanor Copenhaver had brought love again into the life of Sherwood Anderson, a man who required almost moment-by-moment assurance that he was loved and who had until he met Eleanor thought often of suicide as a way out of his unhappy third marriage and his unloved condition. And Eleanor had brought to Sherwood another route of escape from his thoughts of worthlessness and death, for through her concern for the victims of the American industrial system she had given the writer material for his pen, the goal of social reform, and the chance to share her political beliefs and activities.

Thus, saved from real or only spiritual death by his new little radical black-haired friend, Sherwood Anderson at the end of the last day of 1931 set himself to keep two New Year's resolutions: first, he would during the coming year do his best to win Eleanor in marriage, believing that with this fourth marriage he would surely find the right mate to love and reassure him for the remainder of his life; and, second, he would comfort himself daily in 1932 in his longing for Eleanor and comfort Eleanor whenever he, being much older, might die, by writing to her a secret letter each day, a letter that he would seal and place in a cupboard at Ripshin in the Virginia mountains for her to find and to read, one letter each day, for as long as the series of letters might last after his death. The cached letters would allow Eleanor to share, someday, a memory of Sherwood's courtship of her in 1932, revisiting with him in memory that most difficult time in their lives, when he had loved and needed her and when she had loved him and worried about marrying him.

And thus Sherwood Anderson spent New Year's Eve, Thursday, December 31, 1931, in Marion at Rosemont, with Eleanor Copenhaver and her father Bascom and her mother Laura Lu. He awoke in his rented room on New Year's Day, Friday, January 1, 1932, in Marion, Virginia, and wrote the first words of his first secret letter for Eleanor someday to read, responding, in the loving way of an author, to "a curious impulse."

January

Friday, January 1, Marion, Virginia

A curious impulse. Morning in the mountains. There is a grey hill, across which clouds drift. It is cold. Now and then there come flurries of snow.

Dreamed I was some place with a woman. She kept showing me my picture in the newspaper. "Do you not know your picture is in all the newspapers?" she said.

"No. I have not looked."

I was ashamed I didn't know. No, that was not my feeling. I kept thinking—"She will think I am pretending to be more modest than I am." There is such general agreement that to be in the newspapers, at any price, is a good thing.

I awoke in the night and went to my desk. I wrote to Eleanor. I was full of love for her.

Last night I was in her house. She went and sat by a dark window. The wind howled outside. Suddenly she became very beautiful. Something in me hurt, she was so beautiful.

I discussed with Laura Lu the merits and demerits of puritanism.[1] She thought it had certain noble attributes. I agreed but thought it had done more harm than good.

I sat with Eleanor on a couch and we read Clark on the social implications of the law.[2] She had on a red dress and was lovely.

The wind went howling and dancing. It made the shutters of the house rattle. When the new year came I was in bed reading a book called *Kitto's Palestine*. It was odd reading a historian who seemed to take the Bible as literal. It was amusing.[3]

1. Laura Lu Scherer Copenhaver (1868–1940), mother of Eleanor Copenhaver.

2. John Marion Clark, *Social Control of Business* (Chicago, 1926).

3. *Palestine: The Bible History of the Holy Land* (London, 1841; often republished), by John Kitto (1804–54).

Saturday, January 2, Marion, Virginia

Gertrude Stein—a new book by her . . . it in my hand as I go to the bathroom.

Sentences. Words.[1] Sitting on the seat and smoking a cigarette. Success.

Wash it.

A solitary tree on a hill . . . soft colors on morning hills.

Abraham went to Egypt. He was sixty. His wife Sarah was very beautiful.

Breathing exercises.

Joseph Robinson wrote—". . . the visit of one of the kings of literature to his home." That was me. It was in an envelope . . . sent to me by a newspaper.[2]

I showed it to Eleanor. That was yesterday. We rode to the top of Lyons Gap. That was in the afternoon.

Greys. Mist drifting over hills. By accident I bit Eleanor on the ear and hurt her. Tears came to her eyes but she laughed.

She was beautiful, laughing when it hurt.

She read the piece about me as literary king and I felt silly. It was silly. I said—"Don't let anyone see it." I tried to grab it but she put it in the bosom of her dress.

We drove. I tried to sing. "I got a gal in the Sourwood Mountains." I couldn't. I tried to get her to sing it.

We went home and I read aloud to her—Clark—*Social Control of Business.*

In the morning I revised two chapters—the new novel *Beyond Desire.*

It excited me.

It rained all day—little outbreaks of rain—quick showers—grey fog.

Vanity Fair wrote. "Take your Dreiser speech and make a piece for us."[3]

I was horny all day.
I was laughing.
Eleanor was very beautiful.

It is absurd to let yourself be lionized as that man did in the newspaper. He intended it to be nice.

You go to their houses. They make it a special occasion. It isn't nice. They intend it to be nice.

Eleanor and I looked for mushrooms.

I wrote a letter to the Society for Cultural Relations, Soviet Russia. I want to go there—take Eleanor there.

I went to see Frank and Ruth. Had a drink of whiskey.[4]

Afterwards went to my son and dined with him and his wife.[5] Had cooked onions. Onions and whiskey made my breath bad. Was ashamed of it.

1. Either Stein's *How to Write* (Paris, 1931) or *Before The Flowers of Friendship Faded, Friendship Faded* (Paris, 1931).

2. Joseph Robinson, "Sherwood Anderson in Boone," Macon (Ga.) *Telegraph and News,* December 27, 1931, p. 4. Robinson wrote of Anderson as a king of literature and decided that "how to entertain literary royalty so that it will not regret a trip of sixty miles is something of a question." One entertainment for Anderson was the singing of the Appalachian song "I Got a Gal on the Sourwood Mountain."

3. *Vanity Fair,* magazine published in New York City, where Anderson had spoken on December 6, 1931, to three thousand people in defense of Theodore Dreiser, activist writer accused of criminal syndicalism in the coal-mine strikes at Harlan, Ky.

4. Frank Copenhaver, distant relation of Eleanor Copenhaver and a businessman and Democratic politician in Marion, Va., and his wife Ruth, who were among Anderson's best friends in Virginia.

5. Robert Lane Anderson (1908–51), oldest child of Sherwood Anderson, who was living in Marion and operating the two county newspapers that his father had owned; Robert Anderson had married Mary Chryst, who taught English at Marion College.

Sunday, January 3, Marion, Virginia

Two emotional experiences followed by a third.

The first two were in writing, going through something with a character, trying to understand her.

The third in Eleanor's house. It was evening. We had come back from driving. I was on edge. She had been to the hairdresser's. We talked of a trip abroad, seeing people—possibly Russia, Germany, France.

We came home.

There was her father, sitting by the radio. He seemed asleep. Perhaps he was.[1]

I went into the kitchen. There was her mother, cooking.

It was for them. I went with Eleanor into the cellar to get some bottles for Frank . . . for wine.

I do not understand her father's ungraciousness. He bullies everyone by it. At the dinner he was silent and morose.

I took a present to Mrs. Copenhaver—some concentrated vegetable soup. He said, "Where did you get this stuff?"

"Sherwood brought it." Eleanor and her mother explaining hopefully, cheerfully.

"Well. It stinks."

Last night, after a meal of silence, he got up and went again to the radio. There was a man on the radio talking of God. There was an ugly dragging voice.

Eleanor's sister—I thought . . . I could not help thinking . . . suppose she were sensitive. Sometimes I live with her in fancy—years in a strange place.[2]

It may all have been this crass rudeness. Doors slammed, sharp ugly commands to children—

The voice of that ugly man somewhere on the radio. It was as though someone had put ordure in something I was eating.

Eleanor came in. "We have to listen to 'Amos 'n' Andy'—to please him."[3]

I said, "He don't care"—hopefully. I couldn't help it. I was on the point of tears.

Or blind rage. I could have taken him, shaken him.

I would, if I had the right, tell him in plain words, "You have elements of goodness in you but it is all vitiated by your boorishness."

If he does not want me in his house it would be decent and manly to tell me.

Fighting with myself. I held onto myself—went in and listened to "Amos 'n' Andy."

They were particularly dull and ugly. He chuckled. "You can't keep old Andy off the air," he said.

The implication—the advertisements, by a corrupt company, of a probably harmful toothpaste.

The kind of material out of which democracy proposes to make a civilization. I tried to read and was afraid my voice would break any minute.

No doubt I am blind. I am a civilized man. I want to be awake and sensitive. To live in the presence of those voices over the radio it would be necessary to dull yourself.

It would be easy to go crazy.

Afterward Eleanor, very beautiful. Her beauty was a little far away, withdrawn.

Her mother was lovely. She schemed to get her mother off to bed.

Myself torn—"I must not eat in that house any more."

That thought in me. It balanced against love of the two women.

Home. I could not sleep. Read about Joseph in a history of Palestine. Slept.

Queer that this old Jew Jacob—his whole life a record of cunning—should be held onto as a religiously important figure.

Tried to imagine Eleanor beside me. Dreamed of a big hall—many people . . . there was dance and joy.

Joy has as much right to exist as gloom and ugliness.

Fear—suppose, someday, Eleanor and I should have to take that terrible old man into a house and care for him.

In the morning fine snow. My room is pleasant. I wanted Eleanor in there. Every inch of the room in which you live should be thought about. It pays you back.[4]

It is nice to have Maurice in here. He was a civilized, alive sensitive man. I loved him. Odd how—the photograph of Mimi and the blue girl of Maurer seem to talk to each other.[5] Will go away tomorrow. I hate to think of Laura Lu left here.

In the bathroom. A cold bath. Doing my breathing exercises. From the bathroom window I see a hill. It's fun to imagine it the seat of gods.

Woods gods.

River or wind gods.

To pray to in the morning.

1. Bascom Eugene "B. E." Copenhaver (1870–1944), father of Eleanor Copenhaver and a Democratic political figure in Smyth County, Va., a man who did not enjoy the friendship of his wife and daughter with Sherwood Anderson.

2. Laura Eugenia "Jean" Copenhaver, younger sister of Eleanor, mentally deranged and confined for the remainder of her life in an institution.

3. "Amos 'n' Andy," a popular comic radio program starring white performers in stereotypical black roles.

4. Sherwood Anderson had lived with his son Robert in an apartment above the printshop in Marion, Va.; at Robert's marriage, Sherwood had taken a room in the Onyx Sprinkle home in one of the prouder areas of the town.

5. Maurice G. Long (1878–1931), wealthy businessman of Washington, D.C., whose recent death had greatly saddened Anderson and whose photograph he kept; Marion "Mimi" Anderson Spear (1911–), Sherwood's only daughter, then a student at the University of Chicago; Alfred Maurer (1868–1932), American painter whose work Anderson admired and owned.

Monday, January 4, On the Train

On the train going to New York. In my hand a book, borrowed from Mrs. Copenhaver—a history of Ireland.[1]

A business man I know on the train. I am a little afraid of him. He may come to sit with me. He will brag.

At the station I talked with him. He has made a half million dollars by sharp selling. There were eight men, laborers, working nearby. They were not, at the moment, working very hard.

My bags were near. A dog came and, lifting up his leg, pissed on one of them. I was going to New York. "That for New York," said the dog. Like me he prefers the country. I threw a stone, not intending to hit him, but to scare him away. "Piss on New York, if you feel that way," I said, "not on me."

The business man did not think the laborers we saw were working hard enough. They perhaps got $2 a day. I knew some of them. They have large families. Occasionally a worker stopped and leaned on his shovel. "Look at that. That's what's raising hell with this country."

The train filled with daughters of the rich going east to some finishing school. Dissatisfied faces. A mother sat near me. She kept asking everyone—"Have we passed Abingdon?" We had. She asked the question in a loud tone over and over. She explained.

She had wired Gov. Stuart to come to Abingdon to speak to her as she went through. She had told the conductor, the porter, the brakeman. Gov. Stuart lives I'm sure fifty miles from Abingdon. "I'm sure," she said, "he or his son Harry were there."[2]

She was furious that no one had told her Abingdon, Va., was

being passed through. A brakeman finally quieted her. He explained, rather to the whole car, that he had got off the train at Abingdon. "There wasn't a soul on the platform."

The college girls smoked cigarettes in all the sleeping cars, in the diner, everywhere. The trainsmen kept trying to stop them. It was hopeless. We all began to smoke. Soon the air was blue with smoke.

Ben Wasson, of Greenville, S.C., was on the train. He is Bill Faulkner's friend. I had some whiskey and we had a drink.

He spoke of Bill, what he was like, our love for him. He told me the sad and tragic story of the night when Bill's wife had a child—born dead.

He had phoned the doctor to come and he didn't come. Bill could not bear to tell his wife. He sat through the night with the dead child. In the morning he got a revolver and went to the doctor's house intending to kill him. He shot and missed. They put Bill in jail.[3]

1. Probably Francis Hackett, *The Story of the Irish Nation* (New York, 1930).

2. Henry Carter Stuart (1855–1933), governor of Virginia (1914–18) who had business interests at nearby Lebanon, Va.

3. Ben Wasson, who had attended the University of Mississippi, had become an attorney in Greenville, Miss., and had while in New York edited Faulkner's novel *Flags in the Dust* so that it could be published as *Sartoris* (New York, 1929). The death threat by Faulkner is apocryphal.

Tuesday, January 5, New York City

In New York. It is a tense morning, when I cannot relax. John my son is here in a nearby hotel. We breakfasted together.[1]

We went to the Metropolitan. He has been here all week looking at painting.

He had picked out certain things he wanted me to see.

A lovely Vermeer—a girl in a room.[2]

Very still—a soft flow of color.

A rug over a table.

Color like old wine, bubbling softly softly.

The painting was a song.

A still-life Cézanne.

Very thick.

Thick. Thick.

It was smooth thick.

He can make you feel something—a whole life in a painting—I mean the thickness of it, the thoughts, loves, troubles, joys.

A rug on a table—a blue jar.

The table itself.

You can't say what such a painting means.

Degas—a little statue of a primitive brown woman, a dancer. Gorgeous.

Her legs. Her little face.

She would live in you forever.

Rembrandt—a young man . . . the painting of the costume. I got absorbed in the sleeves of the man's jacket.

A feel of cloth as though it had suddenly become the most terrifically important thing in all the world.

Again wine-like color, flowing, piling up, flowing, a river, a wind of color.

We went to a Pieter Brueghel, a harvest scene, but were exhausted. Will go back to that. Will take Eleanor to stand with me while I look at that.

Saw my lecture manager. Suddenly hated him. Would have liked to spit on him.[3]

I am like that. My hatred of business grows and grows in me. I put it back and back.

I say, "They are not to blame. They are not sons-of-bitches," etc. Then suddenly off I go. I am unjust to some particular man.

I want to fight.

"You are a son-of-a-bitch.

"You are a bastard, scheming, money-sick son of a whore," etc.

It's awful.

Afterward I am sick.

I went out into the street. I took breathing exercises. I walked on Sixth Avenue. Eleanor and John had lunched with me. Eleanor was lovely. I had brought her violets. Her eyes are brown and the violets were blue but there was the same good steady fine softness.

Went to see Tom Smith, my publisher.[4] Tom is never slick. He is kind, sophisticated, real.

It is shameful to be even as successful as I am. There were

two almost old men—old unsuccessful writers—waiting in a lobby to see Tom.

I was shown right in. I kept saying, "Go on with your business, Tom," meaning, "See those men."

"But there are always such men there." He didn't say just that. It was implied. It was true.

"But, Tom, I have no business."

"I want to talk."

We did talk. He never saw the old men. Someone must have said to them, "Come back tomorrow."

We went to Tom's apartment. It is lovely there. The rooms have a real tone. My day had been full. Earlier, when I was with John and Eleanor, I was terrifically alive. At such times I see a thousand little things along a street—click, click, click, click, click, click.

Faces, eyes, words caught, fronts of buildings, signs—
Modern civilization.
We are all here—caught, caught.
Let's dance.
Brothers, brothers.
Sisters, sisters.

Tom telling me a story about Dreiser, a misunderstanding between friends.[5]

Talk of the publisher—his duties, etc.

Tom saying—of new writers coming on—"If a young writer—his first book—

"If that is objective—outside himself—he may come on.

"If he writes of himself only from the beginning, No Good."

Tom: "I love women but cannot love a woman."
Myself: "I must always love a woman. Women mean nothing."
I must also love a man.

Took John to Café Royal—Second Avenue and 12th—to dine. Nice. A young Jew came up. "I want to take you some night to dine—with young Yiddish writers, poets, painters, actors.

"Yiddish scenes, food, etc.

"Can you come?"

"Yes."

I'll take Eleanor, if she can go.

1. John Sherwood Anderson (1908–), second child of Sherwood Anderson.

2. Anderson was reacting to art works by Jan Vermeer (1632–75), Dutch painter; Paul Cézanne (1839–1906), French painter; Edgar Degas (1834–1917), French painter; Rembrandt van Rijn (1606–69), Dutch painter; and Pieter Brueghel (*ca.* 1525–69), Flemish painter.

3. W. Colston Leigh, proprietor of the Leigh Bureau of Lectures and Entertainments, of New York City.

4. Thomas R. Smith, executive editor of the publishing firm of Horace Liveright who had worked with Anderson since 1925 on several books published by that company and by Boni and Liveright.

5. Liveright had published several books by Theodore Dreiser (1871–1945), including *An American Tragedy* (1925) and *Dawn* (1931).

Wednesday, January 6, New York City

Rain. Rain.

I went with Eleanor to a store to get special food for her mother.

I was tense before speaking. I was angry.

I had to talk with business men about money. I try not to hate them.

I say to myself, "It isn't their fault."

They are too self-satisfied. They always speak of honor, honesty, etc. I try to be quiet inside.

I get angry and say terrible things.

Dreiser has written a book, *Tragic America*.[1]

It is almost incoherent, the sentences are so heavy and bad.

He is a man. You admire him. He has tenderness for people in him.

I feel like getting drunk.

1. Theodore Dreiser, *Tragic America* (New York, 1931).

Thursday, January 7, New York City

To an audience of women in a Long Island town. This is the club about which I quarreled with my lecture manager.[1]

Here is how such things turn out. I had agreed to lecture. I had been running the two weekly newspapers at Marion. I wrote, for *Forum*, an article about the experience.[2]

Letters began to pour in, thousands of letters from young men and young women. I thought, "I'll go talk to these people."

I had an idea. Perhaps I can interest some of the younger men and women. Something might be done—a few daring country weekly editors. Ten, fifteen, thirty such, say in Virginia—or Ohio, or Texas.

These papers having pretty much drifted into the hands of the petty bourgeoisie. They being dull, doing nothing for community life, etc.

Also I thought, "I'll talk sometimes about machinery, its dangers, etc."

There was an agreement with the lecture man—no women's clubs.

Women's clubs are made up of the wives of the well-to-do suburban people, suburban morals. Dead faces—floating up to you—these dead women.

Fatness about the eyes—no hardness.

Who fucks these terrible women? Do they get fucked?

They are pretty when they get married—pretty in a spoiled way, I'm sure.

They go off fast—candy, gowns, furs, card parties, cocktails. Some of them do have children.

I kept thinking of Eleanor, her hard little body, hard little legs. Of her mother—

She living among these people all her days—not like them.

There was one man. It turned out he was a doctor.

Thinking of Mrs. Copenhaver. "She has lived always among such people as these but in her heart she is of us—the ragtag, the rebels." Loving and admiring her.

From this audience I was altogether detached. I became altogether impersonal—a man standing there—not myself Sherwood Anderson—an actor.

Something more than that. I spoke well, clearly.

What I was saying to upset all these lives—their security.

Thinking of working women trooping out of mills in towns, hard drawn faces.

My own mother—dead of toil at thirty-two.[3]

Is there something buried away in these fat, well-dressed, self-satisfied upper-middle-class women?

They going to church—going to places where they try to get culture.

There are American writers [who] write for such women. Titillating the porch rockers.

These our American ideal.

Thinking of pioneer women in forests, out on the prairies. Abe Lincoln—that girl he loved and who died.[4]

There was a woman there—the chairman told me afterwards. She told me of a man named Cosmo Hamilton being there. She said, "They pawed him over. They won't paw you."[5]

I was glad of that.

She seemed a sensible body. She might have been a middle-western farmer's wife.

She might have gone to barns to milk cows, feed chickens, tended a farmer's garden.

Lying with him at night, hearing farm night noises, planning the year's work.

There was a little woman with upturned lips—gaping vagina. I fled.

Night in the rain, in town, crowd on the street.

I got lost in a subway jam at 42nd.

A Negro man rescued me. He went out of his way to escort me. He is not from the South. He told me, "I was born in Massachusetts."

To be lost in crowds occasionally, drifting, turning into streets.

Rain, workers hurrying homeward, men and women.

Soft rain on the cheeks.

Those women, out there, in their suburb. Husbands coming home from brokers' offices.

Wishing perhaps they were with their mistresses—the wives wish perhaps they had lovers.

1. Anderson spoke on January 6 to the Garden City–Hempstead Community Club, of Garden City, Long Island; he had forbidden his lecture manager to schedule talks to women's social clubs.

2. "The Country Weekly," *Forum*, LXXXV (April, 1931), 208–13.

3. Sherwood's mother, Emma Smith Anderson, who lived from 1852 to 1895.

4. Ann Rutledge, friend of Abraham Lincoln's at New Salem, Ill., who died at nineteen in 1835.

5. Cosmo Hamilton (1879–1941), English publisher and novelist.

Friday, January 8, New York City

I go to my desk in the early morning so am almost writing of what happened on the day before.

It was a rare fine winter morning. After working I walked on Fifth Avenue. I met Eleanor at 51st by the cathedral. Her eyes were very lovely.

We went playing along the street. She went with me to buy a suit of clothes. I got me a dark suit, very nice and cheap. I got me a grey sweater to put on under my coat on cold days. We lunched together.

I wished we could go walk in the park. I wanted to take her with me to the Metropolitan.

I wanted to stand before certain paintings. I know more of paintings than she does, have been more with painters, have thought more of painting.

There is something very delightful to a man in exhibiting what he knows well to a woman he loves.

So he has already thought of sentences that describe his feeling. Some he has got from others. There is a feeling, almost as though he had done the painting.

He is, for the moment, Cézanne, or Rembrandt, or Degas. He tells little stories about these men, as though they were comrades.

I was walking with Eleanor on Madison Avenue, near the Hotel Ambassador, near the new Waldorf—the sun shining, motors in the streets. I had eaten a lot of figs yesterday.

Suddenly. I wonder how many people it has happened to. I thought it would be just wind.

It wasn't . . . a little in my drawers, a most uncomfortable feeling. I didn't tell her.

I hurried away from her—not to the Ambassador or the Waldorf—but to a small hotel on a side street.

You walk in a certain way. It wants to come. It would pour out of you. It is as though you were trying to walk with your legs crossed.

Absurd amusing thoughts. They do not come at that moment but later, when you are comfortably seated, have unloaded. Suppose a President . . . standing up to address the Senate . . . the dignity of the nation must be preserved.

"Why did I eat those figs . . . or prunes?"

Or a preacher in the pulpit.

Or a bridegroom, standing up with a bride . . . to be married to her.

Evening. . . . I walked alone on Eighth Avenue. I went into a bird store to inquire about birds, thinking I might later take one to Bob's Mary. Talk of birds, where they come from, who captures them, etc.

An old fat man, the bird tender and seller, very glad, very willing to talk.

I had thought to dine alone, in a small place . . . a working man's restaurant, among working men . . . having my own thoughts . . . but was prevented.

A young man—an Italian—had been following me along the street. He came and sat with me. Piablo.

"I do not know you."

"But I do you.

"I have been following you along the street, into the bird store, etc. I saw you pass a big hotel—the New Yorker. I thought, 'He will go in there.'

"You didn't. You came here."

He dreams of being a writer. He is young and handsome. He had come to hear me that time I spoke at the Dreiser meeting.

He began saying how much it meant to younger men that such men as myself were willing to speak up for labor, etc.

He is himself a laborer. In some way he has lost the first finger of his right hand. His father was an Italian who became a druggist. He hoped to get rich and so fooled with the stock market. He lost all.

All the time he, the father, wanted to be a painter. Occasionally he closed his drugstore and went up into a room where he tried to paint.

He began selling liquor, illegally. His young son ran about and delivered it.

Later the son—who wanted to be a writer—worked in a speak-easy.

The father went broke and the mother died a terrible death. She got a still and tried to make liquor at home, for the son to sell. It exploded.

She lived three days. There was a poison that ran through her body. The son said, "You could see the white pus everywhere, under the bloated skin."

Her tongue hung out. It was so swollen she could hardly breathe. The house was filled with the noise of her breathing.

The police came and raided the little apartment. They wanted to take her away but could not move her. She died in terrible misery.

The son read poetry. He worked in a speak-easy. He went to school at night and learned to be a wireless operator. He went to sea. He said, "The worst thing is there is no one most of the time to talk to."

The family, two sisters and a younger brother, have sunk into the laboring class. There is a younger brother of whom he is fond and proud. He has married a servant girl.

He came to this one and said, "Hands are nice."

"Why do you say so?"

"It is nice, with your hands, to touch the body of a woman."

The older son—perhaps twenty-seven—cannot now get a job at sea. He says, "There are no places. There are too many operators."

He has got a job as a laborer. "I had to lie to get it." He had to pretend he was married and had children to support.

We talked of George Moore, Cabell, Dreiser, Ben Hecht.[1]

Of the old Greek poets. He thinks he will become a communist.

He has thought of joining one of the gangs in New York, becoming a holdup man.

"I can't have any love life," he kept saying. He said, "You can't feel your manhood and dignity with a woman who is more successful in life than you are."

I took him with me to a hockey match at Madison Square Garden—to see the beauty of the players, their swift and graceful movements. He kept telling me nice little human stories about himself and his family and friends.

1. George Moore (1852–1933), Irish novelist; James Branch Cabell (1879–1958), Virginia novelist; Ben Hecht (1894–1964), Chicago newspaperman and novelist and later a California playwright and screenwriter.

Saturday, January 9, New York City (I)

A rainy day—tramping in the rain. I got three cucumbers and ate them raw. I love them. I had stolen a salt cellar full of salt and had it in my room—for this dissipation. I stole it because I did not know where to go to buy a salt cellar full of salt.

In the morning my bowels ran off—a flood—a Niagara. I was like an old cow in a pasture of green grass in early spring.

You wonder that you can contain all that water.

I went to see Eleanor in the rain. She was in a little dark street—22nd near Fourth—as usual very lovely.

She has the gift of beauty.

It is an evasive thing.

Beauty—whatever it is—comes and lights like that, on persons, scenes, hillsides, rivers—as a bird flies and lights on a bush.

She had got a new coat—very elegant. I wanted her to have a new hat for it. We went into a little nearby place and had tea.

We played along in the rain. I challenged her—running under the noses of automobiles. We walked to Eighth Street where she took a subway.

People hurrying homeward at the dinner hour—in darkness and rain. She had a dinner engagement. I tried to kiss her in the dark shelter of a building. Some drunken man had been there. There was vomit at my feet. She laughed and wouldn't let me.

Went away from her fairly dancing. To Burt and Mary to dine.[1] I hinted for a drink of wine and got it. Mary went off to a concert. Burt and I talked.

He is a rich man. There is always a wall between the poor man and the rich man.

But what am I saying—I am the rich one.

Mary said—before she left . . . it was partly malicious—"You do not live on our level. You are on the heights." I let it pass. The wine was good.

I have given Burt my O'Keeffe, that cost me $300.[2] I didn't want it. It's fun to give things to the rich.

I got Burt to show me his prints. He has invested thousands. We sat a long time over those Daumier, Dürer.

Noted how Howard Pyle got all the good he ever had in him from Dürer.[3]

Burt nice over his prints. He is a lovely old child—more intelligent with his money than the thousands of New York rich . . . very humble—nice, nice.

Hello—Mary came. We had many drinks. Home in the rain. Wet feet.
Thinking of Eleanor's loveliness.

A letter from a young man. It is attached. I wrote this morning. What can I say? "Don't indulge too much in self-pity. It's rotten to be unable to give."[4]

1. Burton and Mary Emmett of New York City. In 1927 Emmett (1872–1935), a wealthy advertising executive at the Newell-Emmett Company of New York City and a collector of art, had lent Anderson money to purchase the two Marion, Va., newspapers in exchange for which favour he collected Anderson's manuscripts.

2. Anderson had known the painter Georgia O'Keeffe (1887–1986) in New York in the early 1920s through her friend and (later) husband, the photographer Alfred Stieglitz (1864–1946).

3. Honoré Daumier (1808–79), French painter and caricaturist; Albrecht Dürer (1471–1528), German printmaker and painter; Howard Pyle (1853–1911), American illustrator and author.

4. Assuming from reading the *Winesburg, Ohio* story "Hands" that Anderson would be sympathetic to homosexuals, the young man had written for personal advice.

Saturday, January 9, New York City (II)

It is a day of lost confidence in self.

Reading the newspapers in a hotel room. Germany getting ready to quit paying reparations. French statesmen being interviewed. "France's sacred right to reparations," etc. They won't dare try to get their peoples to go to war to collect the money for the bankers. Germany will get out of it. They are right. What fools statesmen are.

Fred O'Brien is dead in California. There never was anything in his writing to compare with his talk.[1]

It began to flow. His had been an adventurous life. The last time I saw him we sat on the docks at New Orleans—a Sunday morning. He was already white-haired.

Boats went by—going upriver to Baton Rouge—big oil tankers. There was a Japanese freighter lying nearby. The river was up. Driftwood floated by on the brown water.

Brown water—flowing out of a continent into the sea. Fred talking. He had a lithe strong rather small body. As he talked his face became all alive.

He talked of early days, of wanderings, of ships, seas, islands, island people. Like all writers he wanted some perfect thing—the perfectly balanced immemorial tale told—something that would balance all life—express it all.

He never got it. He was himself something more charming and real than his writing. He didn't want that.

I remember that, from some ship nearby, there came on that Sunday morning the cry of a parrot. Any such sound would start Fred off. He told a tale of three parrots on a beach below a cliff, on some Pacific island.

There was an old brown islander climbing down the face of the cliff.

Some ridiculous thing happened. I have forgotten the nub of the story. Today, reading of Fred's death, I only remember ships and skies, and an alive voice.

Laughter.

Keen love of other humans, brown and white and yellow men.

The modern man—without faith in anything but life. Life going suddenly. Maurice Long going this year—suddenly, quickly.

To fall down in the street dead—while talking to a friend.

To have hold of the hand of a woman loved.

To be walking across a field, as Maurice died, beside a creek.[2]

Here's your earth, sky—one last look. I'd like the sound of a woman's voice singing somewhere, then darkness.

P.S. There should be a breathing space before complete darkness. I'd like bells to ring—sheep to run across a pasture in warm sunlight.

I'd like to walk again, if but for an hour, with Maurice, Fred, Joe Haley.[3]

Bill Faulkner—a little drunk—under the shadow of the cathedral in New Orleans—his telling one of his tales.

Max Eastman laughing.[4]

I'd like the forgiveness of women wronged—if it was wrong. I'd like them to know—I did love—at moments.

I'd like it to happen suddenly, after another hour each with some twenty, thirty, forty men and women known, loved at moments, before complete and final darkness.

1. Frederick O'Brien (1869–1932), journalist and traveler who popularized sea-island writings with *White Shadows in the South Seas* (New York, 1919), *Mystic Isles of the South Seas* (New York, 1921), and other works.

2. Maurice Long had been found on October 18, 1931, dead of natural causes in a ravine on his farm near Ashton, Md.

3. Joe Haley, unidentified.

4. Max Eastman (1883–1969), social critic and editor who was publishing *History of the Russian Revolution* (3 vols.; New York, 1932–33)

Sunday, January 10, New York City

Rain.

A luncheon . . . the International Juridical Association. Sat at the speakers' table . . . Adelaide Walker. . . .[1] Luncheon for a General George W. Chamlee—of Chattanooga—chief council for the Negro boys at Scottsboro.[2]

There is some quarrel between two organizations—National Association for [the] Advancement of Colored People and International Labor Defense (obviously a communist organization).

The general interesting—a quiet, sensible-seeming man. This is a curious, nice kind of courage . . . to take these poor Negro boys' case . . . to associate himself with the communists. Accusations that the communists are, in this case, merely using the case for communist propaganda, they do not care whether or not the boys are saved, etc.

On the other hand—the other organization, obviously trying to keep in with the respectable whites.

At any rate the communists have got this General Chamlee. He seems to be a man.

He told a story. A Negro brought to Chattanooga, while he was attorney general there. Negro accused of killing a white man.

Men from Knoxville sending word. "We are going to charter a train. We are coming there to get that nigger."

The general went to the jail and got the Negro. He hid him in a small inner room in the jail . . . said to him, "I've arranged. I'm going to meet that train.

"If I don't come back you'll know I'm dead. We aren't going to lynch you. We're going to try you.

"If I don't come back I've arranged. A man will pass you a revolver and a box of cartridges. If they get to you you get as many of them as you can before they get you."

The men from Knoxville heard of the general's arrangements. They didn't come.

1. Adelaide Walker, wife of Charles R. Walker, both members of the National Committee for the Defense of Political Prisoners and both associated with other liberal causes and with Theodore Dreiser in the protests at the Kentucky coal mines.

2. George W. Chamlee, prominent Chattanooga, Tenn., attorney who represented the nine blacks accused in Scottsboro, Ala., of raping two white women.

Monday, January 11, New York City

Must speak tonight. I shall be unable to work on the book today. Toward evening will grow nervous and irritable.

The day, yesterday, indoors, in a slump. It may have been no more than eating too much starchy food. No chance of seeing Eleanor.

Was haunted all day by Fred O'Brien, just dead . . . thinking of his charm . . . the talks we once had.

Going about in my hotel room, half-praying, stretching my arms, doing Alys Bentley's breathing exercises.[1]

She says, "There is in the air a mysterious quality of life. You have to reach for it. Reach. Reach."

I reached but didn't get it.

In the evening walked outdoors, felt better, life came back. If we could know what goes on inside people . . . the little sadnesses . . . moments of desperation. The streets dark on Sunday night.

Dark figures lurching along. It was very cold . . . men without overcoats. The morning papers say 800,000 out of work here.

What does it mean . . . in homes . . . little holes . . . children . . . discouraged men and women?

Called Lewis Galantière. He lives at the Algonquin.[2]

Went there and sat until he came in. Bill Woodward and his wife passed, didn't recognize me, slumped in a corner. Thinking of his book—*Meet General Grant*. He didn't get Grant. The book angered me.[3]

Galantière and I walked out to a speak-easy. He is a Frenchman, born in Persia. I think his father had some sort of official position there.

Came to America as a young boy . . . combination of French and American influences. I knew him in Chicago, then Paris. He became a banker, is now with [the] Federal Reserve Bank.

Affectionate, well-read, alive . . . a man of charm.

Although a banker handling millions not money-minded. Not rich. He said, "The figures become just figures. You have no sense of millions, as goods, lands, houses. You sit working out problems . . . theories of finance."

We went to a speak-easy.

I had become alive after a dead day. We talked of love of women, places seen together—a weekend once in the little French town Provins . . . people remembered.

Faulkner, Hemingway, Burton Rascoe.[4]

About Rascoe's father . . . from my own class—cook on a rail-road work train. . . .

He went to Arkansas and got land—struck oil, got rich.

Burton went into the stock market, did nothing else for three years . . . figures, figures. He watched the boards. He made $150,000.

Memories of a party in my apartment in Chicago where Rascoe and Ben Hecht quarreled about Cabell.[5]

Carl Sandburg.[6] Bill Woodward.

Names floating across a conversation over drink. Sinclair Lewis . . . his unhappiness.[7]

Tales of American writers living in Paris. . . .

The American man . . . his curious impotence . . . unable to handle women . . . the coolness of so many American women.

The American woman who works, reads books, goes here and there.

She will not altogether submit to any man. Regarding sex, she says, "I want to" or "I don't want to."

She wants it to mean something to her as a thing in itself . . . a kind of nobility in it.

Man's talk . . . the Frenchman's attitude toward women . . . and expression.

The married woman, after three children, saying to her lover, "You are bad. . . . You have made me feel bad."

He had got her. She hadn't quite wanted to be got.

She had and she hadn't.

Talk of beauty . . . how it comes like a bird flying. It may light on some obscure woman sitting in a corner. She has a crooked nose. Her legs are not straight.

Yet it has alighted on her. She is the most beautiful woman in a room filled with women, too obviously beautiful.

The woman.

"I want that. I want beauty to come into me."

She wants someone—a man—to know it has come.

"The grace of God be upon Thee."

Lewis changing. He said, over the drinks (he had been, when I knew him before, a book man) . . . , he said, "I'm getting away from books.

"I want to sit looking at people, hour after hour, day after day, thinking of them."

There were American men and women, in the speak-easy. The men were all getting prematurely bald.

Something boasting in voices. In a corner a man and woman kissed. It seemed meaningless. Dissatisfied faces.

Talk of Henry Mencken.[8] We walked in the cold streets. I left Lewis [at] his hotel.

Walking alone. . . . "Dare I ask Eleanor to marry me?

"I want companionship. I want to see love come and go."

Tired. Sleep. The room seemed lonely.

1. Alys Bentley, who had conducted at Lake Chateaugay, N.Y., a women's dance camp near which Anderson and his second wife, Tennessee Mitchell, lived in the summer of 1916.

2. Lewis Galantière (1895–1977), with the International Chamber of Commerce in Paris (1920–27) and from 1928 with the Federal Reserve Bank of New York.

3. William E. Woodward, *Meet General Grant* (Garden City, N.Y., 1928).

4. Anderson had known William Faulkner (1897–1962) in New Orleans in 1925; Ernest Hemingway (1899–1961), in Chicago in 1921; and Burton Rascoe (1892–1957) in Chicago, where Rascoe had been literary editor of the Chicago *Tribune*.

5. Rascoe and Hecht had decided to quarrel about the work of Cabell in their columns in Chicago newspapers, one defending and one attacking. See Ray Lewis White, ed., *Sherwood Anderson's Memoirs* (Chapel Hill, 1969), 370–71.

6. Carl Sandburg (1878–1967), poet and Abraham Lincoln enthusiast whom Anderson had known in the days of the Chicago Renaissance, *ca.* 1913–19.

7. Sinclair Lewis (1885–1951), midwestern satiric novelist whose writings about small-town America Anderson did not enjoy.

8. H. L. Mencken (1880–1956), journal editor and newspaperman who had published several of Anderson's writings in *Smart Set* and *American Mercury*.

Tuesday, January 12, New York City

There are days when the will to write words seems entirely paralyzed.

I spoke last night in Brooklyn. It did not go well in me although Eleanor who was there seemed to think it was all right.[1]

There was one charming incident—an old woman coming into a little room after it was over. She at least seemed delighted and said so. I embraced her.

There are certain audiences that set you on edge. Audiences are like people. They have moods. They are too tired—they are smug, dull, alive, open, closed.

Is there something in yourself that closes an audience, or is it so tightly closed you cannot open it?

You are trying to express ideas you have expressed before. They are dead now.

At noon Eleanor and I to see the paintings of Walt Kuhn. They were very alive—freely and boldly painted—with fine abandon.[2]

The room in which they were hung did not tire. It gave you life. We stayed for an hour. The woman who owned the gallery came and told me Mr. Kuhn was coming there. Very likely she had phoned him. I could not wait. I shall go to his studio later.

Eleanor very elegant in a new hat and wearing her new black coat—the day sharp and cold and clear. We dined together at a little restaurant in Brooklyn—a minestrone soup only—and walked in the cold wind-swept streets. Like myself she has lived many places and took me to see a building in which she once lived.

She changes constantly. It must be that anyone you love does. Last night she was a French woman. Suddenly everything about her seemed French.

After the lecture I was not at all tired—a bad sign. I had given nothing.

1. Anderson had spoken at the Institute of Arts and Sciences, Brooklyn, N.Y.
2. Walt Kuhn (1877–1949), painter who enjoyed many exhibitions and won many prizes and who in the 1920s designed theater sets.

Wednesday, January 13, New York City

My brother Karl's birthday. He came to my hotel in the late afternoon.[1] I had been to lunch with Eleanor. I took her violets. She read a long letter from her mother.

Some phrase in it, carelessly thrown off, hurt.

Eleanor told me, for the first time, quite fully, the story of her sister who went insane. I have thought, more than once, of how it would be a marvelous story to write—the story of that family.

They themselves think, I'm sure, that the strong one is the mother. I would make the father the strong, determined one.

I would make him secretly lustful—a man of the flesh not the mind.

Traditions of sturdiness, religion, honor.

Mrs. Copenhaver is not first of all strong. She is alive, vivacious, eager. She must surely have been beautiful. Anything might have been done with her.

To her religion would have been a romance—the Christ, the hope for tenderness . . . worship of her own father in it too.

She might have been led to take life as a lovely sexual experience—touch, nature, lust qualified. To him religion must have meant always final salvation for his soul.

Peasant stock—determined to survive. He is a sturdy peasant yet.

Determined on his own conception of right—inflexible—hard—wanting to be tender and never knowing how.

He got a certain stinging wit. He whipped his wife and children with that sometimes.

He held his wife rigidly for fifteen years. Imagine the dinners on Sunday, long Sunday afternoons. Soil people, sure of themselves, their right. Children had come.

The tone he still often gives his house, his way of pushing, bullying. . . . Elizabeth tried to do just that to me.[2]

All the time sick inside that he cannot be something else.

The uncertain years. The wife wanting to leave. Money closeness . . . his hard determination. Children holding him some . . . religion more . . . her religion, not his. It meant something to save her in the end, as with him. It was something to live by.

I would draw the story up to that girl, the one who went insane. I would make her year a repetition of the mother's mountain year.

Revolt in her. "I'm not going to be held." The mother also, during her year, must have dreamed of a real lover as the daughter did. Any woman would have done that.

There would be the two figures—the mother who broke through . . . to a life of her own in her children—the daughter not strong enough—insanity.

There would be the figure of the father left. There is the terrible story of the son challenging him, in his own house, before his wife, over the noise made eating soup.

So you can't disregard the rest of us—your own peasant ways . . . your virtue, your sureness about right.

The evening at home when the wife and mother is sick. The father to challenge the son about drinking.

The daughters frightened. The son not frightened. The son knowing the father's strength without his brutal sureness. Civilization beginning to temper him.

1. Karl Anderson, Sherwood's older brother, a successful painter and illustrator of periodicals.

2. Elizabeth Prall Anderson, daughter of a prominent Michigan businessman, whom Anderson had met in New York City and married in 1924 and from whom he had been estranged since 1929.

Thursday, January 14, Washington, D.C.

Sunset very lovely in Washington last night. As usual had been a fool. I got it into my head I would have trouble with a young Jewish man, in charge of speaking there.

His name is Bisgyer. I did not know how to pronounce it. I thought, "He'll be impertinent—bossy. I'll tell him to go to hell."

Nothing of the sort happened. He seemed a gentle, reasonable man.

I spoke well last night. I read aloud the long automobile poem.[1] It was full of strange lovely music.

People met—a woman poet, about to publish a book. Nothing at all of the poet in her looks—rather self-satisfied, plump and fair.

A book dealer. He thinks that when an author comes to a city he should go call on the book dealers and shake hands with the clerks. Many authors do it, he says. The clerks remember you and push your books, etc.

A business man . . . he excused all the apparent brutality of business men by saying they were always at a rush, hadn't much time to be considerate. "Rush rush. That's the word," he said.

"But where are you going?" He didn't seem to know.

Some woman—old, watery-eyed, expensively dressed. National Pen Women's Club.[2] She wanted me to speak before a national meeting of these. Pleading watery old eyes.

After I had spoken—the corking little old woman eighty-three—full of life and fire. Came and hugged me. We hugged each other. Made me think of Mrs. Folger of long ago.[3]

When I first knew her she was sixty-five. She didn't believe in God. Later she went to live with her son, a religious man. She was dying at eighty-three and sent for me, on a snowy night, far out in a city suburb. I went at 4:00 in the morning. She had me to her bedside, sent everyone else away—whispered. "I'm dying. Will be dead in an hour. I didn't want to hurt anyone's feelings. I wanted to tell someone. I still don't believe in all this nonsense."

Maurice

Another tragedy. He was such an alive gorgeous creature.[4] He was always having women. He told me once he had never been able to love any of them. He went restlessly from one to another, sometimes having several at once. H[orace] L[iveright] is like that.[5]

Maurice had got rich. One night we sat in his car and talked until 3:00. It might have been his money. "I always think perhaps they are up to something," he said. He kept after them, restlessly. He was not primarily a lustful man.

He got women everywhere, would pick one up on the street. He drank.

When he was a little drunk he would offer anyone anything.

He had a charming place in the country. He took women there. "Do you sleep with all of them?" I once asked him. "For God's sake, no," he answered.

He died suddenly, leaving his estate to his son—a charming young man. He looks like his father.

The father for years had not lived with his wife, the boy's mother. He had provided for her generously.

He had files full of love letters from women, young unmarried women and married women. He knew a lot of rich men. Some of their wives were in love with Maurice.

He was a flaming creature, strong and big.

After his death, one night, the house in the country being

deserted someone broke in. Drawers were opened—the whole house searched apparently. Nothing was stolen.

The son told me about it. We talked frankly of his father's affairs with women.

After the father's death the son, with one or two men friends, went through the father's papers. All the letters from women were burned.

They may not have known that.

The son put a caretaker on the place, a fine old Negro man. He has just been killed.

Someone went there at night, a woman, accompanied by a man. They have found their tracks. The Negro man was found shot twice through the head. His wrists had been slashed with a sharp knife. He had been hit in the head with some heavy instrument.

His body was rolled in a blanket and thrown on a bed. His keys had been taken from his pockets. Again the house was searched—nothing stolen.

The son thinks the wrists of the man were slashed, after he was shot, to give the impression the Negro was killed by some other Negro, perhaps as the result of a private Negro feud.

1. "Machine Song: Automobile," *Household Magazine*, XXX (October, 1930), 3. Anderson had been scheduled to speak on January 12 at the Young Men's and Women's Hebrew Association in Elizabeth, N.J., and on January 13 at the Jewish Community Center, Albany, N.Y.; it is unclear to whom he spoke in Washington, D.C.

2. The International Association of Poets, Playwrights, Editors, Essayists, and Novelists, founded in 1922.

3. Louise S. Folger, who operated the Oaks boardinghouse in Springfield, Ohio, where Anderson lived while completing his high-school-equivalent education in the 1899–1900 term at the academy of Wittenberg College.

4. Anderson was writing again of Maurice Long, his deceased Irish-born business friend who had owned both a farm and a waterfront home near Washington, D.C.

5. Horace Liveright (1886–1933), New York socialite and businessman, publisher of Anderson's books and producer of Broadway plays and Hollywood films.

Friday, January 15, New York State

Dull and heavy from lack of sleep. Two drunken working men on [the] train . . . they quarreling about the prize fight in Chicago between Dempsey and Tunney.[1]

Memories of two women's voices, they talking in low tones about a third woman.

"She has had a lot of men. Can she now settle down to just one?"

I thought I would walk with Mazie Copenhaver.[2] I had things I wanted to tell her. A woman called up.

"I am coming to see you."

"That's nice. I'm going walking with Sherwood Anderson. Come go along."

"No. I won't intrude."

"Oh, do come, do come."

"No, I won't intrude."

"You won't be intruding. Do. Come."

Mazie Copenhaver said it once too often. The woman could not resist the chance to walk with a celebrity—that [being] me. I went along, sullen and sore.

Doctor Johnson—at the Wilsons' house in Baltimore—very charming.[3] She has the charm of a young girl—although she may be fifty-five. We sat together on a couch and suddenly, as she leaned over, I caught a glimpse of her shoulders and the tops of her breasts. The skin was firm, hard and clear. She talked of race horses, the harbor of Marseilles, her girlhood in a little Georgia town, Doctor Watson the psychologist who became famous and then turned business man for $25,000.00 a year,[4] of two young men, when she was a young girl, coming to a little southern town, trying to flirt with herself and [her] sister, her desire to do it—a conversation with a man on a steamer . . . all told with rare vivacity and charm.

Frank Copenhaver in bed in the hospital. Our conversation. His niceness.

On a train going up the east bank of the Hudson, past Albany and Troy. A drunken man in here too. He is asleep, sprawled across a seat with his mouth open. Now and then he half awakes and shouts some sentence, larded with curses. The sentences are incoherent.

1. Jack Dempsey (1895–1983) who, in Chicago, on September 19, 1926, lost the heavyweight boxing title to Gene Tunney (1897–1978).

2. May "Mazie" Copenhaver, Eleanor's youngest sister, who had married Dr. Channing Wilson of Baltimore, Md., a teacher at the Johns Hopkins University.

3. Dr. Buford Jennette Johnson, child psychologist and expert on early childhood education at the Johns Hopkins University.

4. John Broadus Watson (1878–1958), developer of behaviorism theory, who in 1921 became an advertising executive.

Saturday, January 16, New York State

Grey and turning cold—without rain. Was at Skidmore College—in Saratoga. Memories of other days there—with Dave Bohon—the Kentuckian—now dead. There I got the impulse to write the story "I Want to Know Why."[1]

Impression

The little North of Ireland woman in the room—with plenty of IT. She using it on everyone—ambitious, alive, dominant. She is nice yet. There is a feeling she won't be. She will push herself forward in life.

A little alive socialist man with a black beard. He is playing with life—having fun out of it. I asked him, "Why are you so intent on reform in government, in revolution?"

"It's more fun to have a program, something to work for. You have to be serious or you won't have any fun."

Talk with a man about automobiles. I drove his car. Although it had been driven 70,000 miles it responded nicely. "You have a feeling for the machine," I said. "Yes. I love it." He wasn't constantly driving on the brake. He did not constantly jolt and torture his car.

I got to New York and went to Paul Rosenfeld.[2] We had planned to give together a dinner for some friends. He got out a new book of verse by William Carlos (Bill) Williams and read aloud. The book opened with a beautiful poem about the American soil—the virgin soil—the Virgin—not young but old—ravished by the adventurers from Europe.[3]

No real love of her. Talk of how no real love of the soil of America had ever got into Americans. It's the same thing you feel in the man who abuses a car—no connection in such a one between him and the inanimate world.

Nothing between him and rooms, trees, rivers, skies, streets, houses.

Another impression this day. I met a young writer. In conversation he said to me, "I like some of your short stories. They are the best thing you have done," etc.

Another says, "Your *Many Marriages* is the best thing you have done."

Or the novel *Poor White*.

Or *A Story Teller's Story*.[4]

There is an insufferable impertinence in this. If he said it, speaking to another, not to me, it would be all right.

I have living children—two sons and a daughter. Suppose people came to me and said, "Your son Bob is the best of your children."

Or John.

Or Mimi.

It is amazing how many people do this sort of thing—a sort of self-assertion being in it, also—thinking you should be pleased. They do not know how to praise. In the layman it is bad enough but, in the young writer—

A friend says, "I wish you would write another story that would touch me as closely as your story 'A Man's Story.'"[5] The friend knows how to bestow praise.

1. Anderson had spoken to a group called the Key, at Skidmore College, Saratoga, N.Y.; David Bohon, one of the mail-order business clients with whom Anderson worked while in advertising in Chicago and whom Anderson visited in the horse farm areas of Kentucky; "I Want to Know Why," *Smart Set*, LX (November, 1919), 35–40.

2. Paul Rosenfeld (1896–1946), New York music and literary critic who had invited Anderson to visit Europe in 1921.

3. Anderson misunderstood the authorship of the poetry that he heard at Rosenfeld's apartment. The poem in question was not by William Carlos Williams (1883–1963), American poet, but was instead by Phelps Putnam, "Words of an Old Woman," *The Five Seasons* (New York, 1931), 3–5. Anderson's confusion resulted from Putnam's creation of a fictitious Bill Williams, the persona of an ordinary American, to "occasion" the poems by Putnam.

4. *Many Marriages* (New York, 1923); *Poor White* (New York, 1920); *A Story Teller's Story* (New York, 1924).

5. "A Man's Story," *Dial*, LXXV (September, 1923), 247–64.

Sunday, January 17, New York City

Ill with a cold in a New York hotel room. Will not go out today. Thoughts—of Marriage.

They come from hearing a woman make some little slighting remark about her husband. A story—told by a friend.

He is a big attractive man. He was in a friend's house. He and the other man had some sort of business connection.

The house owner was a little thin man with an attractive wife. She was determined to be a good woman.

It must have been hard sometimes.

The husband was one of the kind of men who never sees anything. She went and got her hair done at a beauty parlor, got a new hat, a new dress. He never noticed.

He provided her with everything she wanted, she had but to ask. There was plenty of money. She could have what money she wanted.

She had no children, got into all kinds of activities, tried to write, to be a sculptor.

She was miserable. My friend was in her house, stayed there several days.

He is an observing man. Nothing escapes him.

After a day or two he felt her unhappiness. It was nice for her having him there.

She had many lovely gowns. She kept putting them on.

She was like a child who suddenly has an audience. In her girlhood she had been fond of singing. One evening she went to the piano and began playing and singing. She had a charming voice. Her husband was reading a book.

He thought nothing about it. "Well, she wants to sing. Why not?" As a matter of fact it was the first time for years she had sung.

My own friend, the big man, sat there. He is a man who is aware. You can imagine what he was thinking.

It went on. Perhaps the husband did not want to be disturbed. He got up and left the room. The woman stopped singing.

There was the guest in the house, her husband's friend, not hers. To be sure they weren't really friends. They were involved together in some matter. Let's say they were "business friends."

The man who told me this had been sitting, listening to the woman sing, but got up. He stood by a fireplace. "I wondered why I had been hanging about that house," he said. "I suddenly knew.

"I was so damn sorry for that woman I was in love."

So was she—suddenly—because I thought about her, admired her clothes, listened to her talk.

She walked that evening from the piano to where he stood.

So there was a marriage. She tried to say something but couldn't. She had learned how to bear the fact that her husband had no interest in the little things of life, that meant so much to her.

"He might at least have pretended to be interested while this man is here.

"Not to humiliate me like this."

She might have been thinking something of this sort.

She stood quite close to my friend. Her husband was sitting in the next room under a lamp. She walked into my friend's arms.

He held her. He is quite tall. He could look over her head and see her husband's back.

He put his arms about her, let his big hands come down over her little body.

He kissed her.

If her husband had looked around at that moment. . . . They stood together, their bodies pressed together.

She stepped away from him and made a motion with her hand. He followed her through a dining room into the kitchen of the house. He did not touch her again. "Was it nice, holding me like that?" she asked him.

"Yes."

"Am I nice? Would you like to have me?"

"Yes."

"Well I won't. You know I won't?"

"Yes." Suddenly he understood. She was a resolute woman, a good woman.

She had wanted to know. She had grown afraid. She had wanted to know.

"Yes. You are all right. You've got it."

"You could get me."

They had a drink together, the man and woman, and she cried a little. Then she went away, to another part of the house. On the next morning my friend left.

Monday, January 18, New York City

I am speaking tonight at Columbia University, here in New York—subject, "The Machine."

I was ill all day yesterday and did not leave my room—a sagging—a letting go. Perhaps too many people. I did not leave my room all day.

Thinking—why do I choose to be ill?

It may be a rest time—to get hold again.

I had fruit in my room and ate that.

One of the times of faces. They come running, streaming. Something opens and closes. I am half asleep, half awake.

They may be faces of people I have seen on the street. My mind made no conscious record. Nevertheless a record must have been made. Here they are.

They run. They stand still. They are, for a moment, like portraits framed.

The eyes look into mine. They are demanding something from me.

I am inadequate.

Thinking later—of my attempts at love. Have I been a good lover—at times? If I have will I be forgiven that so often I haven't been?

I read Herman Melville's *Omoo*.[1] It is playful, charming. When I had read almost to the end I put the book down and slept. In my dreams—or in a semiconscious state I went on with the story—from where I had left off. This often happens. I feel myself writing it. It is not myself writing. I am writing now in the tone, the style of another.

Later I pick up the book again—finish it. Afterward I am confused. The story has now two endings, mine and that of its real author.

1. Herman Melville (1819–91), who in 1842 published *Omoo: A Narrative of Adventures in the South Seas.*

Tuesday, January 19, New York City

The story of a woman's death—heard in Gene's house last night.[1] I spoke at Columbia.

I didn't speak well. They said I did but I didn't. Nothing happened between me and the audience. I could not see the people. I spoke into a dark mass.

I like to see it, be afraid of it, anxious, waiting. If something happens, O.K. I like to know.

I was exhausted. Gene came into the dressing room. I had not seen him for years.

We went to his apartment. He had got married. Gene is good. No new impulses are likely to come to him.

There were the two women—his wife and a dancer. The dancer was tall—lesbian-looking, bony. She had long, strong feet. They were bare and she sat far down in a chair—thrusting them forward.

I was very tired.

There was talk of a woman we had both known, how she died. Gene had been with her on the evening before she died. He was the last one to see her alive.

She died in her bed, taken ill in the night alone. She was found dead there.

Gene's story was one I had not known.

There was a party—a drinking party. Gene said the drinks were vile—homemade gin and cheap red wine.

Almost everyone got drunk. It was an icy cold night in winter. Gene had come to the party late. "I had a drink or two of the stuff. It made me a little sick and I quit."

He stood in a little hallway and the woman who died passed him. She went into a bedroom. He heard her fall.

He went in there. She was lying on the floor, terribly ill.

He began working with her. She was grateful. "Gene, Gene," she said. "Don't let them see me."

"What matter if they saw her?" Gene said. He thought the people at that party were just riff-raff. He said so. "I don't know what she was doing there, or I was doing there," he said.

He made her drink water, glass after glass, gallons. He had put her on a bed. Her hair was down.

There was a clatter of drunken voices in the next room. They were alone in the bedroom.

So he worked and worked with her. "I pumped her legs up and down," he said.

She had always been a very dignified woman. I remembered her, tall and with heavy auburn hair. She was straight of figure and had a fine carriage. She had been a famous singer.

She had come down in the world. She had a love affair with a poet. He deserted her. Then her voice cracked.

She had become a teacher of singers. "How had she got there, to that party? For that matter, how had I got there?" Gene asked.

This in the apartment in New York, Gene's wife listening— that dancer sitting there with her long bare feet thrust out. I had known the singer in her glory.

Gene was working with her on the bed in that room when the door opened. A man and woman, half drunk, looked in. "They thought we were making love in there," Gene said.

The door closed. Gene realized what had happened. He and the singer had been friends for years. They were never lovers.

It was one of the messy moments that come into being. The singer also realized. She got painfully out of bed.

"Take me away from here," she said.

Gene took her. He got his coat and took her out of the house where the party was going on. The others at the party grinned. "They had their nerve," Gene heard a woman's voice saying.

The woman he was with staggered as she walked so Gene walked her for miles through the streets. Once she stopped. "Stand here," she said. She went off alone into an alleyway. It was late at night and very cold. "She vomited in there," Gene said. "She was better after that."

Gene took her to her apartment. She was living in poverty. There were a few belongings left from the days when she was rich and successful. Gene sat down beside her. They talked a little and smoked cigarettes.

"Are you all right now?"

"Yes," she said.

"How did you happen to go to that place?"

"I don't know. I was lonely."

"And you?"

"I went. I was invited. I guess I was lonely," Gene said. He sat there smoking a cigarette and looking at her. She had thrown herself down on a couch. She closed her eyes. "She's tired," Gene thought.

She was pale. "She was beautiful," Gene said. He described her as I had seen her when she was a successful woman. She was very still. Gene tiptoed out of the apartment and left her thus. "She may have been dead then," he said. Anyway she died. She was lying there on that couch, just as I left her.

The point was that afterwards . . . the others at that drunken party that night . . . they swore they had seen the two . . . Gene and that singer . . . we had both known . . . once a glorious creature . . . they swore that in the bedroom that night Gene and the woman. . . .

They said there should have been an investigation by the police. Perhaps Gene had killed her.

1. Probably Gene Fowler (1890–19?), popular New York journalist and biographer.

Wednesday, January 20, New York City

Gloom—intense. Walking to shake it off. Reading to shake it off.

I went to Max Eastman. He was charming. 1 was ashamed that I was there.

I saw Selma Robinson, the poet, beautiful—very slender and lovely in a white evening gown.[1]

The girl with strange eyes and a great mop of hair who came to the table. She told a story of Doctor Freud in heaven.

I wanted to go out of myself—my own deep gloom. I couldn't. I fought it.

The story of the woman with the breasts—feeding the child. The actor who came to call.

I remembered the composer Bloch—one snowy night in his house, his talk . . . the old Indian woman with the dry sagging breasts . . . the desert . . . the sense he gave of earth and sky and woman . . . the strangeness going out of his house into the snow.[2]

It is self, self. The little nerves of the back are tight. They won't let loose. The mind won't let loose.

Individuals stand out sharply. There is no feeling of fellowship. Women do not get you. You do not feel their loveliness.

The woman poet came and sat with me. She talked of the girl on the couch, making the men embarrassed—seeds. Max was friendly, like a fine big dog. Stuart Chase came.[3]

There was a flock of men and women. Dancing began. I did not dance. I sat in a corner drinking. I drank whiskey and gin—quantities. It had no effect on me.

A whiff of conversation. I must have started it. Murder. Why do we all love murder stories? Max had an idea—we all want—while we live—the ultimate experience, the ultimate in sensations.

Do we all envy the murderer in his cell? He did it. He knows how it feels.

He has in some queer way lifted himself up to that place.

To stand in a room at night in a country house, like that one Maurice built—wanting such happiness there—I mean Maurice, the builder.

Another night. Maurice is dead now. There has been a murder done in his house . . . in a room where we had all once been so gay.

A man and woman are standing there, over a dead man they have just killed.

No matter who he is, why they have killed him. There he is, lying there before them. There was a struggle, knife thrusts, blows. Then a revolver whipped out.

A man, on the floor now, is shot. He struggles, is shot again, lies still, is shot again.

The dead are terribly unimportant. All dead people look insignificant. It isn't worthwhile killing each other for this experience.

Once I saw a book—actual photograph—presumably—of men killed by the Al Capone gang in Chicago.[4]

All this fuss about such a minor matter. They looked like dead dogs, lying against [a] shed, across sidewalks, in the naked street.

Dust cart—come and carry this away.

The man and woman, imagined, in Maurice's house—the dead man there before them. Never mind why they did it.

I imagine a light burning in the room. Silence. Perhaps a little wind in trees outside. There would be a dead leaf or a page from an old newspaper blown against the house.

The two looking at each other and then at the dead man. If what Max said is true—that we all want to have known some final absolute experience in life—this cannot be it.

They would suddenly hate each other, be afraid of each other. Yes, there is a hell. This is it.

They creep forth, get into a car and drive away. The man drives and the woman sits beside him.

Fast. Fast. Drive furiously.

Slower. Slower. For God's sake be cautious.

For God's sake, let us never see each other again.

It turns out to be ultimate degradation.

1. Selma Robinson, American poet, author of *City Child* (New York, 1931).
2. Ernest Bloch (1880–1959), Swiss-born music composer.

3. Stuart Chase (1888–19?), social critic and economic theorist, author of *Prosperity: Fact or Myth?* (New York, 1929) and *A New Deal* (New York, 1932).
4. Al Capone (1899–1947), gangster of prohibition-era Chicago.

Thursday, January 21, New York City

Diego Rivera—the Mexican painter—a great, fat, jelly-like man with a small bullet-headed woman, on a couch, at Lewis Gannett's place.[1] It is a penthouse, on top an office building. We drank gin—made into cocktails. I did not stay long or drink much. Rivera had little or no English. I could not talk to him. His hands and eyes were nice.

Thinking as I walked of the little shop on 14th Street where a million things are sold. It is a trinket shop with lead soldiers, toys, church pictures, etc. Two huge Greek women—a mother and daughter—run it. They become absorbed in my ring. There is a virgin with child—a mitre. Is that authority? I spent a half hour with them going over pictures. We could not find her. They promised to consult their priest. The ring is evidently Byzantine.

A little dance hall to which any girl may go and be paid for dancing. She must dance with any man who offers. The man pays ten cents. I presume the dance hall keeps five of it. I went and stood against the wall.
There were perhaps twenty-four rather pretty little girls in there. They stood by a wall or walked about. There were not more than ten men. The men looked like young clerks, with a few laborers. There was something about the girls. These are tight times. Can they get here enough for a meal? They must have at least one good-looking dress.

Was with Eleanor in the park—a little park by the river. We had dined and walked down there. The river was dark and strange. A few boats went mysteriously up and down.
There was some sort of excavation going on. We sat on a bench. This in the early evening. It was delicious to touch her.
She had got something on her shoe and I leaned down to brush it off. It turned out to be dog manure. We went to find one of the little drinking fountains, commonly found in parks, so I could wash it away but as it was winter they were all shut off.

1. Diego Rivera (1886–1957), Mexican painter and muralist; Lewis Gannett, journalist who had reviewed several of Anderson's books for the New York *Herald Tribune*.

Friday, January 22, New York City

Dinner in the apartment of my publisher. There was a young man there—son of Seth Low—once famous in New York.[1]

Women came. There was a little woman—very chatty about all the places she had been. You got a notion of a young life spent, hanging about New York. Had seen Eleanor at noon and she had spoken of all the expensive furs she had seen on women coming out of a luncheon party. Eleanor nice, her eyes nice against some pale sweetpeas I had brought her. I had thought I would run into Tom's place, stay for dinner and then leave.

The dinner was sent up from a restaurant, very nicely served. The little chattering woman ran on about her dancing, drinking, etc., until the others came.

With Low a tall handsome woman with strange eyes who told me she was from the East Tennessee mountains.

She was very American—individualistic. There was little talk of socialism or communism except when she brought it up. I said I might go to Russia. "I hope you get sick of it," she said.

I kept thinking of her in fields—or walking along one of our mountain roads, long straight legs, good shoulders.

She said she had been in a speak-easy all night. She had slept all day.

The young Low lives on a farm his father owned. "Do you farm it?" "No." I kept wondering what he did but did not ask.

Bill Woodward and his wife came in and told a story. He was once at the head of a bank that loaned money to school teachers. There were some twenty-five school teachers who borrowed money in one year, all from the same building. There were notes given. The amounts were small—$25 to $100. For a time the payments were all made regularly and then they stopped.

A man was sent to the school. It turned out none of the teachers had signed notes. They were all forgeries.

All by a pretty little woman who was one of the star teachers. She had a gift for forgery—in a few minutes could imitate any signature.

She was in love—with another woman.

The other woman got all the money and went away with a man. She confessed all.

They let her off. The school authorities weren't told. She kept on teaching. She was through teaching at 3:00 and then went to a store, where she was bookkeeper. She did that for years, working like a slave, long hours every day. She paid all back. When she had it all paid she killed herself.

1. Seth Low (1850–1916), who had been president of Columbia University and mayor of New York City.

Saturday, January 23, New York City

My older brother in my hotel room to spend the night. We up early, breakfast in the room.

Talk of the whoredom of American life . . . the rich . . . women . . . wives of rich men. We both know such men and women . . . too many of them.

There is in some way the whole key to our American civilization in it—the emphasis on money and things.

You think of it—its implications. When they discovered America—what it must have meant to all Western Europe. "A new world. A new world."

Riches—a new chance. Read your history.

Those early explorers. Gold lust. Cruelty. Gold pouring into old Europe. Spain.

Then England—land lust.

Land lust in the early Americans, the pioneers.

There must have been something more. Thomas Jefferson and others.

Dreams—promises—hopes. Does it end in the manufacturer and his fat wife?

The daughter. The stock broker.

Speak-easies.

The artist—he has in some way to deal with this world of affairs. They try to get him.

There is dirt everywhere. Money, money, money.

Good, goods, goods.

The artist loves luxury too.

They piss on him. They want him. They want at the same time to dirty him.

The revolution should go deep, deep. Given money this whoredom is inevitable.

It touches everyone, everything. Half the energy a man has must be spent in fighting it.

Sunday, January 24, New York City

Sunday. Rather dirty grey clouds. Thinking of something—a man washed by a woman.

He is full of mistakes, false starts on the way toward love, cruelties, shame.

She has no shame. She is pure and straight. She is strongly sensual. A night. They make love. He gives her he thinks all he has. It is only a beginning.

They lie very still a long time. They begin slowly making love again. It is the woman making love now.

She bares her strong white teeth—she bites, softly, then hard. The next day there are black and blue places, the marks of teeth, on his shoulders.

She is at the same time gentle.

Wash me. Wash me.

Wash me and I shall be whiter than snow.

He feels himself carried away. She has become a white boy running. The little nerves of his body are paths and roadways. She is running, running. He looks up at her.

Suddenly she has become the mother. There is softness in her eyes.

Now the feeling of being washed begins. She is cleansing him. She has dropped him down, down into a deep sea.

He feels himself going deeper and deeper. He is about to die.

Laughter.

Something naked.

Her hands touch him again. They touch, touch. The boy runs in the pathways. Seas, trees, skies, earth.

Why did you live? Begin to live. Now, now.

The clean feeling of the man afterwards. The good of it.

The discussing with my brother—then with the publisher.

Georgia O'Keeffe, Marin, Stieglitz. Marin a man. Sharp face—like an animal. An alive man.[1]

A good day.

1. John Marin (1870–1953), American painter of seascapes and Manhattan skylines.

Monday, January 25, New York City

Very tired. Unhappy. Sunday with my brother Karl—Ray there. Helen.[1] Seeing Van Wyck Brooks . . . dead for years—alive again. A strange story there.[2]

The lady and the ring—Queen of Romania.

The inlet from the sea.

"If you had your life to live over would you change anything?" Not a thing.

Karl's pastels . . . the street—real force. Something new.

The landscape out there.

Karl's strange problem. Interruptions to the conversation at Van Wyck's. Helen laying down the law.

My brutality—telling the story of the Christmas tree.

I am trying to gather all together when I am tired. I can't.

1. Raymond Anderson, Sherwood's younger brother; Helen, wife of Karl Anderson.
2. Van Wyck Brooks (1886–1963), literary editor and historian involved in publishing some of Anderson's earliest stories, who was recovering from serious depression.

Tuesday, January 26, New York City

Awoke with a slight attack of the blues. I had a childish feeling that Eleanor was not interested enough as I told her all the adventures of my day. She was of course concerned with the adventures of her own day.

I came childishly home and wrote a complaining letter. It was not sent. I awoke this morning and tore it up.

I am still planning to go to Russia in the spring. Talked to a man who told me I could collect my Russian royalties in rubles to be spent in the country.

Went to the office of the *Masses*. They are printing my speech prepared for the Dreiser meeting here last month.[1] The beauty of some of my phrases, the balance and the thought will seem strange in that magazine, that goes in so much for loud words . . . strong curses, etc.

Saw Mike Gold.[2] As I went up the stairs I thought, "He will begin by saying, 'You have come in with us at last.'" He said just that.

As a matter of fact I would have said everything said in the speech at any time these twenty years. I have written of workers since I began writing.

Sunshine—a cold clear day. I can hear the sound of builders on a building. There is always something cheerful and nice in the sound of hammers on wood . . . something being built.

1. "Let's Have More Criminal Syndicalism," *New Masses*, VII (February, 1932), 3–6. This magazine followed the doctrines of the Communist party.

2. Mike Gold (1893–1967), Communist editor of *New Masses* and *Liberator*, author of *Jews Without Money* (New York, 1932).

Wednesday, January 27, New York City

Wednesday—soft rain—

Thinking—of self—how it has again and again murdered me. Self pushes itself in. Self gets between you and your work, between yourself and people.

It begins. You imagine some injustice has been done you. It builds up and up. Meet two people who have quarreled. They are both trying to be honest. What different tales they tell.

Money. Sitting on the edge of the bed—dressing—lacing my shoes. I am about to publish a novel. I think up schemes for pushing it. I would know how to sell it.

If it sold I would have money, perhaps, for me, a lot of money. But I remember I had money once before. It almost ruined me.[1]

Saw Alys Bentley who showed me many black cards, on which squares of color had been placed. They were lovely.

We spread them out and played with them. The colors were the musical scale. Alys had a theory. A certain color for the head, the heart, liver, bowels, etc.

She grew a trifle mystical. She was nice just the same.

The business man who sleeps for two hours every noon in his office. A man stands at the door. He tells everyone the business man is in an important conference.

Who with? What are his dreams? He has a couch in there.

The story of the man in the speak-easy—wanting a woman. He says he loves his wife. No fun to fuck her. Likes orgies with prostitutes. The woman he found. Miss Laukhuff.[2]

You tell my brother, will you, what you found me doing. The hater . . . a story.

1. This refers to Anderson's escape from the life of an Ohio businessman to the life of a Chicago literary artist, an escape that followed a four-day mental disorder late in 1912. For discussion of the breakdown and escape, see William A. Sutton, *The Road to Winesburg* (Metuchen, N.J., 1972), 162–205.

2. Miss Laukhuff, presumably related to Richard Laukhuff, a bookseller whom Anderson had known in Cleveland, Ohio; this man was originally an immigrant German organ maker who disdained to work on machine-made American musical instruments. The reference is otherwise obscure.

Thursday, January 28, New York City

I have quarreled with Eleanor—not actually but in fancy. Will the misunderstanding become a fact?

I have been hurt. She has been so absorbed in her own affairs that I do not feel myself a part of her.

It was a tangled day yesterday . . . one of the thwarted emotional days that come. My work moved forward and stood still.

There may be a little movement of some character in a book very difficult to make. Jake has gone on a train from New York to Chicago. In real life he goes and gets a ticket. He is on the train. He is there.

In a book it is different. You must feel the impulse with him, know why he wanted to go there, etc.

You have to be convinced in your own mind he would go to Chicago.

Marriage

Perhaps I want too much. There is no use my shuffling. I want a woman who is my woman.

Your own life may be too much made already.

I apparently do want someone sympathetic to this illusive stuff in which I try to work.

I have missed tenderness too much. My mother was probably pretty harsh. I have built up, in fiction, another mother.

Karl intimates that is true.

My childhood may have been a starved childhood.

I'm afraid it doesn't do me any good to know that there is sterling stuff inside someone—if it cannot come out in little tender constant thoughtful acts.

Such men as your father—sterling men. No graciousness. I can admire them from afar. They are not of my world. If I had to live in a house with such a man I'd kill him.

In the night—Thursday.

I never really know whether you want these notes of my thoughts. So much of my time is spent in a room. The thoughts are my life, I suppose. Perhaps they are only a bother to you.

I have felt a little that I have been a bother to you this week, staying on here, increasing, by so much, the complexity of your life.

I dream of another kind of life for you. Perhaps you will not like it. After all, I do not know, this life with its many complexities, meetings, conferences, etc., may mean more to you than anything I can give you.

It will be so much quieter. I wish I knew the truth. I never see you here that I do not feel I am a bit guilty, keeping you from someone else.

Sometimes I do not see how anyone does anything, trying to do a thousand things.

When I was in business I suppose I was at a thousand conferences. I don't remember that anything was ever done at any of them. When anything was done some man dropped everything else, forgot everything else and did it. That's the way it was in business. I may be all wrong in this. I don't know.

I do think, Eleanor, that you ought to pretty definitely make up your mind soon. If we are going to Russia I will have to point up my own plans. I want, if possible, to go very early in May.

You misunderstand me a little on nights like this too. I did not want to take you to sit in a hotel parlor. I only came up there to take you home.

What was the matter with me the other night was not that you had not given me more time. I seem unable to make it clear.

I'm a hungry man. It doesn't take much to feed me. A few little drops of milk . . . if you could say, "My dear, I love you."

I walk along beside you often very hungry for that. Perhaps it is foreign to your nature to show love quickly and often. These little things—in life—the word said, mean everything to me.

Do I have to teach you to be a lover? I wonder sometimes. I have, Eleanor, times of doubt.

I think, "She doesn't yet know what love is."

I think, "Later, after she has married me, some other man may teach it to her."

To say the little word quickly . . . I make the little gesture, to kiss you on the street. The kiss doesn't matter. I'm not very conventional. I rarely think, "Who may be looking?"

At such a time you say—I can't tell you—a word would take the place of a kiss.

I put the kiss on you sometimes, on your hat or coat. I have so often the feeling that it means nothing to you. Am I right? Be sure, dear.

If we marry will I always have to beg? I want you as lover. I'm not afraid of exhausting love.

There are the little delicate arts of relationships—as between lovers. Do you not think they are worth cultivating, dear?

To make the point clear . . . it is a coming toward me I begin to hunger for now. If you haven't, in yourself, the little hunger, always present, for the warmth of it. . . .

You see what I am driving at. You may really not need me. You will have to put up with so much, my moods, hungers, blue times, faculty of being hurt easily . . . better one big hurt than that I never feel you—soft, yielding thing . . . you wanting the little fires lighted and lighted again as I do.

Why, I have to be honest . . . I am hurt a thousand times by such small things as that your hand never—or hardly ever—reaches for mine—always mine for yours.

That your eyes so seldom seem to need to seek mine.

You ought to think hard, dear. If you can go on without me, if I am not an absolute and daily need to you, you should not marry me.

You may be able to stand alone, without a man. I shall always be needing a woman. I admit it. It seems to me a definite fact now that if I don't get you, finally, as I am trying to say here, I'll end up knowing it isn't in me to get my woman.

Friday, January 29, New York City

Exhaustion after a wakeful emotional night. I got up and exercised. My eyes looked burned out. Went for a long walk. At first stumbled along, nearly struck by several automobiles. The drivers turned to swear at me. Began to feel better. Stopped to buy flowers from a man standing on a corner. He stuttered.

Went into a church. It was nice in there. I knelt down with the praying people. Felt refreshed.

As I came out of the church I met a woman I had not seen for years. I think she used to love me. She rushed into my arms.

I gave her the flowers.

I had begun to feel human again, after a crazy night of wild thoughts. I went to meet Eleanor. There she came along the street, looking lovely. She had bought a flower from the same stuttering man and had brought it to me.

We went into a restaurant and I poured it all out to her, all my wild thoughts, fears, etc. It had been one of my nights of faces. Eleanor's face had come floating, very lovely. Her lips kissed me. That had quieted me in the night.

I proposed to her that she come and join me in Russia next summer, that we be married over there. She agreed.

Returned to this room here and work. At night to dine with Maurice and his woman Pat at a speak-easy.[1] The queer position of a kept woman. Maurice one of the men destined to be hurt. The thirty-five dollars.

The young man named Kraft.[2]

There was a good deal of talk of Theodore Dreiser—his books and his character. We all admired [him]. There were many strange stories of the man told.

I told the story of the man who owned the box factory in Chicago and who committed suicide in the river there.[3]

1. Maurice A. Hanline, who worked as an editor at Horace Liveright's publishing business and who had written *The Sympathy of the Moon* ([New York], 1922) and other poems.

2. H. S. Kraft, New York writer whom Anderson met through Maurice A. Hanline and who proposed that Anderson work with him on a film or dramatic project concerning factory work.

3. "All Will Be Free," *Sherwood Anderson's Memoirs*, ed. White, 372–76.

Saturday, January 30, New York City

The multiplication of words—making sentences, stories, books.

I went to Paul who had a bad cold. He was a little whirlpool of gloom. He has got into the state where he doesn't believe in his own work. Apparently he cannot just go along and live . . . even in ugliness little things do pop up.

A stretch of field . . . the reflection of light on water, two men talking earnestly on a street corner.

The little mill girl from North Carolina who got a trip to New York. Some people met her at the station in New York. She was almost in tears. "I was never so disappointed with anything in my life as I was with New Jersey," she said.

Walking in the rain through wholesale districts—the district of fur dealers.

Hides in windows and warehouses, wild cat, mink, squirrel, cats, rats, rabbits. These centering here—hundreds of thousands of furs—from wild and tame animals. The smell, the sights and sounds.

Taking you back to woods, wild places, streams. Paul should walk more in his city.

The woman on the bed, her shoulders, arms, legs, the soft animal smile as we made love.

Days are good days.

Sunday, January 31, Washington, D.C.

Sunday.

Thinking of Eleanor. I am in Washington. I was drunk last night, very drunk. I could just stagger home to my hotel.

I am here to see Boris Skoirsky—of the Russian Soviet Information Bureau. I shall see him at 12:30. It is 11:00 now.

My head is still light, still whirling, a bit crazily.

There were Cliff and Jean Hill and two other men and two women.[1]

An impression of—The Husband.

That man explaining. His wife, the dancer with the dancing partner.

We went to a dance hall but they didn't dance. The man owed them money and didn't—wouldn't or couldn't—pay.

So they didn't dance.

We danced. Jean and I danced.

I kept drinking. I got drunk. I could just stagger back to my hotel.

I kept having thoughts—relating to men and women—their closeness, their lack of closeness.

Although I was drunk I kept looking at the men and women in the club. I dare say they were well-to-do women . . . it must have been a fashionable club. They were well dressed.

The way the women tried to abandon themselves to the men— some tried, some didn't. The men were so much more self-conscious. I saw a lot. I was drunk but I saw a lot.

Sitting there drunk and giving myself up to something— to observation, impressions. Jean danced beautifully but, after-wards. . . . She was so drunk that she fell off a chair.

I thought of Eleanor—her niceness, the terror and wonder and the challenge of intimacy. It was a good night of thinking— being drunk so—glad to be drunk, being washed by people— getting impressions—sharp—men and women—letting them, letting it, letting myself.

Washing over—in and out—as though dancing.

In dreams deathless.

In life deathless.

A man ought to keep loving . . . never stop . . . just keep on. It's the only way.

1. Cliff and Jean Hill, friends of Maurice Long and residents of Washington, D.C.

February

Monday, February 1, Marion, Virginia

The distraction of getting settled again in my room in Marion. It is bright, cold and clear. I shall go this afternoon to the farm to pack the dishes, etc., to be shipped to Elizabeth.[1]

All day yesterday in Washington I was a little light-headed from having been drunk on the night before. Sometimes when such a drunk ends there is a strange clear clean feeling.

I went to Funk at the hospital in Washington and sat with him for two hours. Other men from Marion came in—Dooney, the long-distance auto driver, a strange shy man who is a clerk in one of the government departments.[2]

There were four shy men sitting about Funk's bed.

It was a long room—about twenty beds—and to entertain us, Funk told of each case—how they had suffered, about men who had died, men with feet and hands cut off.

In the evening took Ruth Dove to dine and we had good talk.[3] I had begun to recover. We went to Cliff and Jean Hill and sat with them until time for my train. Frank Tannenbaum, the writer, was there.[4] He said Americans were too strong individualists ever to revolt against capitalism. It did not seem to me a very profound observation on Americans.

1. Elizabeth Prall Anderson, who had asked that her belongings left in Virginia be shipped to her family home in California.

2. Charles H. "Andy" Funk, attorney in Marion, Va., and commonwealth's attorney for Smyth County (1924–32), who was one of Anderson's closest friends in Marion; Dooney Hester, who in late April, 1929, had driven a demonstration automobile for 1,342 continuous miles.

3. Ruth Dove, another friend of the deceased Maurice Long, of Washington, D.C.

4. Frank Tannenbaum (1893–1969), a writer in Washington, D.C., who had published *The Mexican Agrarian Revolution* (Washington, D.C., 1929).

Tuesday, February 2, Marion, Virginia

Yesterday a day of extreme activity, seeing the dentist, going to the farm, planning the farm work for next year, going to Frank's about wine, seeing Burt Dickinson about the papers in the divorce, talking to Mary, Bob's wife, going out to dine and to call on Eleanor's people.[1]

There is a queer thing in people. You become convinced, as I have, that the capitalistic system is doomed. It has brought real happiness to no one. Here is an intelligent man, or woman—your friend. You talk it over. After a long talk they become apparently convinced. "Yes, you are right," they say.

You go away for a week. Again you talk. It is as though nothing had ever been said.

Most people seem unable to move off one plane of thinking and onto another.

Packing things to send to Elizabeth . . . the sense again of her queer passion for spending money that almost destroyed me. So many useless things. Everything duplicated over and over. There is a kind of dreadful gloom descends upon you in thinking about it.

Talking to Burt Dickinson and discussing Walter Reed Hospital, at Washington, where I went to see Andy Funk, as patient. He went in as a private. I was shocked at some of the things I heard there, as to the careless brutality of nurses and others with privates.

Burt said, "The government has got itself into a hole, wet-nursing every sick private." He really wants, apparently, a civilization in which the common man is treated as, for example, a Chinese coolie. He himself was in the war but got exemption from active service and stayed in Paris. His father was on the exemption board.

At night, in bed, dreaming. I was suddenly in the position of a Stalin in Russia. To reorganize America upon sensible lines. How vast the problem would be. How impossible for a man like me to do anything with such a problem. My brother Ray—who is a fool—would tackle it without a quibble.

1. Burt L. Dickinson, attorney in Marion and one-time mayor of the town, another of Anderson's close friends, who was serving as judge of Juvenile and Domestic Relations Court.

Wednesday, February 3, Marion, Virginia

Rain rain rain.

I had a touch of something like flu—could not work although I was not depressed. I was in the bank. The bank had, by a clever trick of figuring, beat me out of one dollar. They are always doing some such trick. I got mad and in a loud voice began to cheer for communism.

Rain rain. I wandered about in my car. The earth steamed. A letter came from a woman. It pleased me. I am myself always being raped by sights, sounds, colors, smells. I go off. Let someone else go off thus too.

Although it is early February the grass is all green. It was a sensual day and a sensual night. I dreamed all night of running horses.

They thundered past me, the riders leaning low over the horses' necks. I could feel the wind of them.

I awoke occasionally. It was a night of thunder and lightning. The thunder rolled and rolled away, into the hills.

I slept again and again dreamed of horses. I had a hard-on. I awoke holding it in my hand. I dreamed of wrestling with a horse.

At last, toward morning, Eleanor came—very gentle and quiet. I walked quietly with her. I awoke feeling better.

Thursday, February 4, Marion, Virginia

More rain—the river is flooded. I drove down to Henry Copenhaver's mill and then to the Lincoln dam and the Henry Staley dam.[1] Everywhere the waters reddish brown and whirling. Logs and sticks flying downstream.

Above town a laborer's house out in the stream. It was not in danger. The working man's wife, a rather loud woman, was standing on the porch. She had five children, all girls, and they were all barefooted.

A crowd had gathered onshore beside the husband. A crowd had gathered. There they were. Ordinarily they were people leading obscure lives. In the morning the man stumbled off to work and he came home at night tired.

All of these girls in the family, so many mouths to feed, dresses and shoes to buy. If a girl is to get a husband she must have clothes. "Why didn't you get me a few boys? Boys can go to work easier than girls."

There had been quarrels, the man accusing the woman, the woman accusing the man. All day the woman had to work in her little house at the edge of the stream. Her life was passing unnoticed.

But now—the house had become a boat. It was not in danger yet. After all it stood in a kind of backwater. There were a few logs and branches of trees being carried in there. The children were fishing them out of the brown water.

The woman on the porch pranced up and down. She shouted. She laughed. She cried to those ashore who in turn cried to her.

The husband also had become suddenly the center of attention. "Well, well, this is living." All the neighbors were looking. The woman was on a stage. It may be where all people want to be.

"Why, Mary—aren't you afraid?"

"Naw. Naw."

"Can you swim?"

"Naw, I can't swim. I ain't afraid."

She laughed. She pranced. She threw back her head and laughed. It wasn't necessary to shout to be heard by those on shore. She shouted.

The husband shouted. He laughed. People he hardly knew, fellows from over in town, two or three clerks who had come down to the river to see the flood, a young lawyer and the editor of the paper called him by his first name.

"So you are flooded out, Jim."

"Yes, I'm flooded out."

Laughter. They called his wife, Mary. "Jump in and swim, Mary."

Loud laughter. It was an hour of joy for that obscure family.

All day yesterday I was unable to write. I had been reading Dreiser's *Tragic America*.[2] The prose, as is usual with him, was halting, heavy stupid.

It seemed to me he had got between me and words. Made words dead things to me. I tried and tried but could not make words sing together.

I dreamed all night of Eleanor. She is always a sweet clear figure in all the confusion of my dreams.

As I write this morning it rains.

1. Henry Polk Copenhaver (1851–1934), farmer active in local church work and organizer of the agricultural exhibitions at the annual Smyth County Fair.

2. Theodore Dreiser, *Tragic America* (New York, 1931).

Friday, February 5, Marion, Virginia

I'll use up this paper.[1] I wrote to Eleanor. I used a good phrase. I was describing the morning and spoke of fat clouds lying across the sky like logs.

John has a new Bockler, very rich and soft in color.[2]

I saw Eleanor's uncle Gord—a tall lean man with very intelligent hands and eyes. I liked him.[3]

The wind was whooping and howling through streets last night. Today all is silent, grey and still.

I have got into a neighborhood of the respectables. Men of position in the town have got their houses all about here. They are the upper-middle class.

The houses are like the people—heavy, stolid, stupid.

I went in on a couple lounging in their home—on two beds. The woman was in pajamas. There was a sense of flatness.

All her slender bones were flat, her hips extraordinarily small and flat. There wasn't a handful. Am I a peasant?

I thought of Eleanor's firm, round hips—breasts—strong shoulders. I should have had her long ago. I should have bred sons by her. It is such a joy to run the hand over her body.

I was a little mad in the afternoon. The sun shone, after several days of rain. There was a whooping wind. I drove. I got out of the car and walked.

The wind played with leaves. Leaves went dancing—I wanted to dance, shout and run. I got back in the car and drove furiously, running with the wind. I shouted and sang.

I was full of love for Eleanor all day.

1. Anderson, who habitually stocked his stationery supply from the hotels where he lived, was using paper from the Ambassador Hotel, Washington, D.C.

2. Charles Bockler, once a bank clerk in New York City who hoped to become a successful painter, for whom Anderson had since 1928 tried to arrange financial support.

3. Gordon White Copenhaver (1888–1971), carpenter and farmer of Smyth County, Va., and brother of B. E. Copenhaver.

Saturday, February 6, Marion, Virginia

Awoke at 2:00. A hard-on. Read Balzac—a terrible story. It did not help—"A Tragedy of the Sea."[1]

Dreamed of that old fisherman, killing his son.

Awoke again at six. Went and put up the shade. The light just breaking over hills—very soft, clear and warm. The bare trees on the hills, in the early light, were like hairs standing stiffly on the head of a giant.

At night terror about my work, its inadequacy. It seemed weak.

A talk yesterday with Mrs. Copenhaver—men and women. Would, or could, a man ever understand a woman? She thought men like myself both wanted and expected too much of women.

I am amused by the houses near me, where I now live. A rich lumberman, a successful politician, successful in a small way, a sharp, scheming little lawyer, the town treasurer. The houses are so fat and self-satisfied-looking, coming up out of the night. They say so much and so little. There is a terrible price being paid to the stupidity of capitalism.

I was cheered by the receipt of a letter from a working man enclosed. I wrote him.[2]

I have been very very hungry for Eleanor.

1. A translation of Honoré de Balzac, "Un Drame au bord de la mer," set in 1823 and published in 1834; Anderson owned Balzac's *Droll Stories* (New York, [1930]).

2. From a Seattle, Wash., admirer of *Perhaps Women* (New York, 1931) who had written to compliment and corroborate Anderson's description and analysis of factory work.

Sunday, February 7, Marion, Virginia

There is a queer and unnatural dread of Sunday in me. It is Sunday in the small town. Perhaps I do not understand the churches. They are not religious organizations and should not be taken so.

However, the service is confused with religion in people's minds. To live in a small town and not to go to church is to be really outside the life of the town.

In bed I thought of Eleanor, the one time in our experience when she was most disappointed in me. She was hurt, offended. She said nothing. She went and did me a little kindness.

It is a bright, clear, cold morning. I awoke at six and read Balzac's story "Don Juan, or The Elixir of Long Life"—a horror story.[1] I slept again and dreamed of driving a team of fine horses along a paved road.

After coffee I went to the drug store, to sit there while my bed was being made and my room swept.

A woman drove up in a car, her small son with her. She was angry and spoke harshly to the son. I thought—in how many houses of the town do men and women wake up and quarrel on Sunday mornings? They speak harshly to the children. The children must get into starched clothes. They go off to Sunday school, still quarreling.

There are odd things about the service. The other night I went to see a man and woman married at the Presbyterian church. He said, during the ceremony, that he hoped they would live as faithfully to each other as Isaac and Rebecca. That would give the man at least plenty of leeway.

The Presbyterian preacher here has as ugly a voice as I ever heard come from a human throat.

Why do I hate preachers while, at the same time, I pity them? The shiny head of the Lutheran preacher—a kind of hesitating smugness, cultivation of the rich—

An almost entire lack of any facing of the real problems of human life.

Mouthing forever about Isaac and Rebecca and Jonah and other old cunning Jews.

They claiming to be God's chosen people. At the same time these people hating the Jews. What a confusion.

Edwin Seaver—the undertaker—came into the drug store. I thought of his hands pumping embalming fluid into dead bodies. He began to tell how he happened to be a Presbyterian. He was a Methodist and a Democrat who married a Presbyterian and a Republican. He made a deal with his wife. "You be a Democrat and I'll be a Presbyterian—a swap." He seemed content with his bargain. He is in business with his father who remains a Methodist. That way they get corpses out of both congregations.[2]

God give me pleasanter thoughts.
Of the people of an imaginary small town who had learned really to worship.

We live in such a lovely country here. We should return to land worship, river, tree and hill worship. I imagine all the people of a town going in procession, say on a rainy Sunday.
There would be the rain falling on them. Sweet rain. It makes food grow.
The sweetness of winds on cheeks realized . . . the goodness of the sun.
Special days when all went into the fields, in the plowing time, in the seeding time, in the harvest.
Wine under trees, love, games, laughter.
It's ours while we live, the land, the rivers, trees, the skies, the rain and the sunshine. An embrace of love with nature—God in the background. God would be quite willing to stay hidden away seeing people really worshipping in nature.

1. A translation of Honoré de Balzac, "L'Elixir de longue vie," set in the sixteenth century and published in 1830.
2. W. C. Seaver and Sons, undertakers, a long-established institution in Marion.

Monday, February 8, Marion, Virginia

I had got into a dread of my room at night. There were several restless nights. Two or three of my nights of faces came. The faces snapping suddenly into place before my eyes, looking into my eyes accusing, pleading, smiling. The face stays a moment and then goes and is replaced by another.

I have thought they are faces of people I have seen some time, people who want understanding, who want their story told. Such nights of faces are often a prelude to a sleepless time.

I was with Burt in the woods, saw a piece of river I had not seen before, back of the Max Snider place. Max came out, a little drawn, thin, clean farmer. His farm house nestles nicely against the woods in some open fields. He seems a generous kindly man but when Mazie and I went into his woods for mushrooms he went and told Mazie's father—thinking we were doing an immoral thing. Mr. Copenhaver thought it was Eleanor and myself.

That day it rained and Mazie had on a thin summer dress. The rain made it cling to her figure. When we came out of the woods her whole figure was sharply outlined. She said, laughing, "After this you should marry me."

"I'll marry your sister," I said.

The old farmer came out to bring us some apples. Perhaps he also wanted to see Mazie's fine figure.

Burt believes, as I do, that democracy will fail and has failed. He is afraid of revolution, does not trust people. He believes in a governing class. He says, with justice, "You are one of the kind who would stir people up to revolution but, if something new had to be put into execution, I am the sort of man who would be given the job."

We walked along a little bluff along the river, the river greenish-blue, running swiftly—a sense of determined power in it. The sun shone. In the woods it was very silent. We saw no birds, no rabbits.

In the evening Mrs. Copenhaver and I talked. I told of the strange life and death of my sister Stella and she told of the time when she, her husband and children had family worship every day.[1]

They went into a room and knelt by chairs and Mr. Copenhaver prayed or read from the Bible. He was one of the long-winded kind of prayers.

Later they gave up formal family worship and he prayed at table. Still he prayed too long. "He occupied too much the stage," Mrs. Copenhaver said laughing, "so I thought up a scheme."

She did not want to take over the praying herself so she had each child recite, at one meal a day, some verse from the Bible. Eleanor was best at it. Randolph knew but one verse. "And Jesus wept," he said. He said it every day, solemnly. He fairly flooded Jesus out in tears and so the whole thing was finally dropped.[2]

1. The sad life of Anderson's sister Stella (1875–1917) is discussed in White, ed., *Sherwood Anderson's Memoirs,* 103–109.

2. Randolph Copenhaver (1902–82), only brother of Eleanor Copenhaver, was then a medical student at the University of Virginia and later a physician with the United States military.

Tuesday, February 9, Marion, Virginia
To Laura Lu Copenhaver

Dear Friend . . .

I spent the night, when I wasn't sleeping, trying to define in my mind my own attitude toward the locust swarm of liberalism that alighted on our town yesterday.

Perhaps Women.

As you may have guessed my own feeling is that this particular parade has back of it the pushing power of a determined woman. What is she up to?

There is the picture, Charles Walker and his wife . . . New England . . . inherited wealth. There are plenty of people, born wealthy, who do not want to stay in their own class. Society bores them. Most American society nowdays is very like what Mazie found when she did society here in Marion. It isn't different. It's bridge and running about to resorts and drinking, etc. Women are not likely to find the best sort of men there. American men, with anything to them, do not go in for society.

The truth is that men and women are pretty far apart in modern society. Women go in for encouraging men to go ahead and make money. Then, if the man does it, the woman despises him for doing it.

A woman, such as we are talking about, our Adelaide, does not, after all, follow Christ's pronouncement, "Sell all you have and give to the poor." She mighty well doesn't become a coal miner's wife. She marries a man.

What of him? He is one like herself. He is a rich man's son, tired of the rich. He isn't strong. One summer he goes to work in a steel mill. He said to me, yesterday, something to the effect that a crowd of working men in a room were such splendid fellows, etc. I was amused. Edmund Wilson overheard that. I saw him wince. He should go down around the lower drug store at noon when the Lincoln employees are sitting about during the noon hour.[1] Any decent crowd of working men I ever worked among, being told they were specially splendid fellows, etc., etc., would laugh too. They would do more than laugh. "Ah rot," they'd say. Well, something much stronger.

Might as well say you and I and Mr. Copenhaver are splendid. We are? God knows we are not. There you are.

You say, Bob says, everyone says that you cannot do anything without organization. You must have such pushers as Adelaide. I guess I'm pretty primitive. I want to hitch fair Adelaide to a plow, plow with her a piece of stony ground, where the plow keeps jumping out of the ground . . . the collar galling her shoulders, every time she winces me hitting her across the flanks with a whip. "Gittup there, Adelaide. We got to get this field plowed."

The organization of the church becomes so important that what Christ said and thought is pretty much forgotten. People say, "It's the best there is." If it is then some people have got to stand aside. "I won't take the second best. I won't let the words of some preacher confuse me about Christ. I may have a better mind than he has." It sounds egotistical and terrible. Maybe it is.

This is a big middle-class country. Ideals are middle-class. We started that way. Our society was pretty much built upon the idea that every man here had the chance of becoming comfortably well off, a little better off than most of his neighbors. Most working men still cling to that ideal. Such a one says, "If I can't make it perhaps some of my sons can," etc. You get accumulation, the chance of rising above someone else as an ideal of a whole society. That's about where the western world is. We should remember that Christ was of the East, not the West. The East can still conceive of a society not primarily based on goods, on possessions.

The breaking down of the capitalistic system, if it does break down (and I think Marx was essentially right, it will fall of its own weight eventually) will, if it amounts to anything, sweep everything out from under the feet of the present. We will be thrown back. I myself, at my best, believe, not in saving money as I earn it, but in spending it. Why? Because money accumulated makes a coward of me. If I have to struggle to the very end then I have a chance at least of being alive to the very end.

To return to the working man and woman. I think the only right way to look at them is to think of them as people who have lost out in the modern competitive game. The way to do is to think of yourself and Mr. Copenhaver and Eleanor and myself and Mazie and Channing, not as what we are . . . rather lucky on the whole by the grace of God. . . . I've got this quiet room, nice clothes. Someone brings me my breakfast here.

A slight, a very slight shift . . . we are all coal miners and coal miners' wives. I honor my mother and father. If such a delegation as was here, yesterday, had come to our house, when I was a child, had driven up there with a truck . . . perhaps some speeches made . . . they telling us grouped about that we were specially noble people . . . the future was in our hands . . . "therefore this food that you may eat," a movie man standing near watching mother take a loaf of bread. . . .

You've got to get it that way. There isn't any other way. They say, like the book publishers, "You got to get publicity." Why didn't Christ advertise? He should have had him an advertising agency.

The noble Sherwood Anderson, going in a truck, with a movie man, to take his mother Emma Smith Anderson a loaf of bread.

I saw a piece in a paper where some preacher said, "You've got to sell religion like you sell chewing gum." And not only that but his saying it didn't shock anyone much.

I tell you the revolution has got to be deep, deep. I don't know whether we can face it. I honor my own mother. She would have taken a loaf of bread for her children if you had brought it secretly at night, as an equal, one who happened to be luckier than she was. If you had brought it in a truck, under the auspices of *The New Republic*, camera men, etc., she'd have thrown it in your face.

1. Edmund Wilson (1895–1972), Marxist social critic and political activist; the Virginia Lincoln Factory, manufacturer of dining room and bedroom furniture, one of the largest employers in Marion, Va. The social reformers were in Marion to try to convince Anderson to join in their planned demonstrations in Harlan, Ky.

Wednesday, February 10, Marion, Virginia

Warm for winter—grey and cloudy. There are warm streaks across the grey. At the horizon it is heavy and somber.

Yesterday I failed to write. The words would not sing together. There was no march to the sentences.

Went to Mrs. Copenhaver and made rather gusty sentences about the hand-hooked rugs, for her catalog, which she put down.[1] Mr. Copenhaver lay about groaning with a cold. Went and had my tooth fixed. I have reduced three inches about the waist by morning exercises. Have to have my clothes readjusted.

Walked with Jerry Gordon in the evening and he told me the story of his trip here from New Orleans. I recommended he write it but he probably can't. I may do it . . . if Red doesn't go along.[2] The whole picture is nice—the naive and fine attitude toward the world and people, the tramps—the fast freight, the typewriting machine . . . his own awkwardness in getting off the train . . . the camp of the tramp . . . Negro and whites—the young salesmen who sneaked him into hotels . . . the man with syphilis.

His joy in bed . . . the books. . . .

Went home thinking of French style in prose. This has come from reading Balzac and others. Thinking—they are too sophisticated for it.

All human events become slightly unimportant—even the revolution, Napoleon, Waterloo, etc. They get outside of it too much.

There is always a slight smack of superiority. Cabell of Richmond has tried to do it in America.

It all fades into nothingness beside a prose master like Turgenev. I have done better prose myself, more earthy than any Frenchman has done.

Read Turgenev—*Annals of a Sportsman*—the group of boys pasturing their horse for the night by a stream.[3]

All the night stillness and wonder—the sight, the sounds, smells, the very taste of night. No smart Frenchman could have done that.

1. Laura Lu Copenhaver founded and operated, from her home in Marion, Rosemont Crafts Industries, a company that bought and marketed locally made handcrafts such as bed quilts.

2. Gerald Gordon, Marion resident who had worked in the Anderson printshop; "Red" Oliver, hero of the novel *Beyond Desire*, which Anderson was writing in 1932.

3. Anderson was always fascinated by *Annals of a Sportsman* (known also as *A Sportsman's Sketches*) by the Russian Ivan Turgenev (1818–83); the section noted is "Byézhin Meadow." Anderson owned *A Sportsman's Sketches*, trans. Constance Garnett (New York, 1920).

Thursday, February 11, Marion, Virginia (I)

A furor in the printshop this morning. It will end by Bob's firing both Joe and Gil Stephenson.[1] He probably should. They are Bourbons—incredibly stupid. In these times Bob has maintained their wages at a high scale. Joe is a former KKK man and his father is of the same stripe.

Bob has now got a good printer in the job department and they are furiously jealous. They have both been running about town making nasty comments about the crowd who stopped here on the way to Harlan. I am about to come to the conclusion that, as Joe is so high and mighty about the unemployed—calling all who help them Bolsheviks, etc.—he had better be given a dose of unemployment himself.

Old Gil's got plenty of money. Bob could so easily get men in there who would make his own life more decent.

1. Gil and Joe Stephenson, father and son who had worked for Anderson in the printshop of the two county newspapers that he bought late in 1927.

Thursday, February 11, Roanoke, Virginia (II)

Drove to Roanoke. Getting angry with the man in the shop. Joe Stephenson—the little Bourbon—lower-middle-class, spoiled my morning's work.

I went to Mrs. Copenhaver and talked, rather excitedly, saying that I believed more and more in communism because I had ceased to believe in democracy.

I mean only by communism the growth of a governing class. Let it begin with the proletariat. They, having nothing, would be most likely, while in power, to destroy privileges, the rights of property, etc. Take away the right to speculate in shares, etc., or to profit from increased land values, etc.

The right of revolution must always be held most sacred of all rights.

Let a man prove, not by property, not by just being born and growing to a certain age, but by absolute proof, through altruistic service performed, his right to vote—within his party.

Let the party rule.

If you want to know what democracy is you should run, say for a small county office in this country. You will be insulted. You will be patronized unbelievably.

You say that man needs the incentive of money earned, accumulated. There is something in that. We need perhaps a few luxurious lives.

Let a man earn money—accumulate it—by his force and shrewdness. For example the party, the men who have proven their manhood, enough to be allowed to be of the party, must choose a leader.

Pay him a big salary. Why not? When he dies let all he has accumulated go back to the state. Do not let him leave it or by any subterfuge give it to his children.

Let every man know that, whatever happens, he will eat, he will have food, clothes and shelter.

I left Mrs. Copenhaver and, thinking these thoughts, drove here to Roanoke. For some reason, perhaps because I was excited, I drove furiously. I kept drinking whiskey out of a bottle. I arrived in Roanoke exhausted, wanting my woman very much, feeling myself a good deal of a fool. I am reading Philip Guedalla's life of the Duke of Wellington—not too sympathetically.[1] I do not too much like the tone.

I slept hard enough—when I did sleep—but got up stale. I was lustful in the night. I am here to have my eyes remeasured and to meet Eleanor and drive her home to Marion.

1. Philip Guedalla, *Wellington* (New York, 1931); Anderson also owned Guedalla's *The Second Empire* (New York, 1922).

Friday, February 12, Marion, Virginia

A dead day in Roanoke yesterday. I just had life to write my notes. I sat in the hotel room over there reading the life of the Duke of Wellington.

I felt the splendor of his old age. That is to be the test for me now, whether or not I can bring any splendor into age.

I set myself in the morning. I have begun doing exercises when I awaken. I never do sleep heavily. Often I awaken weary from much dreaming, disillusioned too.

I jump out of bed and go through certain exercises. This to have physical activity. I cry to myself, "Money come up. Money come up."

Crying to some slightly tired thing in myself.

"Another day. Up. At it," etc.

It's the only way I know to avoid the day-long slump, week- or month-long slump. I've been through these.

Eleanor was lovely. There was a flame in her. I had got some lovely flowers from Fallon the florist, at Roanoke, who refused to take any pay for them.[1] I was glad. Eleanor was a proud flower.

We went down by a little town, on a side road, where there is a little waterfall on the Roanoke River, near the town of Lafayette, Virginia, a tiny town, nice in the evening light. There was an open space by the river and the fall and we parked the car in there. Eleanor, if she ever reads this, will remember the evening, white house against dim distant hills—such as Charles Bockler would have liked. There were cars moving along a road across the face of distant hills.

Good life. Life was good there.

We saw the light fade. I saw the woman, being beautiful.

Afterward we went on to Pulaski where we dined at the hotel and Eleanor phoned her mother. I was suddenly absurd about signing my name to a dinner ticket. Eleanor was more beautiful than I had ever seen her.

1. Frank Fallon, florist of Roanoke, Va., who was a continuing friend to Anderson.

Saturday, February 13, Marion, Virginia

A queer feverish day. I became, as I often do, too personal. The day passed in a sort of foolish explosion . . . myself thinking of the difficulty of working . . . wearing myself out thus, rather than in work.

Waldo Frank has been beaten up, going with other writers to take food in to the striking miners at Harlan, Kentucky.[1] I was myself asked to go. I made the excuse I was working. I wrote about all this some days ago. Was I letting myself out then?

Is it my duty to participate, actively?

Am I afraid of being killed? Yes.

Am I afraid of being beaten? Yes.

I am afraid of being beaten because there is something I cling to. I cannot give up the notion that goodness is a part of every man as well as evil.

If I became an active participant in a war. . . . I think there must inevitably be a long terrible war in the world between those who have and won't give up and those who have not and can't get.

Some kind of clear-headed leadership in thought must come or our civilization must perish.

I have come to believe now in the failure of democracy, founded as ours is on capitalism. No one really defends capitalism. We have got that far. Democracy is defended but it is forgotten in America that, under democracy, capitalism has grown constantly stronger rather than weaker.

This terrible constant appeal to the mob. It is like a work of art that can be so easily perverted from its true flow . . . I mean the appeal back from capitalism to democracy.

Is democracy—as an idea—then sacred? No, it must go. It has already gone. There is no American democracy. America is already controlled by a small group of men.

Controlled without altruism, with no hope—by entirely cynical men.

The spirit is out of the masses.

1. Waldo Frank (1889–1967), novelist and social observer who had known Anderson since publishing some of his earliest stories in 1916.

Sunday, February 14, Marion, Virginia

Sunday morning—cold and grey. I slept late, having stayed with Eleanor until nearly twelve. She had on a new long red silk dress. She was very beautiful.

Her father sat heavily and grumpily in his chair. He was trying to get his Sunday school lesson. Some voice was coming over the radio—a preachy voice trying to explain the Sunday school lesson.

It was a sockdollager.

The lesson concerned a day when Christ was restoring sight to a man born blind. Someone asked why, if God managed everything, he had let the poor man be born blind.

Never to see the trees, the flight of clouds, the grass, the form of a woman loved, as I love Eleanor.

Christ, it seems, answered that it was done so that the glory of God might be made manifest.

A pretty lame answer. Is God so shabby, so empty of invention, to make his glory manifest, as all that?

The grumpy old man spoiled the dinner in order to get the preacher's lame excuse. He came grumpily to table and repeated, from some newspaper account, the charge that the writers, Waldo Frank and others, had gone into Harlan to get publicity for themselves.

I kept thinking of my own father—a rascal—not providing for his family—drinking—always chasing women—how magnificently courteous he was to anyone coming into our poor house.[1]

With what a flourish he would have received Eleanor, how sharply and quickly he would have seen her beauty.

She might have come a thousand times. It would have been the same.

The virtues of B. E. have become the virtues of a heavy peasant. His wife has been too much for him. The house got nicer after he left. It always does.

Eleanor was very strange, very lovely and womanly. All evening beauty hung over her as perfume over a flower. I could have gone onto my knees to her beauty.

1. Irwin McLain Anderson (1845–1919), whose life is colorfully if not accurately described in the early chapters of White, ed., *Sherwood Anderson's Memoirs*.

Monday, February 15, Marion, Virginia

There is always something nice about Monday—the beginning of the week. It wasn't so when I worked in a factory. Then Sunday had some meaning—a day of rest. Now I am glad to escape the small town Sunday atmosphere—the people marching to church—the artificiality of modern worship.

The conviction growing and growing that money—capitalism—is at the bottom of it all.

Eleanor and I read young Calhoun's book. He is very sound on many things but when he talks of art he is a fool.[1]

I took a new painting, one of my lot, to Burt Dickinson and one to Mrs. Copenhaver.[2] Eleanor and I took a drive out the

Walker Creek road and turned into a new road, coming back by Lincoln Hill. She was very beautiful all day. She had got a little cold and there were some spots on her body. We got out of the car and we went into a wood. Two dogs came and acted rather savage but presently they left. We stood on a little knoll and I made her take breathing exercises to expand her lungs.

It is a grey, chilly morning with rain threatening.

I just want you to know, dearest, how very beautiful you were last night. I had never seen you quite like that. You were more beautiful than I had ever seen you. It hung over you, all evening, like a perfume.

When you are like that it arouses the finer male in me. I feel a new manliness, a new strength.

You must forgive me that I do not understand many things your father does. We are of two different races, as far apart as the poles.

I think of sturdy, Germanic, somewhat rude virtues. I belong, by nature, to a different, more ragtag, irresponsible race myself.

To us the little moment is everything.

When I come into a room, as you know, I live tremendously in everyone in the room. "Be aware. Be aware. Be aware," voices cry in me.

To miss one moment of your own beauty—not to be all aware when it came swiftly fluttering to you—would be to me the last sacrilege.

Your father will remain, I'm afraid, outside my understanding. I promise to be nice. I'll quit speaking of it.

If you take me, as your man, you can count on one thing—I'll catch every little shade of beauty and meaning as it passes through you. I'll even know your thoughts. There'll be a lot of the sturdier virtues I won't ever have.

We'll have anyway many gorgeous moments as we have had.

In spite of my being half wrecked like that, early in the evening, your own beauty quite cured me. You are my healer. You always cure me.

1. Probably Arthur Wallace Calhoun, *Social Universe* (New York, 1932), although this writer was not then a "young Calhoun."

2. Anderson, who occasionally painted, enjoyed at least two solo exhibitions: at the Radical Book Shop in Chicago in 1920 and at the Sunwise Turn gal-

lery in New York City in 1921. He apparently gave some of his paintings to Marion friends and sold others through Laura Lu Copenhaver's Rosemont Crafts Industries.

Tuesday, February 16, Marion, Virginia

Reading Ford Ford's book—*Return to Yesterday*—much about writers. There is a certain tone to Henry James. It fits.[1]

I have something to do this morning. If James had it to do he would write, "I must go get poor dear Elizabeth's dishes shipped," etc.

The only writer in this country I know of who has had that tone is James Branch Cabell. He also would gossip and putter on and patronize others in just that tone—particularly would he patronize women—being, as I am sure James was—on the queer side.

Little airy fairies in big hulking frames. "Poor dear this and poor dear that."

"Etc., as they say," as Dreiser would say.

There is this about Dreiser. You can depend on him. You want an example of a bad awkward graceless sentence and you go to him. You open a book, any of his books. There it is.

And I would not trade him for an even two dozen of the Jameses and the Cabells, for manliness and real power.

It is a grey morning. Thinking of Henry James and his butler, flourishing a knife, had tricked my mind away to Mrs. Copenhaver's girl Viola.[2]

Sturdy, with strong legs. Goodness. I can hear Eleanor's voice on the stairs talking to her. Viola is telling about the affairs of her family, her sister Flora, Flora's husband, a house painter who is no good, the baby, the baby's dresses.

Viola has them all under her broad goodness and they treat her badly. She seems to lose out with men while the thin-flanked, loose-lipped servant girls run off with them.

Trying to think of a world without servants. Why should I? To be a servant would be something too.

In certain moods I think of myself as servant, perhaps to a beautiful woman or a man of parts. I could do it, nicely, I'm quite sure.

It would be the same as being a priest, being thus under the protection of someone. It would be dreadful if you had no respect for the one loved.

Eleanor did something lovely for me and I let her.

It is one of the still mornings when all sounds are terribly accentuated. I can hear the footsteps of men and children on neighboring streets, cocks crowing far off, the voices of people talking in the yards of distant houses.

1. Ford Madox Ford, *Return to Yesterday* (New York, 1932); Anderson never cared for the sophisticated fiction written by Henry James (1843–1916).

2. Viola, a black serving-woman at Rosemont, the Copenhaver home in Marion, Va.

Wednesday, February 17, Marion, Virginia (I)

I have decided early to let this be a disorganized day. I went to Funk's and got wine, for my lunch. I have fruit and Swedish bread and wine—very good—at my desk here.

I feel frivolous.

I got my photo taken for [my] passport.

Mrs. Copenhaver and I got into an exciting discussion about my right to call a bastard a bastard. I had been lighting into the Methodist preacher for preaching a cheap sensational sermon.

I dreamed of Einstein and Mazie Copenhaver. Communism had come and Mazie was [a] waterboy carrying water for men working on a railroad. Dreamed of driving Eleanor in a car in a dangerous crowded place and of being on a freight train beating my way, my companion a tall fine-looking Negress. She wanted to fuck. There wasn't any place. I dare say I would have done it had there been a place.

When I went to call in the evening, Eleanor was heavy and sleepy. She did not get beautiful. Neither did I. She was nice.

In bed I began thinking of her father. He can hear, evidently with pleasure, the finest music. In a moment, afterwards, he can hear, evidently with equal pleasure, the most vulgar music.

He and other men, here in town, go weekly to Kiwanis. How patiently they stand their own mutual performances. Mr. Copenhaver loves to make speeches. He is better than most of them. There is all kind of childish horseplay. They are like rather dull ten year old boys. A sensitive man would presently kill himself.

Mr. Copenhaver talked in the evening of various kinds of trees and of wood. He talked of a fine old log barn his grandfather built. He was nice. Many men are nicest when talking of boyhood.

Dined with Mary and Bob.[1]

She goes too much in pajamas. I do not like to be taken, too much, as a familiar. I like a little fuss made about my coming anywhere to dinner.

The day is grey, wet and cold. I feel frivolous. I'll not be able to work much today.

An evidence of my frivolity I record here. I have recently quit altogether wiping my ass after shitting with toilet paper. It is unsatisfactory. I always have a feeling the stain of the shit remains. I used to find the stains on my underwear. I lay my ass over the washstand and go at it with soap and water. It is much more satisfactory.

1. Here one sentence is omitted by the editor to avoid possible family embarrassment.

Wednesday, February 17, Marion, Virginia (II)

The sun streaming into my room. It a cold clear exhilarating day outside. The day yesterday was too emotional. I was hurt, wounded all day.

I couldn't work. I rode about in my car.

In a barnyard were several rather bedraggled hens. There were two cocks. One got aboard a hen and the other cock came running. He tried to tread the same hen after the first one had finished her. There were other hens but he kept following that one. He seemed to be pleading with her. "You let him. Now let me. I want to feel I am as good as he is."

The divorce papers. The little lies one tells . . . trying to separate—to join again—to make a final joining.

That life may flow through a woman into you as well as directly from life into you.

Reading Mabel Dodge to Jeffers on Lawrence—not liking her so much.[1]

Getting always something—as you do get in everything Lawrence touches, or touching him.

In the evening and this morning, after the exhaustion passed, a good deal of love in me.

1. Much of Anderson's information about D. H. Lawrence came from *Lorenzo in Taos* (New York, 1932), by Mabel Dodge Luhan (1879–1962); he had reviewed Lawrence's *Assorted Articles* (New York, 1930), in "A Man's Mind," *New Republic*, LXIII (May, 1930), 22–23.

Thursday, February 18, Marion, Virginia (I)

I am writing in the late afternoon. It has been a miserable day of failure. The day was cold and clear. All day I felt separated from all life. I was a thing standing alone, unsupported, not in essence nice.

I got out of bed feeling all alive, having been dreaming of D. H. Lawrence. I was with him in a factory. He was nice in there. He felt as I felt. "The possibility of something we all seek, that is communal, is here," he said. He didn't say it like that. He used words more freely, threw himself more into saying it.

I wrote to Eleanor of what happened last night. If she ever sees this she will remember our standing in the dark, in the dining room. I wonder if she will remember the blue dish. I pushed it along the top of a shelf.

I got at something, a little, trying to write what I felt, to Eleanor.

Today I found her sitting on a couch. I was heavy and stodgy. She knew it.

There was no life in me. I kept myself apart. I have been apart all day.

Inside myself I was swearing at myself. "You bastard. You son of a bitch."

I wanted to punish myself.

I am so unmanly at times.

The skies tonight are very lovely. There is a clear wonderful light.

I want to give and give and I do not give.

Thursday, February 18, Marion, Virginia (II)

Dearest Darling Woman,

I am writing this on a grey rainy day in Marion. It concerns your marrying me. I have a feeling that you have still dreadful times of doubt.

We have been to each other what we have been, these last two years. It has been very wonderful to me, lifting me up out of my desperate despondency, the state I was in when I began to love you.

I do not blame you for your doubt. My record is pretty black. I have no way of knowing whether it has been the fault of the women or myself. I can't think clearly about it.[1]

I am pretty sure, most of the time, that the dominant thing in me has not been evil. I can't be sure.

There have been gorgeous moments, gorgeous lovely days. Since you have loved me a little I have done "Mill Girls," "Loom Dance," "Elizabethton," "Danville," the Dreiser and now a great deal of this new book.[2]

It has been a breathing time. You have taken the deadly fear out of me. Life isn't at best very long.

I want you to feel free. It is your life as well as mine.

Obviously—I guess—life with me isn't very easy. I'm not very stationary. I change constantly, run forward, stand still, have moments of courage, dreadful times of doubt.

If you decide against it, dearest one, I swear I will not feel that you have, in any way, led me on. You have always given more than you took. If that happens I'll probably go on being faithful to you in my own way.

I swear I'm not going to spoil your life . . . if I haven't and I don't believe I have. You'll pick it up again where you were when I came hungering to you.

I'll not hang around. I'll not do anything heroic but I can go off to Europe, try to absorb myself in this new factory thing. . . . I want to return to that as soon as I have this book out of the way.

I want to go to factories in Russia, Germany, France and England. I am pretty sure I can sell the notion to some American magazine.

If you decide to be my wife and come with me I believe you can do a lot, getting the slant of the women, helping me in that.

I think there isn't any doubt that you too—this year—not through your own fault—have been carried away from the workers. I myself believe it was intended—to take the sting out of your work.

I would like to have the feeling that if we take a chance to-gether . . . it comes to that . . . we will at the same time and with-out any unnecessary sentimentality—that we will also decide at the same time that we will go the limit, put up with what we have to put up with to get this factory story.

Anything we can do will not be very showy or obvious.

I fancy us being, as far as we can be, impersonal observers . . . trying not to do any grandstand thing, trying to get the story.

It's a good shot, for what years I have left in me of good work.

I think you should bear in mind how much of all that may have been good in my work, these last three years, has been due to you.

But I want to leave you free. I don't think you ought to sentimentalize about me. I think you ought to make your own program.

Having you in my arms, the chance of having you in my arms, coming to you when I am defeated and tired . . . it's lovely. It isn't the test. I know that.

If you do it I want you please to do it only for yourself, because it seems to you the best way of life for yourself, a shot worth taking.

I say this again because I want to impress it on you. I want you to know I mean it. In weak moments I would be coming to you, quite helpless, begging, a child, but thank God that isn't all of me. As they say in the prize ring a man isn't any good unless he can "take it."

1. Anderson's previous marriages were with Cornelia Lane (1904–16); Ten-nessee Mitchell (1916–24); and Elizabeth Prall (1924–32).

2. "Mill Girls," *Scribner's,* XCII (January, 1932), 8–12, 59–64; "Loom Dance," *New Republic,* LXII (April 30, 1930), 292–94; "Elizabethton," *Nation,* CXXVIII (May 1, 1929), 526–27; "Danville, Virginia," *New Republic,* LXV (Janu-ary 21, 1931), 266–68. The Dreiser essay was "Let's Have More Criminal Syn-dicalism," *New Masses,* VII (February, 1932), 3–6; "this new book" was the on-going novel *Beyond Desire.*

Friday, February 19, Marion, Virginia

Finishing 19th. Really morning of the [20]th . . . rain in the night, heavy stupid sleep.

I thought, as I lay in bed, "I'll be ill. I'll be no good."

I don't know whether the boy Red is going to "come" or not. It would be so nice for him to tramp straight forward, across that bridge and die. I may get the feel of it and him and—why yet I don't know.

I've forced too much—been too much the author.

I don't know what I'd do these days if it weren't for Eleanor. I don't give her much. I suppose I'm trying to get a second being, myself and something that I get in her and from her and that is myself and certainly not myself as I am this broken morning.

Saturday, February 20, Winston-Salem, North Carolina

This is stolen stationery. I am in Winston-Salem, N.C., where I came to bring Eleanor. If she ever sees this she will remember the lunch under the laurels—the thick leaves.

Then the hurried drive to Mt. Airy.

The grey day—the excitement.

I have had a futile day of work. It hasn't come off. I worked all morning furiously—then walked. Got into a market street. The people were to me—for the day—all hard, separated things just living . . . so many of them obviously quite miserably.

There seemed a strange deadness and apartness in the people.

I went to the floor of a tobacco warehouse but there was no tobacco being sold today.

A patent medicine fakir had set himself up in there—a rather fat man, of perhaps fifty. He had hired Negroes who played and danced for him. I stood looking.

Thirty years of that . . . the man said to the crowd that he had spent thirty years selling medicine like that . . . cheap little tricking of the people year after year, for thirty years. The idea made me a little ill.

A voice in me questioning, "Does he care? Does anyone care? Will anyone ever care?"

I couldn't stand it. I came away. I can't see Eleanor today. Perhaps I can see her a few minutes tonight. I'm sick with loneliness and a sense of futility.

Sunday, February 21, Winston-Salem, North Carolina

A soft summer rain. Eleanor is here although I have not seen her all day. She is busy with her own work.

I saw her late last night. We drove in the soft moonlight. She was very tired and had a headache. She curled up in a little ball with her head on my shoulder. We were near being run down by a train, in crossing a railroad track.

I had worked all day and again, at the end, had torn up all I had done. I have decided I will for a time leave the end of the novel alone. The day for writing it will come. I slept heavily, even stupidly . . . too stupidly. In a dream I heard a voice praising my story "Mill Girls."

Eleanor and I sat in the car, somewhere, on what seemed a wide treeless, houseless plain near Winston—in N.C. It must have been a yellow sand country. In the moonlight the sand looked like snow.

I was still drawn off to myself. I could not get near anyone—even Eleanor. I began telling of a crazy moonlit night—told of in Mabel Dodge's book *Lorenzo in Taos*. I was in such a state, the whole world so unreal to me, that my own voice seemed not a part of me.

I wrote a note for Eleanor, saying, "I love you." Did I? She was more real than anything else. Even she was somewhat unreal. Even my clothes seemed unreal.

Monday, February 22, Winston-Salem, North Carolina

It rained all day Sunday. All day I stayed in my room working—with an occasional walk in the steady rain, through the deserted streets of this industrial town. It is a huge tobacco, cigarette town. Many millionaires have been made here—off Camel cigarettes. It is said the government receives $800,000 a day in revenue from this town.

It is a controlled industry. Three or four big firms control it. They send their tobacco buyers out to all the little tobacco buying floors.

The tobacco farmers, after the long year's work, scarcely get enough to live on. Labor is miserably paid.

In the meantime huge meaningless fortunes pile up in the

hands of a few. I walked yesterday past long streets of huge build-ings—like prisons. How dreary they looked in the rain.

A story told by a little mill girl. There is an organization here, composed of the wives of the rich. It is organized for the care of the public health. It was decided by the ladies that they could do nothing in the matter of venereal diseases.

It is perhaps something ladies do not care to think about. These ladies however all have sons. The little mill girl said, "They are always after us. They depend upon picking up girls for that purpose among us workers.

"We ought all to get the clap and give it to them."

I went in the evening to drive Eleanor, after her long hard day's work. She was very tired but glad to be outdoors. She curled up on the car seat again, half asleep. All day she had been talking to working girls.

She is in a tight hole too. Obviously nothing will be done for labor until labor becomes strong and demanding. Every effort of labor in industry has failed. Often labor is sold out by its own leaders.

The workers are discouraged and cynical. Many of the little girls, working in these great cigarette factories, are lovely little things. Many of them have minds. They look up to such women as Eleanor, who has been to college—has studied economics. They keep asking and asking, "What shall I do?"

There is no leadership—nothing to say. Once Eleanor believed in the essential goodness of human beings. "If I could only show the men in power," she thought.

I understand. She feels as I used to feel.

Can a man—an owner or a superintendent of a great fac-tory—walk through the factory day after day unaware?

The weariness, the discouragement, the long hours, the mis-erable pay.

He can. He does. They become as nothing to him presently. They are people outside his comprehension. His mind does a little trick. He hears a girl laugh. "See, they are all happy," he says.

He convinces himself that the power given him has some al-most divine origin. The cruelty of man to man is deep-seated.

Eleanor knows and I know that such people as ourselves are not by nature fighters. Only the fighters can really count now.

If for example Eleanor were to begin distributing communist literature among these people within a few weeks she would be turned out of her work. There would be no more opportunity given her to come among these poor girls, doing what she can to make their lives a bit more real. She can't do much.

Tuesday, February 23, Winston-Salem, North Carolina

Yesterday, all day, my depression continued. I could not write. No feeling came into me. I had gone to the one bookstore I could find in the town and there were no books worth reading. I had already got *Scribner's* and the *Nation*. I had read them from cover to cover. In the newsstands there was a great array—detective, mystery, love, movie magazines. At noon I walked among the workers of the great Reynolds tobacco company— "Camels." The streets were crowded with Negro workers at the noon hour. Many women, their lovers present—gigolos, I'm sure, many of them.

The white girl workers do not come out into the streets as do the Negroes, at noon. I liked the soft high voices of the Negro women. They soothed me. I kept walking among them until the noon hour passed.

In the evening late I saw Eleanor, who is working here. We drove to the outer edge of town and parked the car. She was tired but very alive and lovely.

All day she had been with the working girls. She is infinitely nicer always when she has been among them. She tells little revealing things—as that the girls hate working in tobacco.

They say it gives them a bad physical smell. It gets into their hair, the pores of the skin. They run home after work and scrub themselves. They are afraid they will be unattractive to men. How nice.

It is all so human. I am ashamed that I do not write more and constantly of workers. I should spend my life among them.

Wednesday, February 24, Greensboro, North Carolina

Up very early, feeling heavy and futile after a wasted day. I had arranged to take Eleanor in the early morning out of Winston-Salem to the town of Greensboro, where she had work to do. We left Winston-Salem just at daylight.

It was a lovely drive. She sat in the car beside me, in silence, she was drawn into herself. I kept watching her out of the corner of my eye. It is nice sometimes to be thus with another—loved—seeing them far off, lost in their own thoughts.

You cannot connect. It may be you have little to give.

The country drifted past—lovely pastel colors in the eastern sky. We saw the sun come up—red—blood-red. Suddenly she began coming toward me a little in her thoughts and told me of a fear she had been under that had been suddenly blown away that morning.

There was a strike at Greensboro, in the Blue Bell Overall plant, and we went there. The workmen and workwomen were crowded about the plant door and in a nearby vacant lot. We went among them. Eleanor is very quick with life when among workers.

We breakfasted at a nearby working men restaurant, among excited men and women. Presently Eleanor had to leave, to do her work, and I went back to spend the whole morning talking to men and women workers. Heard many tales of long hard days—the relationship between men and tools, etc. There is a curious fineness, a belief in a capitalistic government. I must say I did all I could to disillusion them, wanting to see them more ready for the long and bitter fight they will have to make.

There had been a terrific cut and the employees, unled, had just walked out. The employers had promised, later in the day, to give them some word as to whether or not they could make the cut less severe.

In the afternoon drove Eleanor to Durham and then went off myself to look at Chapel Hill—the state university—and at the new and vulgarly expensive Duke University.

Thursday, February 25, Marion, Virginia

Awoke with a subnormal temperature—feeling dead on my feet. It is due [to] the matter to be settled in court today. It was decided favorably.

But all of this putting of fingers in my poor pie of a life.

It will be good when I leave here—even though I go lecturing.

I spent the day—yesterday—bringing Eleanor home from Durham, N.C. She was tired, after seeing many people. We drove slowly, by a new route—Yanceyville, Reidsville, Mt. Airy, Fancy Gap . . . a land very poor, with poor little log cabins, often beautiful in their simplicity—many of them with only one room. I felt subdued and low in spirits. As we rode along Eleanor was suddenly a young girl, very self-contained, very quiet and beautiful.

Senator Buchanan, the big man of Marion, is dead. It is strange to think of his life, that might have been so fine, essentially wasted.[1]

1. Benjamin Franklin Buchanan, wealthy attorney and businessman of Marion, Va., who had been lieutenant governor of Virginia and who was at his death a member of the Virginia House of Delegates.

Friday, February 26, Marion, Virginia

A gorgeous day. My illness, like so many of my illnesses, was psychic. It was pure nonsense. Eleanor took my temperature and it was subnormal. I grow weak and cannot face the natural consequences of my own sins against life. I want to be reckless and daring. That calls for constantly facing things. I grow weak-hearted. I become ill.

The matter of Elizabeth and myself—settled in the courts. She was at bottom in love not with me and my life but with her own brother and his life.[1] She wanted, poor soul, respectability and safety. She could not have picked a worse man.

I went to see Funk, to drink wine with him in his cellar and talk with him. He explained the trimming of grape vines. The wine was good. We went and sat on the running board of my car and talked of a world in which there would be no great ones, a really communistic life.

Mrs. Copenhaver and Eleanor went riding with me. I dined at Frank's by the railroad tracks and heard the laborers talking of the two brothers, Dave and Frank Buchanan. There would be in it a marvelous story of the Two Brothers . . . showing that in one world the schemer, the trickster, Dave, [was] doing it all for the respectable Frank—Dave the really nice one.[2]

1. Elizabeth Anderson's brother David Prall, who taught philosophy at the University of California.
2. B. Frank Buchanan, recently deceased state legislator, and Dr. David

Buchanan, his brother, retired general practitioner and head of the Smyth County Democratic party. Several pages of an unfinished story called "Two Brothers" survive in the Anderson archive.

Saturday, February 27, Marion, Virginia

This will be Eleanor's last morning here, before the beginning of her California trip.[1] My illness passed quickly yesterday. In the morning I worked.

There was a meeting of school teachers here and a discussion of what kind of literature must be good for children. Mrs. Emmett Sprinkle, a teacher, wife of an automobile salesman, said, "I know one thing they should not read—the books of Sherwood Anderson."

"But who is he?" a stranger asked.

"He is one of our local writers." Mr. Copenhaver was embarrassed.[2]

We went in the afternoon to the mountains, where we had dinner cooked out of doors. I borrowed John's painting of Miss Brickey and have it on my walls.

The day was very beautiful. In the evening Eleanor and I played and tumbled on the floor like kittens. I had drunk two cups of strong coffee and so did not sleep.

1. Eleanor Copenhaver went to San Francisco to take part in labor conferences and to conduct research for writing a report on workingwomen for the YWCA; this work became her master's thesis in political science at Columbia University: "Working Women in San Francisco, California," 1933, directed by Professor Carter Goodrich.

2. B. E. Copenhaver, Eleanor's father, superintendent of schools for Smyth County, Va., since 1901, was sensitive to Sherwood Anderson's local reputation for writing immoral fiction, for having radical ideas, and for having been married three times.

Sunday, February 28, Marion, Virginia

Sunday morning.

Grey, cold and blue—the sky a dirty blue. I hurried up to Eleanor. She was sitting in the window by her father. When I came in he turned at once and turned on the radio. I fled.

The train was late and he went off to Sunday school. I had a chance to go see her again. The whole atmosphere of the house was changed. Eleanor and I danced, we drank coffee.

I ran my car down to Henry Copenhaver's. Uncle Henry and his wife drove down from their house and saw me sitting there. I got out a map and pretended to be studying it.

Eleanor's train came and went—she on the back platform—a gay alive little figure. I was full of tears.

Do I hate her father? No. I hate life that has made him like that ... twelve years old, in his petty insistence on self sometimes. It is a way to assert yourself, to be disagreeable.

Bob came in and invited me to dinner. He bragged about his speech, at Rich Valley High School, was pleased with himself. He had told them—to tell the truth it was all winnowed out of speeches I have made.

I asked him about B. E. "In county politics he's pretty slick," he said. "He gives them the old guff. 'The great thing is cooperation, pulling together,' etc."

Bob says that he told them that the organization of young farmer boys might someday be used as a basis for the farmer's part in an organized society. We were in a new world, etc., and someday the farmer also would have to give up the treasured individuality of the old world, etc.

I let Eleanor, last night—did not intend to—give me, without herself getting.

Is it all illusion that, when we are free, from repression, from fears, I shall be able to give to her, as she now gives?

The evening was spoiled for me by the rudeness of B. E., Eleanor says not directed at me. At any rate I received it, like a blow.

I ate food at the table up there and, at every mouthful, felt that I was eating food to which I was not welcome.

The man sat glum, staring at his empty plate—a great lump apparently of ill-nature. I got it like a blow.

Later I went down into the empty printshop—swore and cried a little. Eleanor must also have been upset. She came through the alleyway in my car and picked me up, going to Piggly-Wiggly, she driving. No fault of hers but pure luck saved us from an ugly smash-up on Main Street. I was full of such a strange mixture of love, anger, resentment and too much self-pity.

Monday, February 29, Marion, Virginia

Was heavy and stupid. Dined with Bob and Mary. I must tell Eleanor the curious story about Bob's refusal to go to New York— and why.

Rode with Funk to see a client. The man and Funk sat on a porch and talked—later by a fence. The man must have been lying. He kept dry-washing his hands nervously.

As regards the conversation—the flow—spoken of by Mabel Dodge—Mrs. Copenhaver speaking of it. There is nothing to be said. The invisible world is peopled by dark terrible ogres. It is peopled by soft singing things. There is no way to tell anyone who does not know. People say, "Be sensible." They may only mean "Make yourself be dull."

Mr. Copenhaver does it for revenge. He is revenging himself because he has not dared meet the challenge given him by his wife.

There were two birds—robins—fighting in a field. I have never seen a more desperate, fierce fight. They seemed wanting to kill each other.

It has become an obsession—my hatred of Sundays here without Eleanor. All the terrible falseness of all modern religious manifestations comes out so plainly.

Religion, in our world, is founded on the egotism that is killing civilization.

I haven't been nice today. Mr. Copenhaver's not being nice last night made me not nice.

Then Eleanor went away. The world has been too empty.

March

Tuesday, March 1, Marion, Virginia

I spent the day trying to say something to Eleanor I thought should be said. The enclosed wasn't sent. B. E. was emphasized too much. It was too much full of self pity.

I have stayed off the novel. I think it will come—when ready.

Yesterday was a bright warm day with birds singing. I spent the entire day in thoughts of Eleanor.

I am however, I feel, getting back on my feet. I'll be O.K. again in a day or two.

The enclosed should be taken, by Eleanor, when she sees it, as a part of my struggle to get clear.

I put yesterday down a wasted day. I was dissatisfied that Eleanor was gone, realizing the blank fully, sore at her father, sore at myself, sore at her. I was in a bad egocentric state all day. I put these [notes] away as a sample of how much I can get wrought up. They will amuse or interest Eleanor someday.

Monday Evening

Darling—

I spent the entire morning, writing to you a letter I will not send. I'll put it in the daily journal envelope and you can see it someday. It tried to state a certain thing I feel about us and that I have not got clearly stated. The letter I wrote this morning was too much concerned with your father.

I have perhaps overemphasized the import of his brusqueness. He probably doesn't much like or dislike me. He wishes perhaps I hadn't appeared. Well, I have.

There is however something else, dear. You said once, "When I marry you I'll explain that you swept me off my feet."

I think you know, dear, that, to many of your friends, I have experimented with other women [and] now I want to experiment with you. I can't quite, dear, let you out on that.

As a matter of simple fact, dear one, you are not a woman to be swept off your feet. I don't believe it can be done. If you take me, and I believe now you will, it will be because you want me and the life with me.

Dear, I want you to put it that way, to Lucy, Lois, your father—all of them.[1] I want you actually to take full responsibility for your judgment about it. It's rather necessary—just because, by all their standards, I shouldn't have you.

You are uncertain about it and have said it is because you are unsure that it is the best thing for me. I think you are honest in saying that but I also think, dearest, that it is a matter that might better be left to me.

I haven't exactly rushed into it with you. I know what I am doing.

There is an inclination in you, dearest, to avoid saying anything you think will hurt or upset people. Your inclination is to say nothing, avoid any open statement. Well, my dear, I think, as regards us, that it would be healthier, better for the future, better for everyone that, if you decide to take me, you let them know, as coming from you, that you are doing it, you know what you are doing, and that in taking a man you are really taking him.

It would at least rather put your lover on his feet. It would make him feel, before your family and all your friends, that you stood shoulder to shoulder with your lover, that all they knew about his past, his mistakes, etc., you knew and that it cut no figure with you.

I think this is rather necessary to marriage. Perhaps I have never really married before. I have got now—very definitely—a notion of what marriage is. There can be times, dear, when, if you marry me, you can ditch me quite as completely by saying nothing as you could by appearing against me. It would be possible and easy to let them think a clever and unscrupulous man had got the best of you and seduced you into marriage against your will, etc.

It wouldn't be true. You are not, in any way, a weak or easily seduced woman. You know it and I know it.

You will know what I mean, dear. There is going to be a question in a lot of minds. When the time comes I don't want you, dear, to leave, in any of their minds, a vestige of doubt that you know what you are doing and that you yourself choose to do it.

I guess it's the difference between a half marriage and a whole one—all the way or half the way.

I went and told your mother how I felt about this. I asked her if she thought it was fair to put it to you in this way.

"Yes, I'd do it," she said.

I also explained to her something of my feeling about your father and she set me straight on that. She said, laughing, what I knew—"Eleanor is solid and square." Then she explained— a woman's mind. There might be something nice about feeling she had been taken by a man—a little against her will and judgment, etc.

Just the same, darling, because of my past, my defeats, I need something else from my woman: When the time comes rather an open standing up with her man. If her friends, her family, anyone doesn't want to take him, as a man, then they needn't expect to take her either.

It's rather necessary although I do not, in any way, deserve it.

Deserving, I guess, has nothing to do with it.

It is all something I have felt, for a long time, I ought to say. It's said. There has been no disloyalty in shirking the issue so far. Now I am, at any rate, an unmarried man. If there has been anything bad about my life I've left uncovered I don't know what it is. I've really tried to make you feel all the things against me. If you come, old dear, I want you to come all the [way]—absolutely. I'm that much of a sport I'd rather love you than not have you that way and so are you.

1. Lucy Carner, Eleanor Copenhaver's supervisor in her work for the Young Women's Christian Association; Lois J. MacDonald, assistant professor of economics at New York University, author of studies of American labor, and longtime apartment mate of Eleanor Copenhaver in New York City.

Wednesday, March 2, Marion, Virginia

The record of these days is too much a record of inability to catch a certain subtle rhythm of life and put it down in the music of prose. Perhaps nowdays it is quite impossible except at rare intervals. There is something in the air, a kind of discord.

The world has to face new problems and is unwilling. Today I talked to Bob Goolsby. He blames everything on what he calls foreigners.[1]

It is the Italians, or the Poles, or the Russians. The South blames the Yankees. I wrote Eleanor about the Jewish clothing merchant who said, "The Russian, socialistic government is all right, better, but the world will not take it."

"Why?"

"Because it is not in style," he said.

There is needed a new mass upsurging of people but it seems a long way off.

I have been for two days in our courts. Saw there no essential effort for real justice. The whole thing has become a game.

Again I have been unable to work. My lover is gone. Perhaps I need terribly and constantly the warm fact of her presence.

1. Robert Goolsby, attorney and real-estate dealer in Marion, Va., who had owned the printshop housing Anderson's two newspapers.

Thursday, March 3, Marion, Virginia

When you have passed fifty-five you must always be prepared, at any moment, to be depressed. You can no longer count on long periods of being at your best. You wait, like a dog at the hole of a rabbit, for good hours, in which a little good work may be done.

The town went fantod. A man and woman, with two friends— evidently all poor people—in a car, and with a small baby, passed along our highway. The Lindbergh baby has been kidnapped.[1] Suddenly everyone decided this was the stolen baby.

There was intense excitement. The sheriff, the mayor and half the town rushed out to a little tourist camp where they had stopped.

On the streets nothing else was discussed. There is a reward of $10,000. Who would get it?

Besides—if it turned out to be true—great publicity for the town. "It would be worth any price," people said. I presume there must be, buried away in people, some feeling also for poor Mrs. Lindbergh but it didn't show much during this excitement.

I went to walk with a lawyer who got into a nice mood, telling of a boyhood love—the love of a very young boy for a girl—her not knowing, his scheming to see her, how he lived on thoughts of her, glowed with them. He was nice, telling the tale.

1. Charles Augustus Lindbergh, Jr , kidnapped two-year-old son of airman and national hero Charles A. Lindbergh (1902–74), being sought nationwide in one of the great criminal cases of the 1930s.

Friday, March 4, Marion, Virginia

A day of rain. I went to Funk in the afternoon and he was trimming his vines. He and I sat in his cellar for a long time drinking wine. My head began to ache. I went to Frank's and ate fish. I was in a discouraged blue mood.

Afterward to the bowling alley where I watched the printshop boys. A lost day.

Saturday, March 5, Marion, Virginia

I tackled the end of the new novel from another angle.

In the afternoon yesterday, after the rain, I went fishing with Frank Authenrieth. He is a restaurateur for the proletariat here— a curious, lean, consumptive-looking man . . . a small gambler and bootlegger . . . very generous and nice. His wife is a little woman with extraordinary big breasts. He has two fine boy children.

We went to sit at the river's edge at Grinsted Mills—a cold, bleak day. The fish would not bite. We built a bonfire. A wild duck flew overhead.

In the evening Funk came and sat in my room. He brought wine. The talk was not good. It wouldn't go.

For some reason he was self-conscious, perhaps because I had rather cruelly challenged him, to quit boosting for the Republican Party. Like most Americans his inner life is one thing, his outer life another.

Sunday, March 6, Marion, Virginia

Reading Schmalhausen's collection of essays—*Behold America.*[1]

A queer run-in, almost a quarrel, with Mr. Copenhaver—who had come home from a meeting of church people quite reactionary.

There was a feeling in the house, when I went up there, not unlike the feeling I found in so many houses during the World War.

People shrink from facing the fact that our individualistic, capitalistic civilization cannot be destroyed without a basic revolution. After our quarrel—or almost quarrel—I felt badly and went back to Mrs. Copenhaver to make my peace.

I went to play about with Doctor Wright, visiting with him in his car the fish hatchery, the proposed airport here, a little tannery east of town. I like him and he amuses me.[2]

Burt Dickinson went with me and we got cress, Burt for his house and myself for Mrs. Copenhaver—to help make my peace. Eleanor has reached San Francisco. This morning there is snow and the whole world, from my window, for the first time this winter is white.

1. Samuel D. Schmalhausen, ed., *Behold America!* (New York, 1931).

2. Dr. George Wright, physician (1918–22) and superintendent since 1927 at Southwestern State Hospital (for the insane), located in Marion since 1887.

Monday, March 7, Marion, Virginia

It was bitter cold with a high wind all day. Worked in the morning. In the afternoon went to Mrs. Copenhaver and we had good talk. She looked somewhat tired. There has been a heavy storm to the east and trains are delayed and telegraph wires down. Went to walk with Funk and suggested to him the idea of making a case history study of our county courts . . . to show what happens to poor people in the courts, what motivates the lawyers and officials. He seemed interested. He has a desire to write, is dissatisfied with the trickeries and mercenary turn of the law. He may do it and it may be a relief to him.

Tuesday, March 8, Marion, Virginia

The extreme cold is passing. I am still reading the book of critical essays *Behold America*. Got a new life of Lincoln which I loaned to Funk.[1] The hills, seen through the window, look like great shaggy dogs lying asleep.

The day was spent in work in my room. I went to Mrs. Copenhaver and later to Funk. Took some paintings to Mrs. Copenhaver.[2] Funk was in a nice mood and talked of the attitude of the Northerners, living in the South, toward the South.

The fear I would not sleep was on me so I took a sleeping pill. My mind is absorbed in the later end of the novel now.

1. Emanuel Hertz, *Abraham Lincoln: A New Portrait* (New York, 1932).
2. Anderson took to Laura Lu Copenhaver for her walls at Rosemont and for her sales through Rosemont Crafts Industries paintings by himself and by artist friends.

Wednesday, March 9, Marion, Virginia

Will soon be starting on the last month before I can see Eleanor again. Went to bed very tired—after a day of writing. It is cold and grey this morning—more like an early January than a March morning. The peach buds have all been killed this early. On the maple trees, in front of this house, the leaves, before the freeze, were as large as squirrels' ears.

Frank Copenhaver arrived home from Florida and I spent the evening there. He looks well. Poor man, he suffers terribly from asthma. He is a good liver and has brought home some delicious Bacardi.

In the printshop when a tramp printer came in. He was of the rascal type, half-beggar, half-thief—the petty-larceny man beyond doubt. He began to lie and I got him a chair and sat with him to see the lies grow into big ones.

Nevertheless he leads a miserable life, sleeping in jails and flops. He claims to have married a woman with several children. He has a trick of making sores, etc., on legs or arms to help him in his beggar's trade.

A letter from Eleanor that made me happy.

Thursday, March 10, Marion, Virginia

Colder than any day and night of the winter. Again I worked. In the afternoon I went to Frank and we tested our wine. The apple wine—made by putting fifty pounds of raisins into fifty gallons apple cider and letting it ferment, turned out to be excellent. It is a light yellow dry wine, with a delicate nice flavor.

Frank talked at length of the Buchanans—B. F., Doctor Dave and John P.—and told me of a strange dream.[1]

No letter from Eleanor.

In the evening to dine at Bob's. Dinner good. Mary very sweet. Mr. and Mrs. Copenhaver were there but Mr. Copenhaver ran off to his prayer meeting and the movies. As usual Mrs. Copenhaver was charming. She got the ugly wooden plaques down off Bob's walls.

1. John P. Buchanan, Marion attorney, state senator, and son of the late B. F. Buchanan.

Friday, March 11, On the Train, Southwest Virginia

On [the] train, between Marion and Roanoke, on my way to Detroit—to make the first of my lectures—on newspapers and on machines. Went to Mrs. Copenhaver before leaving, to see her and Mr. Copenhaver and to see the room with the paintings. The room looked delicious. It is nice the way light in a room has quality because of what it meets in the room.

To Frank to get a quart of whiskey.

Unable to work, thinking of the talks I am to make.

Anyway am tired. Shall be lazy on the train and try to think of the talks.

After Roanoke shall be going toward Eleanor.

Saturday, March 12, On the Train, Central Ohio

In the flat lands of central Ohio, on [the] train from Columbus, Ohio, to Detroit, where I am to speak tonight. It turned colder in the night and I shivered in my berth. The morning papers, got at

Columbus, are full of murders, kidnapping, robberies. It seems strange, when the effect on everyone of a capitalistic civilization is so very obvious, that there is not a cry out of people's hearts to put an end to it. No cruelty that can possibly develop in a communistic society—incidental to getting it under way—can compare to the constant everyday cruelty of our present capitalistic, individualistic society.

An example is Lindbergh—a man the whole people have apparently tried to honor. His whole life has apparently been made miserable, all privacy taken from him, his child stolen.

The whole capitalistic thing should be fought as long as a man has breath to fight.

Now we have an example of a whole nation quite helpless before its gangsters.

I have been reading, for perhaps the twentieth time, Turgenev—*The Sportsman's Sketches*. It is prose—lovely, quiet, assured. It has color, balance, smoothness. It may be impossible to write such prose now.

There must have been, at bottom, something quiet and nice about that life. Turgenev went to Paris. He returned home, to his Russian estates. When he went forth, gun in hand, the man was hunting something more than game. How patiently he listened to the words of the poor Russian peasants, noting the expression on faces, the color of eyes, the clothes worn.

Read the piece called "Byézhin Prairie"—for something perfect in sense of skies, fields, night coming, the mystery of night, the boys—so sharply caught—and the coming of day. It is a rare, a beautiful painting.

Sunday, March 13, Chicago, Illinois

In Chicago—where I arrived on an early morning train from Detroit. I spoke in Detroit at the Athletic Club there—a huge middle-class thing—fat, rather decaying men. The president of the club is named Trix. He is a manufacturer and, I dare say, inherited wealth.[1]

He is the sort of man who, had he been fortunate enough to be born poor, a worker, or some sort of adventurer, would have been first-class, a real comrade.

I think, after the club got me booked, they were sorry. I am gradually acquiring the reputation of being a radical. On all sides the ugliness of our capitalistic system becomes more and more apparent.

In Detroit there had been an ugly incident a few days before I arrived there. The communists had got up a hunger march and some three thousand men had marched. At present Detroit has a liberal mayor and he permitted the march.

The town of Dearborn is very close to Detroit but is a separate town corporation. It is practically a feudal stronghold of the Fords. When the hungry men, in marching, reached the corporation limits of Dearborn the police were lined up along the road. They shot off tear gas but the wind blew it away and the march proceeded. Then the police began to shoot and shot down four of the hungry men.

I saw the funeral on Saturday—thousands marching in the streets with revolutionary fervor. Thus the revolution will come someday—a little more cruelty—

More and more.

And then at last.

I spoke at night, making my speech as ominous and threatening as I could. I was ashamed of the well-dressed audience.

1. Herbert B. Trix (1891–1977), president of the W. M. Chace Company and in 1932 president of the Detroit Athletic Club.

Monday, March 14, Chicago, Illinois

George Daugherty came to me at my room in the hotel and brought some whiskey, the gift of Marco Morrow.[1] He told me an amusing story of Mrs. Copenhaver—at Marion—when the two crooks were selling her two fur coats—evidently stolen. George thought she knew it and at the same time didn't want to let herself know it.

I talked to Mimi, who is to marry Russell Spear—in three weeks—about a wedding present and we decided on paintings.[2]

Went to see Ferdinand Schevill whose wife Clara was ill and in bed.[3] It was a day when I was very conscious of Eleanor all day.

I kept thinking of her in Chicago and wishing I had known her then.

Ferdinand, Mimi and I dined. He also got caught, a little, in the stock market. He did not lose much there but has lost $20,000, the savings of a lifetime, by loaning it to people [who] cannot pay it back.

My nerves were weary from Detroit. It is no good this speaking to businessmen. I do not feel at home with them.

1. George Daugherty, whom Anderson had known well after 1900 in the advertising business in Chicago; Marco Morrow, another friend from Anderson's years in Chicago advertising, who had become an editor of Capper Publications of Topeka, Kans.
2. Marion "Mimi" Anderson, who on April 2, 1932, married Russell Spear (1904–83).
3. Ferdinand Schevill, professor of history at the University of Chicago, and his wife Clara remained longtime friends of Anderson's.

Tuesday, March 15, Evansville, Indiana

I am in Evansville, Indiana, where I am to speak before a men's club tomorrow evening. A long afternoon's ride on the train. I wrote a "Travel Note" for Bob.[1] I have been dull. The cold bleak weather in Chicago depressed me. I should have worked all afternoon on the train but hadn't the heart.

It is a bleak time in a bleak year. Listened to two workingmen talking in the smoking car of the train and was forced to realize they were of about as low mentality as the businessmen I have been seeing.

I liked however the brakeman on the train, an old white-haired man with a shrunken mouth. He had something rather jolly and interesting to say to every station master along the route. At Terre Haute a young Negro, paralyzed and unable to move his legs, was trying to get aboard the train, helped by an old woman, probably his mother, and the white-haired old brakeman called to some of us white men and we all went and boosted him on.

I noticed later that the old brakeman kept going to him and trying to cheer him up. Once I went out on the back platform of the train and there was the brakeman and a Negro porter standing together and singing. I had also heard them singing together on the station platform in Chicago.

1. "Travel Notes," *Smyth County News*, March 24, 1932, p. 3.

Wednesday, March 16, On the Train, Western Indiana

It has turned warmer. I am on a train, traveling from Evansville to Urbana, Illinois, to speak at the state university. It was hard work speaking last night. I didn't like myself. I was in some way too pretentious, too fakey. I never know what makes me that way.[1]

I become excited and when I am that way I am too sensitive to people. Perhaps they are fakey and it makes me so. When I am not nice inside I get tired outside. I am so today.

1. Anderson spoke March 15 at the Temple Men's Club in Evansville, Ind.; on March 16, he spoke at Theta Sigma Tau, University of Illinois, Urbana, Ill.

Thursday, March 17, Chicago, Illinois

The day was soft, warm and pleasant. I rode up from Evansville to Danville, Illinois, through an absolutely flat prairie country. It was like a quiet sea, the same sense of mystery in the distance, calling, calling. A few farmers were plowing in their huge fields. Others were going across fields with horses hitched to long bars of wood that knocked down and flattened last year's stalks.

Was two hours at Danville. A few days before some unemployed men from Decatur had been there trying to organize the Danville unemployed to make their protest more effective. They were brutally thrown into jail for saying things that have been said in dozens of newspapers, in magazines and even on the floor of Congress.

Friday, March 18, Chicago, Illinois

Had brought my daughter Marion down to stay with me at above hotel.[1] She had an adjoining room and in the night the moon attacked her. She had violent cramps. A hot water bottle relieved her.

We had spent the evening with Roger and Ruth Sergel, two of the nicest people I know.[2] Ruth was very beautiful all evening—a barred dress across her strong figure brought out all of its beautiful strong lines. You feel love in that house.

In the late afternoon—at the hotel—Ferdinand Schevill came and we had good talk. The room in this old hotel is very lovely and the outlook over Grant Park and the lake very beautiful.

I have been seeing too many people. It will be good to get on the train tonight for Tucson, Arizona. Here the people beat upon you—clutching and clutching. It is a result of our civilization. All the youngsters want something. They believe you have in your pocket a golden key that will unlock the door. You cannot possibly convince them of your own confusion, your own helplessness.

1. Anderson was staying at the Auditorium Hotel and writing on hotel stationery.

2. Roger Sergel, one-time teacher of English at the University of Pittsburgh and then, in Chicago, executive with the Dramatic Publishing Company; Sergel and his wife Ruth remained friends of Anderson's throughout his life

Saturday, March 19, Chicago, Illinois

I spoke here yesterday—rather well perhaps.[1] Afterward I had a rather bad reaction but not, I'm sure, from the talk. It was from seeing here, again after many years, the faces of men with whom I used to work when I was a young man.

With a thump it brought it home to me—the unsuccessful, defeated men and the successful ones, all in the same boat—all engaged—all these years—in this senseless money-making civilization. It makes them all such terrible children. There is what Paul Rosenfeld used to call the terrible American mouth.

The heavy faces, the cruelty—like boys to one another—the little pretentiousness of those who have made money.

There were women there. Again, as always in a crowd of successful or partly successful Americans, the women were so terribly much more alive, more vital than the men.

1. Anderson lectured to the Advertising Council in Chicago, where he had worked in advertising intermittently from 1900 until 1922.

Sunday, March 20, Kansas City, Missouri

Sitting in [the] train in Kansas City station. It is still cold. Last night at Chicago, at [the] railroad station—I was very cold. Perhaps I was too tired.

There was the emotional thing—leaving my daughter—she going off to get married.

Then I had another exciting experience.

I went with Justin Smith to a club called the Caxton Club and there was Bernard Faÿ—translator into French of my *Horses and Men*—and Victor Llona—translator of *A Story Teller's Story*—two of the most delightful men I know, both in Chicago without my having known they were there.[1] Faÿ got up and told the crowd I was the greatest living American, etc.—in the French way—very charmingly put however. Then Llona talked in the same way and I was both embarrassed and of course pleased.

A man doesn't know what to do. He would like so to believe such words.

Both men went off with me to my hotel room and spent the afternoon.

It was a day of men, men, young men, old men—personalities beating in on me. No escape. I was very, very tired when I got on the train. When I see my daughter again she will be a married woman.

1. Henry Justin Smith (1875–1936), Chicago newspaper reporter and editor and then assistant to the president of the University of Chicago; Bernard Faÿ, French professor of American culture, who had in the 1920s translated several Anderson stories into French; Victor Llona, Frenchman who had translated Anderson's *A Story Teller's Story* as *Un Conteur se raconte* (Paris, 1928–29).

Monday, March 21, On the Train, Western Kansas

It is possible I have been passing through a mild case of flu. On the other hand I may have been seeing too many people. My nerves have been on edge.

At Topeka Marco Morrow came to the train to see me, bringing his wife. She is a strange, hard little thing. With all his adventures with women she has held him because she had a child by him. It has been, I fancy, a hollow victory for her.

There are not many passengers on the train. In the club car a gang of fat, well-fed, expensively dressed men have been talking and drinking largely and amply all day. They look like steers, bred for beef. There is the steady thump of coin in all their talk—coin, interest, investment, 2½ percent, 12 percent, etc. The Pullman conductor keeps trying to sell me the upper. He is persistent. I have however clung to my sales resistance.

The flat western Kansas plains, all day—sometimes softly undulating, sometimes very flat. The farm houses are far apart, each with its little group of planted trees. This land should have produced its own kind of poet. Turgenev could have made it live. Am no good today.

Tuesday, March 22, Tucson, Arizona

A weariness—that goes far down into me—sometimes takes hold of me. I am a man whose roots are in nothing. It is, I'm sure, partly, at least, the effect of my time and place. I am in love with life and, just now, life is not alive. I have a feeling for simple poor people. But they also, in my time, do not want to be simple poor people. They want to rise, be as ugly, as stupid as those oil men I saw on the train today.

This is a bright, green, smart town, here in the desert. I got off the train, train-weary. It was a cold dusty ride down from Chicago. In a queer way the place reminds me of Reno, Nevada.

There are many Mexicans in the streets. I hear the language spoken in the halls of the hotel.

There were two letters here from Eleanor. I love her. I am constantly ashamed, thinking how little I have to give her.

Wednesday, March 23, Tucson, Arizona

My illness is passing. As usual I think it was psychic. It is an illness of the spirit that gets down into the physical part of me.

Went to an old Indian mission here, escorted by a newspaper woman, and wrote a piece for our weeklies—not very good.[1] Saw many Mexicans and Indians, I'm sure about the nicest people here. There are too many vulgar rich Americans about.

Went to the Mariston Chapmans.[2] Found them broke and discouraged. Writers also are being punished for the sins of the capitalists—and their own sins.

The desert at night was very exciting and lovely. As usual, when I have a lovely or exciting experience, I wanted Eleanor here to share it with me.

1. "Travel Notes," *Smyth County News*, March 31, 1932, pp. 4–5.
2. John Stanton Higham Chapman (1891–1972), who with his wife Mary wrote novels under the pseudonym Mariston Chapman.

Thursday, March 24, Tucson, Arizona

At Tucson. There was a terrible woman. I have friends here—the Chapmans. This woman—named McCormick—called me and invited me to go driving in the desert with the Chapmans. When the event came off it turned out the Chapmans were not going.

The husband drove and I sat beside him. He wasn't a bad chap. The wife was one of the kittenish fat sort. She had a camera and kept taking my photograph, snapping it, a dozen, two dozen times.

Click. Click.

No matter where I went, what I tried to look at, there she was. I wanted to be like John and shout at her, "Quit it, you bitch."

I spoke at the university to a fine audience and spoke well. Like everything else it has a technique. I am learning it.[1]

In the evening, afterward, ran off with two delightful Irish scholars—professors here—and their wives, equally delightful. We drank and told stories.

1. At the University of Arizona Anderson's lecture topic had been "What Has Happened to American Newspapers?"

Friday, March 25, Tucson, Arizona

I have just written Eleanor a long letter about Marco Morrow and his son—at school here.[1] I have been out on the desert all afternoon with the boy in a car. He is a nice, rather shy boy but I think does lack some of his father's great personal charm. He is like his mother who is not charming.

It is an odd story, Marco's passion for a son and the strange adventures it has led him into.

In the morning, before going out into the desert with the boy, I went for a long walk down in the Mexican quarter. The little stores are all owned by Chinese. There were many soft-eyed children in the street.

In the afternoon I went with Dick Morrow across the desert and into the mountain, getting up to where the trees began. I was in a quiet, rather tired but happy mood all day.

1. Richard Morrow was a student at the University of Arizona.

Saturday, March 26, On the Train

On [the] train from Los Angeles to Salt Lake City. I had two hours in Los Angeles but in the night had got a cold in the head, making me, at this writing, quite miserable.

Yesterday I went, with three other men, to a Mexican town south of Tucson, Arizona. Immediately we began to drink the Mexican drink called "tokela" and were soon quite drunk.

We had got into a violent discussion—led by the publisher of the Tucson morning paper—on the capitalistic side and myself on the communistic side. It kept up all day, both of us keeping our tempers but neither sparing the other.

There were bars and gambling establishments everywhere, in the Mexican town, the Mexicans, men and women, lolling in the street, quite attractive, don't-give-a-damn-looking people.

There was one very attractive woman, the wife of a professor, and a very charming witty Irishman, named Walsh.[1]

In Los Angeles, quite miserable with my cold and having two hours to wait. I walked and got into a street of employment offices, great crowds of the unemployed standing about.

They seemed quite desolate-looking but the warm climate made their plight seem less terrible here than in the East.

1. Padraic Walsh, a mathematics teacher and later an accountant of Tucson who remained friends with Anderson for several years.

Sunday, March 27, Salt Lake City, Utah

In Ford Madox Ford's book *Return to Yesterday* I read of a long time of depression and ill health he once passed through. The doctors got hold of him and he became very careful and exact about food.

His strength all went. He could not work.

Reading this has put an idea into my own head—that I have been, recently, too much as Ford was. I'd better chuck it. I have thought too much of my health, my food, inability to work just now, etc. I'd better be thinking more of living.

I am to be here until Thursday evening—speaking three times at the university here.

Left Los Angeles at 10:00 a.m. yesterday—suffering, as I thought, from a bad cold. It may only have been too much tokela—if that's the way to spell it—drunk at Nogales—in Mexico—south of Tucson. I was swaying and my eyes watering. I did not eat until evening—contenting myself with consuming oranges and drinking barrels of water.

The train went over a high rugged mountain, labored over, and dropped down at once into Death Valley.

It was a scene of utter desolation—great stretches of moving sand. I got in with a tall lantern-jawed man in the observation car who was a railroad dispatcher on a desert division of his railroad. We sat all afternoon talking—he telling me stories of the desert, of the loneliness, of the beauty of the desert at night in the moonlight and of the terrible sand storms.

The sand flows itself into great dunes and these move across the desert. The railroad and highway departments have to build breaks against it as against floods of water.

It was very hot. Already the desert had begun to blossom, the strange and lovely desert blooming that comes with the spring rains.

We got to Las Vegas, near where the new Boulder Dam is being built, at 8:00 p.m. and I went to bed and to a long healing sleep. The desert air or something had quite taken my cold away.

Monday, March 28, Salt Lake City, Utah

It has been a cold grey day. I'll be glad to go from here to Los Angeles and the sun.

Took a long walk through the streets, visited the Mormon Temple and Museum and shall prepare one of my travel notes for the paper.[1]

I am to speak here tonight. As usual, when I have to speak, I am rather nervous and upset. I prepared a statement, giving a kind of synopsis of my lecture here for the University of Utah yearbook.[2]

Wrote a lot of letters and saw newspaper men.

1. "Travel Notes," *Smyth County News*, April 7, 1932, p. 2.
2. Anderson's précis of his University of Utah talk, "America: A Storehouse of Vitality," has not been located.

Tuesday, March 29, Salt Lake City, Utah

I was told, by a very clever woman, when I was at the University of Arizona, that a Mormon audience was the hardest audience in the world to speak to.

It may be true. At least, although I held them last night while speaking, I had a very queer dissatisfied feeling about it all afterwards.

I wonder if it is not this . . . that these people know—subconsciously—that their religion is even more ridiculous than most religions. They cannot perhaps believe that you respect them.

I went in the afternoon with a professor, a funny little Ohio man who has spent his life looking up documents about Shakespeare—a question of dotting I's and crossing T's in old manuscripts—the sort of thing known as scholarship. A dull life truly and a dull man but he has prospered. He had an expensive car and took me up into the hills to where I had a grand view of the Salt Lake Valley spread away and could imagine Brigham Young and his starved followers coming out into this great Valley with the Salt Lake at the end.[1] It was a heroic, terrible experience and it is too bad that it has not worked out into something a bit more noble.

1. Brigham Young (1801–77), president of the Mormon Church, who in 1848 led a group of religious migrants from the Midwest to Salt Lake City.

Wednesday, March 30, Salt Lake City, Utah

Here as everywhere—educated young men—young professors, etc.—who are wearily sophisticated. Why—for Christ's sake? What about?

It is the "life is an empty cup" notion. I spoke here, in the evening, and went out to the house of some professors—young men with whom I had spent the afternoon drinking beer. In the evening we drank beer again—and talked. It would be better if such young men went to be tramps or farm hands or laborers. They have got themselves all dead inside with life-weariness and constantly infect and reinfect each other. It may be that, appearing constantly before youth—not really having much to give— they have taken on this sophisticated pose to impress. Alas, they have impressed themselves.

Among them—as almost always—a few incipient perverts. That goes, too, inevitably, with the young professional class.

Thursday, March 31, Salt Lake City, Utah

Drove, with two older professors, to the Utah State Agricultural College, ninety miles from Salt Lake, down through the long Salt Lake Valley—along Salt Lake and over a mountain into Cache Valley. The road runs along under the mountains. There are deep gullies up into the hill, down which come the fresh mountain streams that furnish the city water and water for irrigating the whole valley. The hills are bare of trees. Often the summer rains, when they do come, in this semi-desert country, are torrential. In a half hour a whole mountain side drains off into a small creek and it becomes a raging torrent. Great rocks, as large as this desk at which I am writing, are carried down hill and rolled and tumbled by the rushing stream out into the valleys and often houses are swept away.

We climbed up over a mountain where the snow still lay deep and drove into Cache Valley. It was a cold grey day. We were driven by the daughter of one of the professors, a handsome girl, married to an aviator. I sat with her, on the return trip, and she told me many interesting things regarding the life out here.

Note—the water of Salt Lake is so heavy—25% salt—that it is dangerous to dive into it from any height. "It's like diving into cement," the handsome girl told me. Several have had necks broken, trying it.

My impressions of Mormons have been got largely from reading—Mark Twain and Artemus Ward.[1] Humorists are never very fair. They have to be funny.

It is so obvious, everywhere out here, that Brigham Young was a great man. His stamp is on everything.

The Mormons tell you all sorts of amusing stories of his ability, his shrewdness and his hard common sense. Unconsciously you find yourself loving the man, having caught the feeling from them.

There is a widespread impression of the Mormons as a rather grey, drab people. As a matter of fact, as compared with most Americans, they are gay. At the agricultural college I had one of the best audiences I ever faced, youth, all alive, eager, full of fun. It was a curiously fine emotional experience speaking to them and I spoke better than ever in my life, I think.

You have to take this public speaking as an actor takes playing a role. It's the only way to get any fun out of it.

In the evening several of the big men here, publishers, bankers, Mormon bishops and plain newspaper men and professors, gave a big men's banquet for me at one of the expensive downtown clubs. We sat for several hours having fine, rather daring talk.

1. Mark Twain (1835–1910), who devoted four chapters (13–16) of *Roughing It* (1872) to the Utah Mormons; Artemus Ward (1834–67), who developed two humorous speeches on the Mormons—"Artemus Ward Among the Mormons" and "A Visit to Brigham Young."

April

Friday, April 1, Los Angeles, California

The ride down from Salt Lake was quite wonderful. I was very tired and had not slept. On the train were some engineers going to Boulder Dam at Las Vegas. There were two businessmen, getting drunk all day. They were drunk when they got on the train and all day got drunker.

It was a crack train but there were few people on it. I had been, during the days in Salt Lake, so surrounded by people that it was a great relief to escape them. I spoke to no one on the train. I was interested to see what books people read. I went through the train looking. Not one person read an intelligent book.

In the afternoon we went through Nevada and Rainbow Canyons, the train laboring slowly up the mountain sides and then plunging into these canyons. They were smaller editions of the Grand Canyon I once saw. The canyons were made by a small creek, called Beaver Creek. It was a little insignificant stream but, as the hills all about are bare, when rains do come the water all rushes madly down to the creek bed and the little stream becomes a raging torrent.

In these canyons all is color. There is a riot of just those colors that most excite me—yellow and red with all the shading between the two.

Saturday, April 2, Los Angeles, California

The matter of money easily becomes an obsession. Once you begin to think of it it is amazing how it thrusts itself out at you everywhere. When a new building is to go up it is announced, "A new million-dollar theater will be built."

Such and such a man is to get so and so many dollars next year for playing baseball. I wonder constantly if, just in the matter of its descriptive value, it means much. To me a million dollars—the words written out—a million-dollar building, a million-dollar theater, etc.—means nothing. I read such a statement in a newspaper. Something flashes through my mind. Well, it must of course be something gaudy. My mind does a little trick—"a cut-back"—there flashes into my mind the memory of some gaudy building I have recently seen. Why, the building I am now thinking of costs perhaps ten, perhaps twenty millions of dollars—not one million.

There have been a good many deaths among rich men lately— a surprising number of suicides. It is obvious that making money, accumulating money, gets a man, in the end, little enough satisfaction. When the revolution comes, as it will of course, the same sort of men who now run the world will still run it. You have to allow, to the more successful ones, executive ability. The pure dreamer could not, I'm sure, run a railroad. The masses of the people, led by the dreamers, will have to compel the men of executive ability to work for all. It won't be an easy task. That would be the purpose, I presume, of such an organization as is, in Russia, called the Party. Given a free hand the executive mind would again become the acquisitive mind. Why? Because money is the tangible evidence of power. With money in hand the power may continue after the ability has worn out or it may be passed on to a son—even though the son may be of no account. He may or he may not be. He should not be handed power in the shape of money but should be made by society to prove himself.

Sunday, April 3, Los Angeles, California

Los Angeles—a fake, tin-pan civilization. My lecture manager has tricked me. He waiting until I got away out here and then rung in on me three or four women's clubs.

I stayed outdoors most of yesterday and in the evening came in and read a book. It was sold me as a sort of history of the

Russian Revolution. It might have been the layout for a movie, having in it just that fakiness and cheapness—false sense of drama characteristic now of our movie art.

Nothing could induce me to live in this atmosphere out here now.

Once it must have been nice here, in the early days, the Mexicans raising cattle and sheep here—the dusty plains with the mountains in the distance. Now it all seems fakey.

The center of the town is bright enough. There are many tall buildings. Then come the endless streets of little bungalow houses, cheaply constructed, covered with meaningless and vulgar decorations.

It must be that into this country come empty-headed girls from all over the United States. They hope no doubt to make the movies. Whether they do or not is, I suspect, largely a matter of chance. It depends, I presume, upon what man they happen to sleep with, whether or not he has money to shove them forward.

There are innumerable straw blondes. Perhaps they make them here. The movie houses are crowded. It is like the cowboys—what few are left back on the plains. In reality the cowboy is nowdays but a farm hand herding tame cows and steers.

But do not think he does not read, eagerly, the cowboy tales of gun-toting daredevils. All the book stores in the cow country sell nothing else but such tales.

Did I say book stores? There are none. The cowboy books are sold in country general stores, in railroad stations out on the deserts.

Monday, April 4, Los Angeles, California

Again I went to look at Los Angeles. I went to the doorman of the hotel and asked him, "Where can I ride on a street-car—what part of the city would be most characteristic?" but he did not want me to ride on a street car and began telling me of the sightseeing buses.

"But I do not want that," I said. "There will be a man shouting out unreliable information. I will be taken to see the homes of movie stars." He seemed offended. "I thought you wanted to see something characteristic," he said. He assured me the barkers on the sight-seeing buses were very reliable. "We have never had any complaint," he said.

I took a bus and rode. This was however not a sight-seeing bus. There were flowers everywhere. Again I saw many straw blondes. We must have gone into a fashionable movie section. There were many antique places, dress-making establishments, places for rejuvenating the human face, beauty parlors, etc. I rode far out toward a place called Beverly Hills . . . thinking, "It is odd—how the attention of all America has been centered on this spot." The houses passed were surely not shabbily showy as are the houses of the retired farmers who come here. In another part of the country they might look quite comfortable and nice.

I am prejudiced. Every instinct in me calls out against the whole South California civilization. Perhaps I hate what has been done here to the movie art, the terribly false sense of life that has gone out from here.

In the afternoon to a professional ball game—very nice to see—men doing a nice thing superlatively well.

Tuesday, April 5, Los Angeles, California

Los Angeles. People, people, people.

I spoke three times. It is too much. Every little nerve in my body cries out this morning.[1] I want Eleanor.

Upton Sinclair—not a real revolutionist.

John and Anita Loos—broke by the Depression. Back making pictures.

Fred McCormick. Ben Hecht's father and mother.

Count Borosini.[2]

More people. I am infinitely weary—too much—too much.

1. Anderson spoke at the Jewish Institute in Los Angeles, the Pasadena Lecture Course in Pasadena, and the Institute of Technology in Pasadena.

2. Upton Sinclair (1878–1968), novelist and reformer, active in seeking political office in California; John Emerson (1874–1956), actor and movie director, childhood friend of Anderson's; Anita Loos (1894–1981), novelist and screenwriter, wife of John Emerson; Fred McCormick (d. 1951), journalist much involved with reporting news from China and the U.S.S.R.; Joseph Hecht and Sarah Swernofsky Hecht; Count Borosini, European aristocrat whom Anderson had met when returning from Paris and who, while living in Pasadena, Calif., had

invited Anderson to visit—an invitation that Anderson declined on the excuse of needing to read proofs.

Wednesday, April 6, Los Angeles, California

I cannot abide the rich. I do not like to be in their houses. If we ever get a civilization out of which economic fear is taken then—if there are men of special talent—let them have what luxury they need or want.

An impression—Upton Sinclair. He is like most socialists I know. After all he spends his time associating with the rich or the well-to-do. His books have a tremendous circulation abroad—among poor socialists. He is unlike Theodore Dreiser in that you feel no human tenderness in him. Such a man marshals facts against the rich. There are enough of them, God knows. I dare say he believes in a personal devil—personified in some rich man.

He goes in for all the American fads, is hot on foods—eating oats—Prohibition, etc. You feel in him no sensuality—no lusts.

Back of this kind of a man you will find usually some rich woman. She is having a good time. Her husband is dead. She gives to causes. Sinclair will have his hands on some such a rich fat old woman. Bah. Balls.

I felt badly about John and Nita. They came to hear me speak. I did not know they were in the audience. I talked of just the things by which they live.

They make motion pictures. During the World War I used to be with them sometimes. They were making what were called Kaiser pictures. The whole idea was to feed war hatred, make everyone feel that all Germans were hopeless rats, etc.

Now they have a German boy as chauffeur. They are sentimental about the Germans. They are as bad as Sinclair. Just the same I hate to hurt them.

The best thing is to plan to stay away from the rich all you can.

Note. When I wrote *Marching Men* I had a correspondence with Upton Sinclair.[1] He wrote long letters. I had represented working men as human. There were among them liars and cheats, fine fellows, rather cheap ones—all kinds of course. It was Sinclair's contention that, even if all this were true, nothing should be said. "The working people have had rough times. If they have any faults they should not be mentioned." That was his point of view. How corrupt. Bah. Balls.

1. *Marching Men* (New York, 1917).

Thursday, April 7, Los Angeles, California

I saw last night a display of vulgarity such as a man seldom sees equaled. I had been engaged to speak on modern machinery and its effect on human life before a club here calling itself a book and play club.[1] What its members have to do with books and plays I don't know. They were, for the most part, vulgarly rich Jews. I sat beside the chairman who had perhaps heard me condemn somewhere the lives of the rich so he told me he did not want to be rich. All he wanted was to be safe—to be assured of a bare living—say $12,000 a year.

There was a man there named Pond—a son of the Pond who in another generation managed so many artists who, because of the need of money, had to go lecturing.[2]

Mark Twain did it to pay his debts, under the elder Pond. Poor Mark Twain!

So this son of the elder Pond, being at this place, was asked to get up and speak before me. He spoke for a full hour, indulging all the time in cheap jokes at the expense of the artists his father had managed. He made every one of them out either a fool or a cheap vulgarian. He went on and on.

As for the artists about whom he was talking (it will be borne in mind he was only trying to amuse a crowd of rich Jews. I dare say they enjoyed it. I myself burned with indignation even when he spoke of such second-rate artists as William Allen White and Irving Bacheller)[3] . . . as for the artists about whom he was speaking most of them are dead.

It is strange about these rich, feebly cultured Americans, Jews and Gentiles. In spite of themselves they have respect for artists and yet how they love to have them represented as damn fools.

At last, after an hour of this man's gabble, my turn came and I arose. I refrained from saying much about this man, merely saying that, having heard the viewpoint concerning artists expressed by this businessman, it would be interesting to hear one of the artists express an opinion of him, but that I would not myself dirty my tongue with it, etc.

1. Anderson had spoken to the Book and Play Club of Los Angeles on "America: A Storehouse of Vitality."
2. James Burton Pond (1838–1903), lecture manager for such notables as Mark Twain and Henry Ward Beecher.
3. William Allen White (1868–1944), well-known newspaper editor in Emporia, Kans.; Irving Bacheller (1859–1950), American author of romantic novels.

Friday, April 8, Los Angeles, California

Leaving for San Francisco late this afternoon. I spent the day at the MGM Studios—lunched on the ground and walked all afternoon about the place. . . .

A queer impression. I must write of it for the papers.[1] I was with John Emerson in his car in the late afternoon and we rode through many acres of what they call the sets.

Here thrown upon a great open field were fragments of Russian villages, a college campus, the street of a small middle western town, the entrance to a large hotel, the prow of a ship—half a street car, a jungle village, a mine, a street in the suburb of a city, an armory.

These but a fragment of what I saw—all artificial, all papier-mâché.

Here in this place you get again the ruinous thing about American life. I talked to a writer who is out here. What about the people? "The nice people," he said, "are the mechanics and the machine people—in other words the workers."

Went for the evening to dine—at Pasadena with a Mrs. Crane— the plumbing Cranes—very rich, very nice, very sad. Went with Upton Sinclair and wife. They are a story too—a strange pair— Sinclair a little priest of socialism. Mr. Crane had three children destroyed in the Iroquois Theatre in Chicago.[2]

1. "Travel Notes," *Smyth County News*, May 5, 1932, p. 6.
2. Probably Mrs. Charles R. Crane, who with her husband had in 1925 founded the Institute of Current World Affairs; in Chicago, on December 31, 1903, a fire at the Iroquois Theatre killed at least 571 people.

Saturday, April 9, Los Angeles, California

I am writing in the railroad station at Los Angeles—having come here early from the train—much earlier than there was any need to come—this to escape the herds of people clamoring to see me. The phone has jangled constantly for several days. It has been an invasion. One poor little girl waiting in the lobby of the hotel from 7:00 until 11:00. I think it must be because there are so many thousand unoccupied people out here. They have nothing to do. Several caught me in the lobby of the hotel. They had really nothing to say.

"I wanted to meet you."

"My wife is outside. She wants to meet you."

Several people say, "I read such and such of your books."

It really puts me under no obligation that they buy and read my books. I must take it for granted they wanted to.

I spoke at a big women's club here. It is unfair on the part of my manager. I was not to have such engagements. I have nothing against them. It is pounding on a stone wall. I am glad to have the money, however.[1]

A man waiting outside the club door. He was a German going into publishing. He was wanting me to give him a manuscript—for nothing—just any little thing. It was hard to shake him off, he being like a hungry dog to a bone.[2]

I am going to Eleanor. Will see her in the morning.

1. Anderson had addressed the Friday Morning Club of Los Angeles.
2. The German publisher was possibly Erich Posselt.

Sunday, April 10, San Francisco, California

I am writing up my daily notebook a day late as I was away on a trip all day Saturday and Sunday. It resulted in the most delightful two days of my life. In a rented car I went with Eleanor across the ferry from San Francisco to Oakland at noon. It was a gorgeous day—gulls flying overhead, the sea green and the sky blue. We drove out along a great highway that goes down from San Francisco and Oakland to Yosemite but just beyond the town of Tracy we turned out of the great highway into a smaller one. This highway ran south through a flat valley—as flat as the Illinois corn country but all irrigated. Great herds of fat Holstein cattle wandered through knee-deep grass. There were few farm houses and the farms in this great valley must be huge. They are evidently run by hired labor and there must be, in this particular section, a great many Mexican laborers. All along the road we saw blanket stiffs (itinerant laborers—each with a blanket roll on his back) walking the roads.

The towns are small and well built, great dairy barns and white houses set far back from the road among eucalyptus trees.

There were flowers everywhere. The golden glowing California poppies, lupines, and many blossoms I did not know. In the distance beyond the great flat valley, in all directions, the hills, almost bare of trees, softly rounded and reminding of our Virginia hills—except for their treelessness. In some of the fields yellow daisies grew so thick that the whole field was golden. Then there would be a soft rounded hill in the distance on which some blue flowers grew so thick that the whole hill was blue.

It seems to me I could write forever about the day—the soft warm graciousness of the air, the fields and the sky, the air of plenty, the vastness of the great sweet open country.

Monday, April 11, San Francisco, California

This bay section of California is the place for the nature lover. What an inevitable place for a city and how gracious and striking the city is.

I have too much to write of. It is very strange to me that two years ago I thought my life was all lived. I was saved from all that by a friend. There had come over me a kind of spiritual impotence. I thought it had become physical also.

A friend came. Little precious black-haired friend, I love you. If this ever comes to your eyes, after I am gone, remember the Saturday and Sunday with your dear friend in the great valley, remember the little town of Patterson, the tiny roses by the door, the palm trees, the houses.

My own night of dreams. My restlessness. Believe in love, my dear. Remember the long lovely day that followed, yourself sunning yourself in the prune orchard—the booths in the fishmarket—

Believe, darling—believe. Love is its own justification.

Tuesday, April 12, San Francisco, California

San Francisco. . . . It is interesting to find myself and my proposed speech here absolutely ignored by the newspapers. Obviously the newspapers of the city are very reactionary. I was called by my lecture manager who wanted to send the newspaper men to me. Only one came. We had a talk but he printed nothing. The other newspapers—until this morning at 9:00—as I am now writing—have sent no one. I am much afraid there will be no audience here.[1] At the same time in the papers here today there is a column about the western poet Edwin Markham.[2] It makes of course no difference to me but the affair must be rough on the man who has hired me to come here.

Nothing is more strange than the situation into which America has got. Is this my egotism? I think not. At least my voice, as to conditions in America, now has been heard. My position in American letters is of some small import. It is, as anyone can see, a rather remarkable power given the press—that they can thus pretty effectively cut a man off from the public.

I am somewhat stale this morning, perhaps as a result of being too much alive all day yesterday. The beauty of the day and the city kept me aroused all day. I kept dreaming all day of this city as a free city. Will the time come when it is free?

Once there was some tradition of freedom here. Trade unions were strong. Now for a long time they have been defeated. The city, the universities, the whole state is absolutely under the thumb of money.

In the meantime Tom Mooney—proven pretty conclusively to be innocent of the crime with which he is charged—is still in jail, after sixteen years, and the papers today carry in big headlines Hoover's foolish and childish offer to work as President for nothing.[3]

It was charming to be with Eleanor in the Chinese restaurant with the little park below and the bay in the distance.

(I submit the enclosed as a sample of egotism.[4] I have read it over and am amused. It is so evident that I am hurt because not much newspaper attention is given me.

Surely it isn't because of any of the reasons stated. Why indeed should the newspapers be much concerned with me?)

1. In San Francisco, Anderson was to address the Peter D. Conley group on "America: A Storehouse of Vitality."

2. Edwin Markham (1852–1940), poet of the American West, author of *The Man with the Hoe and Other Poems* (1899).

3. Thomas J. Zecharia, known as Tom Mooney (1882–1942), convicted of murder by bombing at a "war readiness" rally in 1916, is discussed in White, ed., *Sherwood Anderson's Memoirs*, 542–45; President Herbert Hoover had offered to serve his country for the token salary of one dollar per year.

4. The enclosed letter, from a Catholic schoolteacher in Sioux Falls, S.Dak., expressed disagreement with Anderson's ideas of masculinity in *Perhaps Women*.

Wednesday, April 13, San Francisco, California

You will always find plenty of aspiring writers in a country like this to which people retire when they have got a little money ahead. Here it doesn't cost so much to have a little shack by the sea. There the sea is. There is plenty of climate. People of this sort are retired or are the sons and daughters of retired people.

There are also wives of rich men who have literary aspirations, etc.

These people form groups and clubs. Times like these are very comforting. They are hard up but so are the magazines. Editors are often quite polite. If they do not want a manuscript they write a polite note. "Your story, or your article, was fine. Alas we could not use it because . . . ," etc.

What a comfort to the aspiring writer. He runs about. He is comforted. He, or she, goes to see friends, taking the letter along. I walked with a man of fifty still clinging to all that.

I cannot quite understand the antique craze. A man showed me a small iron reproduction—he thought—of a thing by Cellini.[1] I thought it quite ugly. He had got it off an old Italian woman and was as happy as a child. Anatole France had this craze.[2] All of the Pralls, Elizabeth's people, had it. It is at bottom, I think, a clinging to the past, to what is dead.

My day did not go well and I had no audience here—a pitifully small group of people. It is hard to speak to a few scattered people in a large hall. The actor in you is dissatisfied.[3]

Went, in the afternoon, to Tanforan—a race track near here, by the sea, to see the horses run.

In the evening with dear Eleanor, after the speech, to a big hotel. People all about were drinking but we had nothing to drink. She was very lovely in a shining red evening dress. We danced until after midnight, joyously. She dances with fine, soft, easy grace.

1. Benvenuto Cellini (1500–71), sculptor and goldsmith of Florence.
2. Anatole France (1844–1924), who had won the Nobel Prize for Literature in 1921 and who had turned to writing nostalgically about his childhood.
3. Anderson addressed the Women's City Club of Oakland.

Thursday, April 14, On the Train, Northern California

I am on a train, going from San Francisco to Portland. Last night I spoke in Oakland and it would have been a quite silly performance—talking to fat, upper-class, change-of-life women but that some kids came over from the University of California and I felt them alive in the room. The room needed it. It was heavy with the poison of dead rich ones.

A man came from Mills College to introduce me, a nice man but a trifle ladylike. It's silly hearing these introductions, a man getting up and telling what a great man you are—how significant and all that nonsense. You sit gazing at the floor enduring it. "Balls," you want to shout, sending a ribald laugh across it.

It's a lovely morning. California is all green yet, at this time of the year. There is a vivid golden streak of yellow daisies in the field beside which the train runs. Round sensual hills in the background.

I have just written a long letter to my lover.

I was haunted all night by the newspaper woman who came to see me at my hotel yesterday and later appeared at my lecture quite drunk. She is a successful trick writer—detective stories, I think—is clever. Lately she has had trouble. Her man has left her.[1]

She is sensitive enough to feel dirty about her work. Jesus Christ but the tricksters sure do pay for their foxy little literary tricks, selling out their own imaginations, getting dirty inside.

Then drunk—boasting foolishly if they are men, crying if they are women.

I'd have taken that one into my arms—a hug anyway—only

she wasn't good to the feel. A woman whose flesh is no longer sweet. How rotten.

Down capitalism. It has so many little subtle ways of selling people out.

1. Nancy Barr Mavity (1890–1959), author of detective novels, an editorial writer for the Oakland *Tribune*.

Friday, April 15, Portland, Oregon

I got up very weak. There was rather a tense time in San Francisco being so near Elizabeth—afraid of something embarrassing for us both.

Then also seeing Eleanor again—after so long.

All the trains are but half loaded.

We rode, all through the early part of the day, through a great flat valley. There was color everywhere. In the great fields men were working with tractors. It was all an irrigated country.

I was at the back of the train all day. The brakeman back there, an old man, was literary. He discussed Eugene O'Neill with me.[1]

I was a bit foolish about eating—ate too much.

There are many things I would like to write about all the country I have seen.

Beside the tracks all day were fields of yellow poppies and purple lupines.

At 3:00 p.m. we began to get into hills—strange-looking bare hills down which the rain had cut gullies so that they looked like the faces of wrinkled old women.

We were following the Sacramento River, going toward its source in Mount Shasta, and could see the snow-covered mountains in the distance.

The train wound and twisted its way up through the hills along the river bed. The river down below in the valley had been a wide, peaceful-looking navigable stream but now it was a rushing torrent.

There was a big, bearded Russian on the train with cruel eyes and a cruel mouth who kept taking notes.

Once in the night I awoke and there was heavy snow beside the tracks. We passed into Oregon at 9:00 a.m.

We had got down into another great valley but not dry as are the California valleys. It was early spring here and the fruit trees were all in blossom. I awoke early after a weak, restless night, the result of too many emotional experiences—seeing too many people, etc. We began running along the Willamette River. The spring salmon run was on and although it was early morning many fishermen were out, in boats, after the big game fish.

At Oregon City there is an elevator taking the working part of the population up to a hill—or high plateau. There were many logs in the river and big paper mills. The brakeman—an incipient communist—began talking of Russia.

1. Eugene O'Neill (1888–1953), most accomplished twentieth-century American dramatist, not especially close to Anderson.

Saturday, April 16, On the Train, Western Oregon

There was a school man who took me riding in his car. We drove out along the Columbia River Highway. It is a magnificent drive. I could not understand most of the things the man told me. He turned his head from me and talked just above a whisper. Later I found out that he was partially deaf so he probably did not hear what I said to him.

He was like a good many men I meet. He may have heard of my reputation for radicalism. He had, I must fancy, got excited about the idea of having me, then he had grown afraid. The result was he did not give my appearance much publicity.

He talked quite radically but left me alone once, for a half hour, in his [office]. I went quickly through his books and some of the papers on his desk. They might well have been the books and papers of the most conservative of men.

In the school house—when we stopped there for a moment—they were getting off declamations about George Washington—a lot of terrible tripe. When we came off and were setting off on our own drive he came upon some boys, sneaking away from the silly declaiming, and sent them back. He wasn't so nice about it, calling them quitters and poor sports. I thought they were sensible to get away from that kind of thing if possible and told him so. To my surprise he agreed with me. I fancy he is one of the sort of men who takes the point of view of anyone he is with.

There was marvelous scenery to be seen out along the road we took, water falls, streams falling off a high bluff to the river below.

The fall of water was, at one of the falls (we passed six in a thirty-mile drive), nearly six hundred feet.

The water falls from the great height in a fantastic way, forming strange designs as it falls, the forms constantly changing.

I was tired, not having slept on the night before. I had something like a chill.

Newspaper men came to see me and I went with one of them to a radio station—to go on the air. He was to ask me questions. When we got into the sending room we had to wait while a professional man, an announcer, talked about what he called "Skippy Cakes." It's some sort of cracker and if children eat it they will become just like a character called Skippy, who is in a newspaper comic strip and has recently been in movies. The whole talk, presumed to be addressed to children and mothers, was unbelievably silly. Thank God I got out of advertising writing before the radio came. I felt very silly doing my own little bit.

The evening was not a success either. I was tired and not well. It was a dull-faced audience. I hadn't the power in me to shake them out of it.[1]

1. Anderson spoke to the High School of Commerce, in Portland, Oreg., on "America: A Storehouse of Vitality."

Sunday, April 17, On the Train, Northern California

After my talk at Portland I went to a radio studio. It was one of the strangest places I ever entered. In a small room there was a noisy orchestra. Performers kept coming. They had barely room to stand. A claque had been brought in—some fifty people crowded against the wall. They stayed there for hours in an uncomfortable place—men and women, shouting and clapping hands when they were told to do so.

There was a man and woman, the woman rather coarse, both the vaudeville wise-cracking type. The jokes were like this. She is singing in a coarse voice. He: "What do you spray your throat with?"

She: "Ashes."

At a sign the claque began to laugh heartily.

The whole thing was like that. I stayed two hours. The announcer kept dragging in my name. I kept watching the claque. There were at least a hundred more men and women outside a glass door, anxious to crowd into the room—to be near these poor second-rate artists. "Is the claque paid?" I asked. It seems they are not. They seemed to me insane people to voluntarily spend an evening so, in the hot close room, filthy with noise.

I awoke very ill. Could just get out of bed. It took me an hour and a half to dress. My head ached and I wanted to vomit. I walked outside in the cold early morning and gradually the feeling passed.

I am on a tourist sleeper and like it. There are no rich. I slept for a time. We got into the mountains and passed through glorious forests. There was still six feet of snow on the mountain top. There was a snow storm.

Monday, April 18, San Francisco, California

I have finished Bismarck's life, by Emil Ludwig. It must be Ludwig's best work.[1] He is writing about a man loved, feared, understood. He writes carefully, never being smart. I think I had better send it to Eleanor's mother. She will herself never have time to read it now.

These books are reprinted now and sold in drug stores at $1.00. It is a fine thing. To be sure there is mostly nonsense sold.

It is too bad that Eleanor cannot have more leisure. Her work must scatter all of her thoughts and impulses terribly. I would like to have her quiet for a long time. It would be good for her.

I returned from Portland and she and I went to Sausalito, to Fred O'Brien's girl—Margaret Watson. We went over [on] the ferry—a beautiful morning on the bay—and climbed over hills to Margaret's house. She has got up rather a hodgepodge of a book, about Fred's fragments from his life and many letters. She wants me to write an introduction to the book. I presume I will.[2]

There was a doctor there—a grey thin man without much warmth, a scientist, I think I shocked, saying that such things as had happened to Fred could only be wiped out by an economic revolution, etc.

The doctor took us to drive and then we walked out onto the rocky promontory called the Golden Gate—the Pacific rolling in there.

Eleanor and I went back to the boat and then walked a little about the fish wharf but she was cold and tired, it being her sick time.

We went into her office and I read in the book of Fred's while Eleanor rested on a couch. We dined at a Chinese place and I took her to her hotel early at 10:45. I wanted to dance but she was too tired.

1. Emil Ludwig, *Bismarck: The Story of a Fighter* (London, 1930). Ludwig had published biographies of Goethe, Lincoln, Napoleon, Schliemann, and Jesus.
2. An anthology of letters and autobiographical writings never published.

Tuesday, April 19, San Francisco, California

A day of women—first Margaret Watson, about Fred's poor book, a talk with her at lunch. A woman after her lover is dead. I said frankly to her, "Begin now," I said, "thinking of getting another man."

It was amusing to see the look of human relief in her eyes. She feels herself, I dare say, she has mourned all she can.

In the afternoon, an attempt to work on the book. Then a long walk, on the Embarcadero here, and to see Mother Jordan—at the White Angel Jungle.[1]

The sight of thousands of men, quite destitute, each with his tin plate. There are no table utensils. Many of the men have made spoons of wood.

There is this woman. At least what she is doing is direct and human. There are no questions asked. Any man or woman, no matter what race or color, may come and get food.

It is rather as dogs are fed. I watched it all with a queer feeling inside me.

Then to see Elinor Mordaunt, the English writer, at her hotel.[2] I like and didn't like her. She is rather a grand old adventuress, I dare say. I do not at bottom like women writers.

With Eleanor in the evening, she very tired, very warm and soft and human in her tiredness. I wasn't as nice as I should have been.

I held things up a bit too tensely—on the mental plane.

We began to dance and I was nicer. I love her.

1. "Mother" Jordan, former ship's stewardess, organizer of the White Angel Jungle, one of the waterfront charities helping to feed the homeless and unemployed during the Great Depression.

2. Elinor Mordaunt (pseudonym of Evelyn May Mordaunt, 1877–1942), English author of detective novels.

Wednesday, April 20, San Francisco, California

At work again on the novel. Went to lunch with George West and the bookdealers here, Gelber and Lilienthal—also Elinor Mordaunt, the English writer, went with us.[1] We lunched in a speak-easy and I was not very gracious as during the lunch, without meaning anything personal, I managed to say both that I didn't much like women writers nor the English.

We sat until 3:00 over wine. Then I came back to the room at this hotel, tired from the excitement of conversation and from the morning work. Eleanor came at 5:00 and I went with her to a department store to get lining for her new blue suit, she menstruating and looking pale and tired but lovely. I took a drink for her and we dined in a nice place in an alleyway, all we could eat for forty cents—fine food too.

I went back to my room and saw Eleanor at 9:30 and we decided to go out to the beach.

It was a mistake as she was chilled by the cold wind.

I got twelve bottles [of] a good chablis and took two bottles to Eleanor's hotel.

1. George West, liberal editor of the San Francisco *News;* Leon Gelber and Theodore M. Lilienthal, of Gelber & Lilienthal, bookstore owners and publishers in San Francisco who had in 1925 published Anderson's *The Modern Writer.*

Thursday, April 21, San Francisco, California

A day of work. In the afternoon went to Ocean Park here to see the fish in the aquarium.

It was cold outdoors.

In the evening took Elinor Mordaunt to dinner in Chinatown.

To be remembered—the story of the sailing ship—outside Sidney harbor in a fog—the drunken crew—beached cargo—officers ashore—the man who fell down the hatchway.

Saw my Eleanor late in the evening and we were both tired. We went to sit in the big empty lobby of the Palace. She hurt my feelings but I was only silly.

I was tired and so was she.

Friday, April 22, San Francisco, California

Very tired. A fever of writing—on Red—has been on me for three or four days . . . all I have going into it.

I have sprung a charlie horse in my hip and am lame.

I went to dine and dance last night with Eleanor. We were both very tired. She thought I was bored. There were very few people in the Chinese dinner-dance place. I was only tired, like a race horse, after a hard, grueling race.

It is harder and harder to hold the pace. I must hold it.

Saturday, April 23, San Francisco, California

Raining. I have been going at top speed for several days and will rest. Have a charlie horse in my hip. The fleet—some one hundred twenty vessels—are coming into this harbor this p.m.

Went to lunch with Eleanor yesterday after working excitedly all morning. In the early evening with Leon Gelber and saw Albert Rhys Williams—who has been a lot in Russia.[1] With another man, a painter, and two women we went to dine in a Spanish restaurant—somewhere back of Chinatown here, in an Italian district. Lots of red wine.

Talk very good. There is always something. People make too much of you. If there is another writer present, to whom not so much attention is being paid, you are nervous, fearing his feelings may be hurt.

I don't think Williams was so. I think he was generous and nice enough not to be.

Got, from Edmund Wilson, [a] copy of a manifesto—to be signed by several writers and issued May first. I signed it.[2]

1. Albert Rhys Williams (1883–1962), acquainted with Lenin and author of several books about Lenin and the Russian Revolution.

2. *Culture and Crisis: An Open Letter to the Writers, Artists, Teachers, Phy-*

sicians, Engineers, Scientists and Other Professional Workers of America, published by the League of Professional Groups for Ford and Foster, who were the Communist party candidates for president and vice president of the United States.

Sunday, April 24, San Francisco, California

Yesterday a cold grey day here. I went with a man named Dannenbaum—editor of a Jewish weekly—to lunch. It's a racket, I guess—this Jewish weekly idea. In boom times he made a lot of money—he told me $2000.00 per month. He lives expensively at an expensive hotel. He seems a nice fellow—wants to write. Now his racket isn't much good any more. A lot of good rackets are falling to pieces now.[1]

For some reason I can't be sad about it—even about the thousands of people out of work. I am becoming more and more a revolutionist. It is only so I guess people can learn to hate our capitalistic, individualistic American civilization.

We went to see the fleet come in, the American Pacific fighting fleet—submarines, torpedo boat destroyers, cruisers, submarine destroyers, airplane carriers, battleships—long, grey, unlovely looking vessels, very ominous.

There was the city with hundreds of thousands of unemployed, all of these terrible modern social problems, and before them strutting this queer neurotic thing—the imperialistic war strength of America—costing more each year than all education in America.

Costing each year enough to feed all the hungry, house all our people comfortably, build great roads—make a new and a real civilization.

1. No one named Dannenbaum published books during the next few years.

Monday, April 25, San Francisco, California

On some mornings the mechanisms of pulling yourself together are complex. The woman who makes your room is late. Lawrence may be right in thinking it better to do it yourself.[1] When she comes she is too slow. Mine here is a heavy Swedish woman. She tries to be conversational. She is built like a truck horse. She has got it into her head that I am another Swede.

My day was fragrant all day with Eleanor although I only saw her for an hour before bedtime. She went to Berkeley and I to the bookseller Gelber. He took me to a young Italian painter—come up out of the working class—who is caught by the beauty and shapes of machines.

There is something implicit here. We spoke of it. The Italian boy very quiet and sincere. There was an idea suggested—the need of a new religious impulse.

Why should the factory and the farm not become the new church?

Take the ownership idea out of property, farms and factories—give workmen the feeling that in making things for others, raising food for others, a religious act is being done.

The factories the new cathedrals. This young painter getting something of all this in his work. I bought a painting—a workman and his wife and child—the velvety, lovely tones of working-men overalls, a factory in the distance, hills.

His name is Valenti Angelo.[2]

1. D. H. Lawrence occasionally wrote of the value of cleaning work, as in a letter of July 20, 1920: "I live in pyjamas, barefoot, all day. . . . We do our own work—I prefer it, can't stand people about: so when the floors must be washed (gently washed merely) or when I must put my suit of pyjamas in the tub, behold me in *puris naturalibus*, performing the menial labours of the day. It is very nice to shed so much." *Letters of D. H. Lawrence*, ed. Aldous Huxley (New York, 1932), 514–15.
2. Valenti Michael Angelo (1897–?), Italian-born artist and in 1932 an illustrator of books for the Grabhorn Press in San Francisco.

Tuesday, April 26, San Francisco, California

Cool. I wore my heavy suit. A hard day for Eleanor. We had lunch together and then dinner. She is getting in, with Mildred, the report of the work here.[1]

There is a young university student has done a pamphlet of my Dreiser.[2]

I read Edmund Wilson on Marx; Flaubert and Shaw.[3]

I sat all day with young Valenti Angelo's painting before me and wrote of it.

It has been one of the days when Eleanor is most beautiful, something very dear and lovely in her. All day I have felt baffled because I cannot work twelve or fifteen hours a day.

In the evening not nice. I went with Eleanor far out somewhere while she got a fitting for a dress. I let myself get hurt horribly by some little flippant thing she said.

(Written to Eleanor. Not sent.)

Eleanor,

Someday I'll hand you this.

About a lover. A man gets very lonely. He works with elusive stuff that is always getting away from him.

I don't want you to do anything ever you do not feel but if, in the midst of things, now and then, you would stop—even for five minutes—write me a little note, let me know by telling me little things about your feelings for your lover, if you have them. . . .

Often such a minor thing will throw me back up on even keel again.

Does it have to be that you are always the shy one? There is such a simple matter as a kiss given. You will never know, dear, how many times I have waited, wanting you to say, "Kiss me, Sherwood."

Of course, dear, not wanting you to say it unless you want the kiss.

It's hard to explain. When I really work the hours fly with swift wings . . . when I can't work they drag. A day becomes a century.

Sometimes I am the central station out of which a thousand wires run, gathering up impressions. Then wires all get disconnected. They whip about, loose ends of wires, in me.

A moment of happiness makes a day for me sometimes. Sometimes when I come to you I grow perverse. I am so hungry for you to make the first step toward me that I can't make one toward you.

Then I pick up some little thing and am hurt by it. It's a little technique—if you want to help an often-puzzled man.

Remember it will always have to be me who must feel he has the least to give.

I am, after all, the one—in our team, if we make a team—the one who has been pounded most.

Sinned most.

Kept faith the least.

Lived longest and hardest.
Have all over me old scars that get to hurting nights.

Just to ask of you, beg of you, to try to remember that there is never a day, an hour that I do not need your help to be nice.

1. Mildred Esgar, colleague of Eleanor Copenhaver in the Young Women's Christian Association study in San Francisco.

2. Printed by James David Hart as *Dreiser* ([San Francisco], 1932).

3. Edmund Wilson, *The American Jitters* (New York, 1932); Gustave Flaubert (1821–80), French novelist; George Bernard Shaw (1856–1950), Irish dramatist.

Wednesday, April 27, San Francisco, California

I did not work on the novel but went off again into the thoughts aroused in me by sitting all day facing the painting of workers done by young Angelo. I wrote until my bones ached and I felt like a woman who has just had a child. I have suddenly determined that I will do a book, if possible, while I am out here. Was not out much. Had an engagement to lunch with a Mr. Barry and at the last minute, feeling very high with writing, I ran out on him.[1]

Went to a restaurant where a group of judges were dining and drinking. They went out and the waiters, customers and the proprietor began to cuss. The cook came from the kitchen to curse them. These men, sending others to jail and then so openly, blatantly breaking the law themselves.

Saw Eleanor for a hurried hour in the midst of her rush. She was lovely but seemed tired. Back to my room to write again and was so excited I had to dope myself to sleep.

1. John D. Barry, liberal columnist for the San Francisco *Examiner*.

Thursday, April 28, San Francisco, California

To Ted Lilienthal's house for a stag dinner of some eight or nine men—a retired naval captain, a rich sculptor, a young farmer, rich young banker's son, some radicals, Albert Rhys Williams, journalists, Ted, myself and one or two others.

We all made Williams the center of the evening because he was the man of us all who had seen much, from the beginning, of the Russian Revolution, knew personally Trotsky, Lenin, Stalin and all the great figures.

Williams was corking. He is a man of real class. How human he made all these men, doing all these really world-shaking things. I myself had got, from reading only, this picture of Lenin as a rather cold, inhuman man. He does not appear so in Williams' version of him but, on the contrary, a very human, determined, clean, courageous man.

In the whole party—at Ted's house—only the rich sculptor made an ass of himself. He kept thrusting himself in, could not bear that Williams and not himself should be the center of attention. Williams was never rude to him but I was.

Williams' story of the young revolutionist, running up a flight of stairs, in the midst of the great revolution, to dictate, to a girl from San Francisco, a message to the revolutionists of the world.

"Brother workers of the world. . . . "

Stopping to scratch his head. Laughing. "I dare say we'll all be strung to lamp posts in two or three days."

Back at it grinning.

"Brothers of the world," etc. It was a glorious evening. Williams made it so.

Friday, April 29, San Francisco, California

Again a furious day of work—not on the novel but on the new thing—"I Accuse."[1] I hope to finish that here. I worked in the morning until I was trembling.

In the afternoon went to sit in a little neighborhood park—all the people seeming far off.

The memory of other such days in me—time, life, a floating thing. I needed Eleanor's most tender side.

In the evening with her down to the Pacific. To sit on sand, watching the waves—then to dine at the crazy rooster place with the slides. We danced until eleven.

1. "I Accuse," a lengthy unfinished work that Anderson described as "an indictment of all our crowd—writers, painters, educators, scientists, intellectuals in general—in a time when the world so needs leadership into revolution." *Letters of Sherwood Anderson*, ed. Howard Mumford Jones in association with Walter B. Rideout (Boston, 1953), 258.

Saturday, April 30, San Francisco, California

The day before May Day. Labor Day.

The manifesto to be issued tomorrow—Wilson, Frank, Brooks, Dos Passos and others.[1]

Wretched at breakfast with Eleanor.

The problem coming up about her father . . . it did not seem to me she felt it as our problem, but as her own—

Leaving me out in the cold. Went to Miss Mavity last night—two men, newspaper men and their wives—Miss Mavity and myself. I liked the man Levy—a Jew—managing editor of the *Oakland Tribune*.[2] He is the cynical man—the newspaper type, his cynicism carefully built up, nursed, held onto—to sustain him, help him do what I dare say he has to do every day.

Play the game of the capitalists who own the press.

Himself really at bottom the dreamer—the man wanting to be [a] poet.

Not daring yet.

A little ashamed, brusque, the poet, in spite of everything, still alive in him.

Unhappy coming home.

Unhappy this morning.

May Day in America—1932.

Labor Day.

1. John Dos Passos (1896–1970), American writer associated with Anderson in several political protest statements.

2. Harold M. Levy (1894–1959), copy editor (never managing editor) for the *Tribune* from 1932 to 1959.

Eleanor Copenhaver, *ca.* 1928   *Courtesy Sherwood Anderson Papers, New-berry Library, Chicago*

Sherwood Anderson, 1932   *Courtesy Sherwood Anderson Papers, Newberry Library, Chicago*

New York - Tuesday - July 26-32
I would like to put down here, every day, if it were possible, something - a sentence or phrase picked out of the day just gone that would make that day remembered.

There are no two days alike - thoughts - feelings. Happenings that induce thoughts and feelings -

There are too few days at least. I'd like to hold onto some one little thing out of every day I live something worth. wing it off from all

2

after days,

It might be some thing
even in Eleanor's eyes — a
silent moment with her.

The way clouds hang
over a building.

An old man asleep in
the park. The nights of
him —

trying to go into him —
be him, just for a mo-
ment

in order. that my life
not be limited to my life —
this effort to enrich it
always, forever going
on.

Ripshin, the Anderson country home in Southwest Virginia   *Courtesy*
Sherwood Anderson Papers, Newberry Library, Chicago

The Andersons among the Copenhavers, 1937. *Left to right:* Mary Emmett, Eleanor Anderson, Katherine Van Meier, Eleanor Wilson, May Scherer, Sherwood Anderson, Randolph Copenhaver, Laura Lu Copenhaver, Mazie Wilson, B. E. Copenhaver, Channing Wilson. *Courtesy Sherwood Anderson Literary Estate Trust*

Sherwood and Eleanor Anderson, 1937   *Courtesy Sherwood Anderson Papers, Newberry Library, Chicago*

Sherwood and Eleanor Anderson's last photograph, February 28,
1941   *Courtesy Sherwood Anderson Papers, Newberry Library, Chicago*

Eleanor Copenhaver Anderson, 1978   *Courtesy Gene Dalton*

The Anderson grave, Marion, Virginia   *Courtesy Sherwood Anderson Papers, Newberry Library, Chicago*

May

Sunday, May 1, San Francisco, California

Sunday, Labor Day.[1]

I have been looking at the morning papers—nothing at all said of labor. For a week the papers have been full of the navy. Today one whole section of the paper given over to a naval ball—dead-faced society dames, empty-faced naval officers.

Labor itself without much self-respect, making no demands. Apparently the day of labor is a long way off.

With Eleanor to the young painter Valenti Angelo where we dined. There is a lovely baby girl with a big head and soft Italian eyes. She played riotously about. Leon Gelber and his wife came.

Valenti talked of his father—the Italian man gone out to Brazil. He came home after several years, walked into the house. In his hat he had concealed a great pile of gold pieces. He threw them on the table. The story of the man who bought the horse to beat the automobile. Eleanor very tired and sleepy. I went home and could not sleep, wanting her. I had to sit up and read half the night.

1. Labor Day is celebrated on the first day of May in communist and socialist societies.

Monday, May 2, San Francisco, California

To Angelo with Eleanor to have her head done and I could hardly keep my own hands off the clay. I have looked at her so much and with so much love that every shadow passing over her face is a living thing to me.

She is very sensitive. Constantly her whole face changes. This young sculptor had seen her on the evening before. He had said

to himself, "I can get her almost without looking at her again."
When I got there, ahead of Eleanor, in the early afternoon, he
had tried that and had got nothing. It was amusing. Presently
she came in and sat down. He began looking at her. I saw the
amazement come into his eyes. "You do not look at all as you did
last night," he said.

It was amusing, perhaps, a bit hard on her to see her sitting
there, Angelo and his wife and myself in the room. You do not, of
course, ordinarily look at the head and face of another in this
impersonal, critical way. She was embarrassed of course, but this
young Italian and his wife are such charming people—soon I
think she was at ease.

He worked rapidly—was not concerned with getting an exact
likeness. He wanted to get the essence of her. We all kept laughing. My own fingers kept wanting to touch the clay.

He was nice letting me make comments and suggestions. The
mouth, the nose, the modeling of the throat, the shape of the
head. I think he got something.

Tuesday, May 3, San Francisco, California

Breakfast with Eleanor who had on a new blue suit. Her eyes
very clear and her skin clear. Something in the blue cloth lent a
new clearness to her. It was all cold and yet alive.

I am a little stuffy, have an attack of the hives.

The day is dark with rain promised. The flowers in my room
have faded.

I went with Eleanor to dine last night and then we went to her
office while she read my "I Accuse." It will be nice if, for a time,
she will be willing to help take some of my doubts away. Now I
am—and have been—in terrible doubt about everything I do.

I have escaped the kind of people who look up celebrities very
well here. I still hope to get something done.

Wednesday, May 4, San Francisco, California

Yesterday—pretty dead. Something dead in the air—or was it
in me?

I worked on the "I Accuse" book. Later I went with Leon Gelber to see Fremont Older, a huge old man.[1] Talk of Tom Mooney in prison. This afternoon I am to go out to the prison to see him. Older struck me as old, tired, confused, believing in some vague thing he thinks of as sweetness and light. I may be mistaken. He may have hardness in him. Tired desire for a better world.

Back with Leon to his bookshop, saw Orrick Johns, the poet, Albert Rhys Williams and George Creel. Creel a little filthy slick man.[2]

Saw Eleanor. She seemed removed, far off. We dined and went to the beach. We were both tired. I had a headache. I tried to be playful. I was a little vulgar, not very nice.

An unsuccessful day.

1. Fremont Older (1856–1935), editor of the San Francisco *Call-Bulletin*.
2. Orrick Johns (1887–19?), writer, Communist labor organizer, and editor of *New Masses;* George Creel (1876–1953), journalist and labor organizer, during World War I the director of propaganda for the United States government.

Thursday, May 5, San Francisco, California

To the great prison here, San Quentin, with Leon and Ted, to see Schmidt and McNamara, the Times Building explosion men, and Tom Mooney. A curious experience.[1]

I should do it someday. Someday soon I must begin writing my memoirs. I shall make it a big book, put all in.

These men however deserve a book of their own, an extraordinary thing—to be locked up thus between walls for life.

The effect on them.

The great prison.

The flowers in the yard.

The Warden.

The Church.

The Department of Justice man.

Schmidt—alive. J. B.—his words like sudden pistol shots.

The Warden—shrewd, horse-trading politician man.

The death chamber.

Mooney—the saint, the child with the toy—himself, the martyr.

Leon. Ted.

Rich and Poor. Grim walls.

Grim is a good word.

Later with Nancy—the tough eager speak-easy—Nancy drunk.

The drunken pretty girls. The car in the street.

Eleanor far off.

1. M. A. Schmidt and James B. McNamara, who were convicted, with others, of bombing the Los Angeles *Times* building on October 1, 1910, in a labor- management confrontation that killed twenty people.

Friday, May 6, San Francisco, California

Breakfast with Eleanor. She had a headache, also heavy with sleep. Trying to talk to her, a medley—Proust, Wilson, Michael Gold, Mussolini, Gaston Means—she getting ideas connected with one name attached to another.[1] Cannot come out of the heaviness of sleep. I always come popping.

Amused, tender toward her, loving her.

Yesterday a passion of work, on the novel, lasting all day. At five I began to drink and the drink helped. I stayed in in the evening to work. I had undressed and gone to bed when Eleanor came by and I made her wait while I dressed and went to sit with her in the park. She was very beautiful.

1. Marcel Proust (1871–1922), French author of truth-seeking autobiographical fiction; Edmund Wilson; Benito Mussolini (1883–1945), Italian prime minister and Fascist dictator; Gaston Means (1879–1938), gambler and convicted extortionist who died in prison.

Saturday, May 7, San Francisco, California

Got, from Leon Gelber, Trotsky's *Revolution* and awoke several times in the night to read it—a restless night.[1] To the Palace Hotel here to hear Lincoln Steffens talk—bitterly disappointed.[2] The room was full of business men and he flattered them calling them artists, etc. Talked of revolution. I am to go and see him later.

In the afternoon to the old Barbary Coast here to Ivy's place to get some grappa.

Took several drinks.

With Eleanor to Leon's house where we dined. Valenti Angelo and wife.

The head of Eleanor. It was in the plaster and had lost something he had in the clay. He had been trying to work without her present. The reshaping of the head was good but he had lost something personal to her

1. Leon Trotsky, *The Russian Revolution*, trans. Max Eastman (New York, 1932).

2. Lincoln Steffens (1866–1936), journalist who had specialized in exposing American political and business corruption and who had recently published *The Autobiography of Lincoln Steffens* (New York, 1931).

Sunday, May 8, San Francisco, California

The day in my room —on the novel. It flowing rather excitedly.

A letter from John, talking of all the currents that flow in on a man now.

Saw Eleanor and dined with her at the little carry-out place in the alleyway. Stayed a great deal in my room writing and reading Trotsky on the great Russian Revolution.

Monday, May 9, San Francisco, California

The interest of yesterday centered about the evening at the house of Angelo—making a new head of Eleanor.

She sitting there before us all. It is a difficult head to do. The face is extremely sensitive and changes constantly, Leon and wife with Valenti's wife in the room.

A discussion sprang up regarding the merits of Lee and Grant, I going for Grant because he seemed to me, as soldier, a truer realist. It is peculiar how a bit of worship of Lee—one of the dullest men that ever lived—clings to all Southerners.

It is also somewhat in Eleanor—the result of training. In that family also a clinging to the notion of aristocracy founded on family. Eleanor is not to blame. She has less of it than the others. It is so easy to see how it came about. Without the pretense of aristocracy no civilization could have stomached slavery. It's a way of getting honor without earning it.

Lee is the grand type—mouthing about his own personal willingness to give up his personal slaves, etc.

He fought for a republic—in the declaration of principles of which was written, "Slavery is the foundation on which we rest," etc.

Oddly enough, just for that reason the man lost.

At least Grant knew a man was a man.

Lee was too insufferably good. In thinking of him one can never quite escape the cry—Nerts.

Tuesday, May 10, San Francisco, California

There is a workman at the side door of the hotel here. I came though that door after being out to breakfast. He has three gold front teeth He is shining the brass on the door. He smiles. I note the shiny metal in his mouth and on the door.

Day of work indoors. After the morning work I had a headache. Slept. Read Trotsky's account of [the] Russian Revolution. Headache passed. Dined alone and went with Eleanor to [the] office of [the] *Western Worker*—communist weekly.[1]

Stayed until nearly midnight, listening to account of many factions of the *Western Worker*.

1. The *Western Worker*, newspaper published by the Communist party in San Francisco from 1932 to 1937.

Wednesday, May 11, San Francisco, California

It takes courage and fortitude in another to stand me when I become, as I often do, escaped cock.[1]

Flare of life playing in me—ideas, self-assertion and just the same great awareness of others.

Went with Eleanor and Ted to Lincoln Steffens, at Carmel. No sleep the night before. Just the same riotous flare of life in me.

The road, color, Eleanor, Ted.

Jeffers and his tower.[2]

The determined, rather cold wife.

The twins.

Thoughts of that household. Mabel Dodge there, writing of D. H. Lawrence.

Jeffers not understood. Poet[ic] Lawrence. Cold—wanting to be strong, warm.

Brutality.
Stiff, small, sly, fighting for honesty through cleverness.
Eleanor, all day like a little boy.
Ted warming in others.
Orrick Johns.
Flowers, colors, conversation.
Straight legs of Steffens' wife, liking her.
The child.
My own approaching age.
All day—just the same—escaped cock.

1. Referring to D. H. Lawrence, *Escaped Cock* (New York, 1931).
2. Robinson Jeffers (1887–1962), American poet who had built a stone tower at his home at Carmel, Calif.

Thursday, May 12, San Francisco, California

I hate it—myself. I love it—myself, when it works. It doesn't work too often. Damn it—myself.

The rather fat, misshapen woman—not much woman—alive, forward thrusting, wishing she were woman, wishing she were man. House by the Golden Gate, one on Belvedere, sail boat.

She would be wonderful, as workman, running a loom in a factory.

Spent the afternoon with her and Eleanor.

Eleanor gets suddenly nice. She is very sensitive to people. People know it. She gets full of people. They live in her.

When she has been long with rude, pushing people she gets them in her, spoiling her for the time.

The fat rich Virginia woman. Very vulgar. Black satin dress, the white hair, feeling it is partly faked.

Brag, brag, brag, fat one, pull your stays tighter. Mrs. Preston Watson—fat old woman child. Your flesh has got coarse.

Brag of John B. Floyd. That pretentious, vain little popinjay politician man.

My mind is stripping your lousy little vain soul, Mrs. Preston Watson.[1]

Whiskbroom windbag.

Give me power and I slay your kind—against the fence
with them.

Or get tender about the poor little bragging lambs.

Oh Christ—

1. John B. Floyd (1806–63), governor of Virginia (1849–52) and Confederate
general whose wife was daughter of United States congressman Francis Preston;
Mrs. Watson was justly proud to be connected with these prominent Virginians.

Friday, May 13, San Francisco, California

Was to have left here today but Eleanor can't go until tomorrow. Worked in the morning and then, with Strong, the lawyer,
to the restaurant on Telegraph Hill to lunch.[1] Too expensive. Fifteen dollars a table d'hôte—as good a one could have been got for
fifty cents.

Paying for exclusiveness you don't want.

We climbed to the top of the hill to see the fleet go out. Majestic funeral procession.

To the Chinaman's to get a box for Mary and one for Eleanor,
lovely little inlaid boxes.

To Ivy's to sit with Nancy. Drank gin all afternoon. Nancy got
a little drunk. She writes detective stories so we talked of murder
all afternoon. Good conversation after seeing the fleet.

The drunken man who wanted his hat, wanted to fight.

Kept drinking. Didn't get drunk. Nancy's man has just died
and she is all hurt and tender. Drunkenness was good for her.

To Ted's—Valenti, Margaret, Kate, Leon, Ruth, Ted, Eleanor.
To the Basque place. Eleanor was strange and lovely in a new
satin blouse. How I love life. Wine in heavy cups.[2]

To Leon's apartment. Most conscious of Eleanor and Ted's
wife, with the straight nice figure, mannish voice, mannish
movements.

She rich and slightly self-conscious among poor people.

1. Strong, unidentified attorney, probably working on behalf of imprisoned
labor leaders in California.
2. Eleanor Copenhaver hosted this dinner at a poor people's restaurant in
order to make a political point with Sherwood's well-off companions.

Saturday, May 14, San Francisco, California

Leaving for the East tonight. With Leon Gelber to the shop of the Grabhorn Press. This is where Angelo works to make a living. Amazed at the smallness of the place . . . that out of this little place has come so many big beautiful books. The whole place is hardly larger than a hotel room. Saw the exquisite *Leaves of Grass* and other books they have done.

It's odd—my own acquisitive instincts aroused in me. Wanted all the books. When I go to see the collection of a big collector, who has them all, I want none of them.

Worked all morning on the *Beyond Desire*. Dined alone—with a nice couple, at whose table I accidentally sat. Had an interesting conversation.

Got a hair cut. The talk of the barber—about his wife, the house in San Diego, his craze for her, trying to break into the house, how he lost her, etc.

Went to escort Eleanor from her office to the hotel. She very lovely. Wrote her a long letter. Didn't give it to her.

Sunday, May 15, On the Train to Portland, Oregon

Wrote the story "Dive Keeper." Perhaps not very finished as I wrote it in a rush.[1] Eleanor kept phoning saying she might not make the train to Portland but I was quite sure she would. She is always slightly alarmist and inclined to exaggerate. When she means ten minutes she says an hour. "I was at the telephone for an hour," etc.

Could not work on a long thing. There was the distraction, last-minute things to do, to be thought of, packing, etc.

When I had written the little thing "Dive Keeper" I went to Ted. I felt a bit lost all day, not seeing Eleanor at all.

Ted was alone. I felt like drinking so we began drinking wine. We opened one of the small bottles of whisky and drank that.

Ted talked a good deal of Leon—Leon and wife in relation to his wife—one man born rich, the other poor.

The man born poor a little reluctant about giving up a certain advantage he has—or believes he has. He is even a little afraid that Ted may be as revolutionary as he is.

The emphasis put on the fifty-cent place where Eleanor gave her dinner. Ted and his wife both made a bit uncomfortable, etc. I had hinted at all this to Leon but he does not really want to give up a certain advantage over Ted he thinks he has.

Talk of Valenti and Ed Grabhorn.[2] Ted tried to give me a very beautiful fifty-dollar book. I wouldn't take it although I wanted it. I felt a curious greediness and had to fight it.

Saw some wonderful Russian photographs.

In the afternoon couldn't work. Didn't want to see anyone after Ted. Went walking. Went into a movie—*Salvation Nell*. Its ineffectiveness made me a little ill.

Should have known it was Eleanor's time. She always gets very strange—a kind of tenderness and gentleness in her.

On the boat. My luck not to have run into the Pralls while here—embarrassment. I had already done that woman enough harm.

At the station. The last boat. Eleanor not there. My heart stood still. Then I saw her in the distance—her peculiar walk—a little jerky, very alive.

The utter lovableness of her.

1. Only one page exists of "Dive Keeper," a story concerning a newspaper woman whose lover has died.

2. Edwin Grabhorn (1889–1968), founder (with his brother Robert) of the Grabhorn Press of San Francisco, publisher of finely printed books.

Monday, May 16, On the Train

Much breakfast discussion with Eleanor as to whether or not we came by the best route. We passing through the states of Washington and Idaho in sleep, myself in an upper berth.

My nose stuffy. It is hard to work on the train in the midst of mountains and rivers flying past. Things outside the car window keep calling.

Thinking all day of a new style into which my writing has fallen lately. It is broken, jagged, fragmentary. Often a word is made to carry the burden of a sentence. It all hurries forward. Often sentences have no beginning and no end.

But this broken, fragmentary kind of writing seems to be natural to me now. I have tried to reject it, get rid of it. I seem unable to do it.

Now I shall try to let it flow on as it comes, so naturally—to see if it becomes, say in a long piece, intelligible. It is the only thing I can do now.

Tuesday, May 17, On the Train

Eleanor should remember the day and night. During the day I wrote a piece intended for *New Masses* on the advisability of the writer now coming out boldly for communism, not for the good it may do the cause of communism but for his own good.[1]

Shall not soon forget the evening ride, particularly one half hour on the back of the train, the giant and strange hills, as the train rushed down through a gorge—the hills seeming to fold in behind.

I am always lying to myself. When a man has passed fifty physical charm, in his physical person, has passed. He is not going toward strength, which is beauty in the male, but toward decay.

He does not want to admit that. The thought frightens him. It frightens in particular the man who is a life-lover, whose dream is to squeeze the last drop out of life.

Little things remind him. For example, I went to get a haircut. The barber said, "You have a lot of hair for an old man." I hated him.

I dreaded going to a barber shop after that, let my hair grow too long. At last I did go. The new barber said the same thing to me.

It is ridiculous that such a chance remark should send a man walking and fighting off gloom for hours. How right the Russians are in treating all men as children.

There is at last a chance . . . some men have done it . . . for a man to go on growing in mental strength and richness to the last. He may be fortunate, may be killed in an accident, not have to suffer the terror of slow decay.

Some whim—my childishly begging Eleanor to be attracted to my person . . . as though it could be got in that way.

Then when she did come toward me sudden fear that it was just kindness in her.

My own physical life, physical expression of life always being made real or paralyzed by these hidden sources in me I don't understand.

Showboat Quillin—prize fighter on the train. His nice, soft, brown skin and nice eyes.[2]

Suddenly thinking of Funk in the night—after I had lifted myself up to my upper berth and could not sleep. He is lower-middle-class. Something in him goes toward communism but such men would always go slowly, hesitatingly . . . because of his few possessions. Perhaps only the utterly destitute man could go freely—he and the men like Wilson, the true clear intellectual aristocrat.

I used to think Paul Rosenfeld that but now Wilson has taken his place—not necessarily in my affection—certainly in my regard.

Wilson, writing of himself, in the thing in *Jitters* called "The Author," when he tells of his own people, his experience of life, achieves suddenly something that never used to be in his writing. In the page or two about himself is suddenly clear, sweet art—such as I have never seen in his prose before.[3]

Thinking in the night of what if any value I might be in a communistic state. It would lie in the field of invention in the world of ideas. When I was in business, in offices, there was always a flood of ideas. Anyone of a dozen—or a hundred of them—might have made me rich but I could never be an executive, to patiently put them through.

There is a plausibility that might have value. In business it was always being used to my own advantage, afterward making me seem to myself dirty. It might possibly carry propaganda into the world of fine art, as Wilson did in the pages referred to above.

Ted Lilienthal said to me, "You make communism seem right and logical. Leon antagonizes me too much. He acts often like a dog who has found a bone and doesn't want anyone but himself to gnaw at it."

1. "A Writer's Notes," *New Masses*, VIII (August, 1932), 10.
2. Showboat Quillin, unidentified.
3. Edmund Wilson, "The Case of the Author," *The American Jitters*, 297–313.

Wednesday, May 18, Stillwater, Minnesota

At [the] house of Henry and Katharine. Liking them both.[1] Very much amused and interested in two sisters' relationships, all the infinite little byplay of it. Eleanor changes in mood and feeling as often as I do. She can keep any man absorbed in her.

The day—last one on train from California—full of grey thoughts, feeling of defeat. Eleanor was never so lovely. I had her love—perhaps because all day I felt myself so unworthy of it.

1. Eleanor Copenhaver's sister Katharine and her husband, Henry Van Meier, a physician in Stillwater, Minn.

Thursday, May 19, Stillwater, Minnesota

Realizing the impossibility of really working here. I must get away from the flow of new impressions. In Marion there are old customs—old places.

We talked all morning at the doctor's house. I exhaust myself talking, taking up some theme and developing it.

We went for the afternoon on the river—the town, rising on a hill from the river, very lovely in the evening light. Eleanor caught a fish.

In the evening the visit of the Methodist preacher, a very boyish, nice man. His wife precise, tight, egotistical, self-satisfied. There was no warmth in her.

The joy of living in a strange town with strange people. The day a happy one.

Friday, May 20, Stillwater, Minnesota

We all went fishing—in a place where a small river had widened out into a lake, driving through a beautiful country to get there. There was a strong wind blowing across the lake. Eleanor turned out to be the champion fisherman.

Afterward I went to gather wood to build a fire for supper out of doors. The moon came up over the lake. In walking about I absent-mindedly called Eleanor "Elizabeth."

It must have brought up in her all my past, the women to

whom I have attached myself, trying to find happiness, etc. There was a subtle change in her but I did not know what it was. I am very sensitive to her. These changes are noted almost instantly.

The evening was a sad one. It would be so with any woman I loved now. She has to accept too much. I on my part am too sensitive because it is I who have used. Muddled all the past, made horrid blunders, been cruel.

There are little things happen. I had sung a foolish song and Eleanor said, "I should learn some parlor tricks myself," the implication being that I was one of course who carried these little tricks about. The saying was not intended as it sounded. I began to grow sad. The trouble with anyone marrying me is that I will always be supersensitive on this one subject—my failure in marriage. I get hurt when there is no reason. I want too much, someone always to be tender and careful about hurting me. I have no right to ask it.

Saturday, May 21, Stillwater, Minnesota (I)

A day in the house. Much talk. No work. Eleanor and I went fishing and caught a great many small fish very rapidly. Voices across the small lake. The green countryside. Henry in the hospital. The strangely dead-seeming head nurse.

Hurrying home for dinner. The cocktail. Katharine's unskill. The glasses. Strange misconception of fineness. Eleanor's confusion. Or is it my confusion?

How are we ever to make an end of smugness if we do not begin with self? Are all principles to go overboard when it comes to one of our own?

The dinner. Katharine telling of the family that moved from house to house, couldn't pay house rent. Henry's smartness about poor people. As they talk visions of my own mother floating up.

The doctor's wife—Mrs. Farr—her deep vulgarity. Her flesh not nice. Pretensions. The conversation laboriously kept on herself . . . killing all conversation. There is a fire in me wants to burn such people. Atmosphere of the room in which we all sit. I begin to get a sore throat, headache. The room, full of doctors, full of ill health.

Where am I? In modern society where do I belong?

Eleanor's uncertainty, love of sister, fear for her. Her own sweetness of person. As soon as she arrived here she instinctively went to Vera in the kitchen. Vera, besides Eleanor, the sweetest person in this house.[1]

The doctor that looked like Maurice. This one caught, uncertain, looking around, wanting approval. At that he may well be a skillful surgeon.

Farr—the scientific man. Neither hates nor loves his wife. He cries, "Work. Work."

The situation where he faced Huey Long.[2] His cowardice and failure there. Lack of social sense although an employee of the state. "None of my business, I can't be discourteous," etc.

Queer feeling about Katharine. She should not have said what she did say of Henry. Accuses him of being low-class, even incestuous with his own mother. I understand now why Randolph doesn't believe her tales. She told that and of Henry's being thrown out of hospitals and schools because he was tenth-rate and then—the next moment—she is in his arms, kissing, calling him "darling."

The other doctor's wife—long neck, rather sexless, tired. She terribly confused by the respectability all about. Tired perhaps in trying to think her way through.

Myself too talky. I should note everything, let my mind always expand, take in every phase of everything and then, when it does no good to talk, let my mouth remain shut.

Every middle-class person I see makes me prouder of my own humble upbringing.

1. Vera, serving woman in the Van Meier home.

2. Huey Long (1893–1935), powerful Louisiana politician and United States senator, whom the Van Meiers' physician friend must have tried to oppose, probably over public-health policies.

Saturday, May 21, Stillwater, Minnesota (II)

This is the day after the evening spent with the two doctors at the Van Meiers—myself got rather ugly afterwards—Eleanor tired, packing. . . .

In the evening the other silent doctor. An unsatisfactory day to me.

The hour alone by the river. Eleanor's coming there.

Sunday, May 22, Columbus, Ohio

Notes written late in the day—after seeing Eleanor off on the train to New York. I was very unhappy in Katharine's house. The last day there was hard and Katharine disliked me. I had been too frank with her—speaking plainly and bluntly to her as I sometimes do to her mother.

She not having any of her mother's swift response. She told me quite terrible things about her husband and then, an hour later, I saw her hugging and kissing him.

Perhaps afterwards she disliked me because she had been too frank.

I was miserable in the night—creeping off to my berth and lying there, quite miserable, like a defeated boy.

Not nice to Eleanor in the morning. Finally I began to talk to her. It took the form of an argument against and for Katharine and her life. I didn't want the talk thus. I wanted merely to feel the warm outgoing of love and trust from Eleanor toward me.

Finally it came and immediately I became well and happy.

Monday, May 23, East Radford, Virginia

At East Radford, waiting for the train to Marion. Awoke with a pestering cold—throat tight, body heavy, inclined to sneeze and sweat.

Columbus, Ohio, very depressing. Eleanor very lovely when the train left from Columbus. Our long lovely time together at an end.

I rather dread going home. Perhaps my cold is but a protest in me, a giving up temporarily. I'll miss Eleanor, Leon and Ted.

The summer uncertain. I want now to plunge into work. The day yesterday, with Eleanor on the train, the stop at Chicago, dodging about, my disagreeableness for the first two hours after the train left Chicago, that passing.

The Ohio country on Sunday. The feeling of depression in Columbus. The *State Journal* there, very depressing in its assumed cheerfulness.

I slept heavily, in a dead way. This will be a lost day for me.

Tuesday, May 24, Marion, Virginia

In bed all day, ill with a bad cold. Grace brought my food from Bob's house. I read Woodward's book *Money for Tomorrow*.[1]

I read innumerable letters, mostly silly.

The ride down from East Radford to Marion very, very lovely. In spite of illness I am reviving my love of this country.

1. Grace, a serving woman at the home of Robert L. Anderson; William E. Woodward, *Money for Tomorrow* (New York, 1932).

Wednesday, May 25, Marion, Virginia

Still in bed quite ill, restless. Had Dr. Willis Sprinkle in. Liked him. No fever, a strong heart, he says.[1]

Read Van Wyck Brooks' *Emerson*.[2] Think the way it is told fits the man, all thought, dreams, intellectual dignity. Little or no lust, sin, all the things that have blotched and colored and made my own life. It is my own experience that, in a bad cold like this, you always feel most miserable just before you start getting well.

1. Dr. Willis Sprinkle, general practitioner since 1930 in Marion, Va.
2. Van Wyck Brooks, *The Life of Emerson* (New York, 1932).

Thursday, May 26, Marion, Virginia

Still quite ill but I must be better, as I suddenly looked out the window and saw hills that seemed like Eleanor's breasts—the way they rise so nicely from her body when she is lying down.

I began reading George Moore's *Hail and Farewell!* again—which would be bad if I were going to work in the next few days.[1]

Doctor Willis gave me some medicine that makes me dopey so I close my eyes, sleep a little and then lie in a comatose state seeing very majestic sentences, flush and warm and full, like the day, outside my window—these sentences coming out from under my hand as though my own hand were apart from me and writing beautiful things with which I had nothing to do.

1. George Moore, *Hail and Farewell!* (New York, 1925).

Friday, May 27, Marion, Virginia

A big day in Marion. The whole town out parading for the one-hundredth anniversary of the county. Eleanor's mother had written a pageant to be played at the fairgrounds. The day has been cloudy with rain threatened all day but now—at 2:00—it has not yet rained.

For weeks the children have been parading—waiting for this great day.

Even as I write it begins to rain. Too bad. There will be a great scampering.

I went to the Campbells' yard to see the parade. Many floats. It was lovely, but as I remarked to John, who came after the parade to my room, it is strange and sad that all the celebrations in America—so young a country too—are always in celebration of the past.

Yesterday was spent lying in my room or walking about in my room. I haven't for a long, long time had a cold so deep-seated. I have been reading George Moore's *Hail and Farewell!*, such a very delicious book.

There the rain is—great drops. I can see the children, all in white, scampering—up at the fairground. It is very quiet in town, with all the folk gone up there.

At the parade I was very sad to think there was not one float or banner expressing any determination at all about the future. How glorious it would have been to have seen just one banner saying, "Down with economic fear."

"Let's build for the future."

"Away with hunger."

I wonder sometimes if people know how deeply I am out of sympathy with all this about the past. It seems to me that people look at me a little strangely, saying to themselves, "What is he thinking now?"

I am inclined to stir them up saying, "Tomorrow. Tomorrow. What of tomorrow?"

But perhaps I only fancy they care.

It rains hard now. Too bad that the pleasure in the past is so spoiled.

158

Sherwood Anderson's Secret Love Letters

Saturday, May 28, Marion, Virginia

Yesterday the day of the great celebration of the birth of the county, with parades, pageants and speeches, but I saw nothing but the parade.

A man named Bell—a lawyer, came from Chicago. He formerly lived here but went to Chicago and got into politics. He told the people here that the Russians had killed ten million people without cause, good people all, and urged a war on the part of all capitalistic people against the Russians to exterminate them.[1]

1. Hayd Bell, attorney, referring to the millions who died in the Stalinization program in the U.S.S.R.

Sunday, May 29, Marion, Virginia

A long discussion at the Copenhavers', myself on one side and against me Mrs. Copenhaver, Mr. Copenhaver and Jaybird.[1] Mrs. Copenhaver's anxiety that I not stir Jaybird too much. Myself still weak from the cold. Myself against the church and all against me.

Mr. Copenhaver's attitude toward my little blue girl. The little explanation I gave him in the room. Her attitude toward him. Dictating letters.

The talk about flowers and nature. What I said to Mrs. Copenhaver. Giving Jaybird subject for the sermon. My cold almost gone.

1. The Reverend John Jacob "Jaybird" Scherer, brother of Laura Lu Scherer Copenhaver and pastor of Monument Avenue Lutheran Church in Richmond, Va., and an officer of juvenile court there.

Monday, May 30, Marion, Virginia

When I was in bed in the night and heard the Sprinkle twin come upstairs and to bed I had a sudden desire for her. It amused me.[1]

Sunday was Sunday.

Went with Emmett Thomas to his father's—a fine old man.

Emmett swore at some children who ran across the road, saying he should really run them down. It shocked me.[2]

Then he began to say that they were children of a man living on the county.

Went to Frank Copenhaver who was ill and gave him and Ruth an outline of the communist philosophy.

It seems to me that my attitude toward Eleanor these days is nicer and more real than it has ever been before.

I must have a real talk with her about marriage when she comes home this time.

I am going to try dictating from the book this week to see how it goes.

1. Mary Sprinkle or Evelyn Sprinkle, daughters of Dr. Onyx C. Sprinkle, Marion pharmacist at whose home Anderson was renting a room.

2. J. Emmett Thomas, who owned and operated the Mt. Carmel Mill in Smyth County.

Tuesday, May 31, Marion, Virginia

A bright warm summer morning and the month of May gone again. For some reason I was afraid of the town and myself yesterday. My day got upset and the effect of my cold had not gone away and all life was a little stale.

Eleanor's mother called me to come and meet her cousin Paul I had heard preach—not liking him.[1] By the magic of Mrs. Copenhaver though I was made to like him.

At once she took all the pretense out of him and made him talk normally and nice. Only now and then did he become the actor and begin to preach.

It was too bad for Eleanor's mother, as she was tired and afterwards—when I ran in to see how she did—she was down with a chill.

1. The Reverend Paul Scherer, pastor of the Lutheran Church of the Holy Trinity, New York City.

June

Wednesday, June 1, Marion, Virginia

For the first time I tried dictating from my first draft and I hope it may work. I hope to go further today. I presume it is the effect of the summer cold on me but anyway I was very depressed yesterday after working.

I went out along the highway in my car and into a side road where I spent two or three hours lying in the sun.

Later I went to Frank's where I stayed to dine. I got rather drunk there. Andy Funk told me a tale of the boyhood of Jay Scherer—a tale repeated from John Buchanan—that, even if it were true, made me dislike not Jay but John and after him Andy for repeating such a tale after all these years.

It was a day of disgust with life such as I do not like.

Thursday, June 2, Marion, Virginia

The dead days follow each other very, very slowly. I think I must still be ill. Something in me is very, very dead.

I tried to work. Whether or not it all amounts to anything I don't know.

Then I went fishing. I was in the place called the gorge. It was very still in there, a lovely evening really. Not a leaf stirred. The water was blue and clear. I only caught one small fish. Nothing seemed very real to me.

Before that I was on Mrs. Copenhaver's porch listening to her talk to a young workman. It went on a long time. Her mind was playing. What life there was in her.

I dined late with Andy, in a small restaurant—bad food—and

he talked of Jim White Sheffey, how he cheated people, how his money went.[1]

Then of himself stealing twenty-five cents from a German to get a supper. I slept heavily, in a dead dull way.

1. James White Sheffey, Marion attorney and brother of Mrs. B. Frank Buchanan.

Friday, June 3, Marion, Virginia

This is the day of Eleanor's arrival from New York with Lois. Perhaps I will not dare see her as Lois hates me.

I spent yesterday walking about in the sun or sitting on benches weak and sick. In the afternoon I went with Mary to work in her garden. On the way home we found the old woman with the crates of chickens staggering in the road.

Went to sit with Miss May who has a broken knee.[1] Andy Funk told me the story of the country girl met in the road. They were driving in a lonely road and as she seemed to respond to some advances he made he asked her outright.

She consented at once and they went into a wood where she lay down. They were on the side of a sloping hill and it was a very difficult and painful position for him.

However, having started, he did not want to stop and so went on to the end but at the end was exhausted.

She was lying there smiling, with a queer look in her eyes. "I should be polite," he thought. "It was very nice," he said. "Will you, sometime . . . will you again?"

"Yes," she said softly.

"When?"

"Now," she said.

He said he was so exhausted he was quite helpless.

"What a fool I was," he said. "I should have waited until I was leaving her. A man is so silly when he asks at the wrong moment."

Andy Funk talked of the man who wants but one thing of a woman. He will go to any length. At last he gets it but, no sooner has he got it than he is at the end of all desire for her.

1. May Scherer (1873–1967), dean of women at nearby Marion College, maternal aunt of Eleanor Copenhaver, who shared the Copenhaver life at Rosemont.

Saturday, June 4, Marion, Virginia

Eleanor and I to the farm—where we stayed while she looked through the books there. She found a lot of copies of *transition* we brought home.[1] We had a beautiful day together. There had been enough rain to wash the dust off the trees and bushes and the whole country was like a young girl getting up from refreshing sleep. I worked on *Beyond Desire*. I was very happy all day . . . a contrast to the sadness of the day before. The more I am with Eleanor the more I love her. We have loved for three years now and it grows richer. I am gradually getting into her hands the thing I want to save.

1. *transition*, avant-garde magazine, published in Paris (1927–38), that specialized in encouraging experimental writing.

Sunday, June 5, Marion, Virginia

Eleanor is here and everything is nicer and better. I went to get her at Radford and she looked very strong and well and lovely. It was lovely to be with her.

When I had got home and had left her at her mother's house and had then returned to my own place here the Mariston Chapmans came.

They are very sad people, Mr. Chapman an ex-mechanic, with all the fingers of one of his hands cut off, and she tubercular. She is really the talented one. What he does in the matter I don't know. It is a strange picture the mind makes—the two of them sitting over the typewriter at work. They work at night, drinking black coffee, like Balzac, but are not Balzac. Once he told me that she has all the ideas, does the writing, etc., and that he takes what she does and tightens it.

They fall in the bad hole of not being cheap and popular nor good enough to stand out as artists. Life here is likely to be very cruel to that sort, overpraising when they first appear and then forgetting.

I offered them my Ripshin house for the summer, at no cost to them, but, on account of the illness of the rest of the family, they cannot move.

They are in a pretty sad way.

Monday, June 6, Marion, Virginia

Up rather late—a bright still dry morning with huge spongy white clouds.

Mrs. Copenhaver, Eleanor and I had a long drive yesterday—in back-country roads—all the country crying out for rain.

Thinking all day of Eleanor and my relationship with her. It changes like a painting as you work on it.

She is very still inside just now and I think I am really coming to feel all her right to be just herself—outside any relation to me—its own value—sweetnesses. It may be that at last enough defeats have come to me to really wear away a little my egotism and leave me alive to her and others—a real lover.

Tuesday, June 7, Marion, Virginia

Got up in the early morning and after breakfast went almost immediately to Eleanor. With the three women sat on the front porch and talked while Sunday [Church] School went on. Mr. Copenhaver at Sunday School. I calculated about when he would return and left.

It seems to me Mrs. Copenhaver is cruel to him but perhaps he is not very sensitive. I can't tell. She is my best friend here, having the most alive mind of anyone about but, if I tell her of some little thing that happens to me, she retells it in her husband's presence. This makes me, for the moment, a spotlight figure and makes him angry. I have repeatedly asked her not to do it but she goes on doing it. Does she want to punish him for letting his mind go cold and dead?

Eleanor was very strong and lovely. I came home and wrote, then went to Bob to dine. Thinking of the strange visit of the Chapmans. There was something they wanted of me they did not ask for.

We all dined out of doors in the little road that goes through Mr. Copenhaver's mountain farm. He always runs about gathering up plants, in which his wife is not interested. He is at his best in nature but even in this his mind had no real curiosity. With a little study and his natural aptitude he might have known a great deal. Knowledge evidently doesn't attract him.

At the same time I hate to see him hurt or made to feel pettish.

Eleanor and I walked in the long valley to the round house and picked wild strawberries on the way. Her small, broadening, sturdy figure was very beautiful with the background of hill and the soft evening sky.

Wednesday, June 8, Marion, Virginia

I have put off writing up my journal until after my morning work, having slept very late. Now I am exhausted.

Mrs. Copenhaver, Eleanor and I went off to Ripshin in the afternoon yesterday. Mrs. Copenhaver very alive. Jay Scherer with his son Jack and his daughter were coming. We ate on top of Iron Mountain and in the evening Eleanor and I drove through Mitchell Valley—coming home to talk to Jay and Jack. Eleanor will remember that drive, the dark, the twisted moon, the silence, ourselves, what a lovely thing happened to us.

Thursday, June 9, Marion, Virginia

I am to start off this morning, to drive Eleanor down into North Carolina, to a camp of working girls there—a camp to which I do not dare go myself, because there would be gossip, etc. The radicals are often the worst gossips in the world.

Yesterday much with the Copenhavers—and much talk of their family—the two Jacks, etc.[1] I managed to get away with Eleanor for a trip to Wyrick Springs for water—then to Wytheville to look at some little mink furs. The day and Eleanor both lovely. She in a simple cloth dress—red, with little white dots. I saw a little farm woman going along the road very like Eleanor but didn't say so. The Copenhaver stock is really strong peasant stock, like my Italian grandmother.[2] There are the good solid hips, good shoulders, strong neck. In Eleanor it all topped off with a very finely shaped head. The father has a big head too but it is not so shapely.

Thinking that, to the type of man like Mr. Copenhaver, literature, the arts in general are as much a mystery as the figures of

Einstein. These minds will not go forward. They are better proof than the so-called criminals of the inefficiency of democracy.

I worked well in the morning yesterday. Thinking at night of Eleanor, that she probably has a finely developed sense of word rhythm, color, etc. It doesn't matter. She has a mind alive to ideas. I can supplement the other in her.

Agreed, with Robert Dunn, to give my name to the communist organization for relief of political prisoners . . . to be shirt front for the real workers.[3]

Was very happy all day—in work and in Eleanor.

1. The "two Jacks," Eleanor Copenhaver's cousins Jack Scherer and Dr. J. Hamilton Scherer, both of Richmond, Va.

2. Anderson liked to think that one of his grandmothers was of Italian heritage. Neither Margaret Austry (1830–1915) nor Isabella Bryan Huggins (1806–96) was Italian.

3. Robert W. Dunn, of New York City, who had asked Anderson to head the Prisoners Relief Fund, under the auspices of the International Labor Defense.

Friday, June 10, Marion, Virginia

Did not work but drove Eleanor most of the way toward Asheville. She will remember the little sandy place under the overhanging bank—the fishes playing in the stream and the dense woods going up from the opposite bank of the stream.

I left her in a kind of dream and drove the one hundred twenty miles home in three hours, so I had to do a lot of mountain driving with many curves and pass through several towns, I must have driven some stretches at terrific speed. I'll never get over being a child. I played I was a steamboat pilot piloting a steamer. There is always a kind of playing with life and death in such driving.

I dined with John and Bob and to bed to read Darrow's life Mrs. Copenhaver sent down to me by a maid.[1] She was entertaining the Buchanans. Darrow's book very fine, simple and direct—the feeling in it I have from talking to him—that he is one of the best and truest men I ever met. At bottom his philosophy is "Let it alone all you can." It is good to get this honest straight man's slant on so many old labor struggles in America. He recognizes absolutely that it is a war.

1. Clarence Darrow, *The Story of My Life* (New York, 1932).

Saturday, June 11, Marion, Virginia

Rain after a long dry time. Perhaps there will be mushrooms. I spent the day—after the morning's work—over Maurice's clothes. It brought back memories of my dead friend that hurt. He went in for fancy stuff. There must have been at least a thousand dollars worth of clothes I finally sold outright to Pat Collins for $125.00.[1] Will send the money to Charles Bockler. That would please him. I got out of it for myself four new ties, eight good shirts and a blue overcoat—rather warm but swank. I had a headache from drinking Bob's beer which I must give up.

1. The clothes were those of Maurice G. Long, Sr.; Preston "Pat" Collins, an Anderson friend in Marion, Va., an attorney and at one time judge of Juvenile and Domestic Relations Court.

Sunday, June 12, Marion, Virginia

The town seemed extraordinarily empty with Eleanor gone. Her personality invades everything, makes everything sweeter and better. Most of all her father's house seems empty. Her mother took me into her room.

I went with John into the woods. I like his mind, alive to everything in nature. We dug about close to the ground speaking of the life cycle of moss and ferns. With Funk in the evening to ride and talk. I stood on the street for a time talking to Marvin Anderson who bragged of getting working girls cheap these days. He told several stories I thought illustrated most of all his own filthiness.[1]

1. Marvin Anderson, an insurance salesman in Marion, not related to Sherwood Anderson.

Monday, June 13, Marion, Virginia

The day was hot, still and stuffy. After work in the morning I felt exhausted. I went to dine with Bob and John, Mary being still gone. They both said they felt as I did. Rain was coming. Dark clouds covered the western sky.

We went to Mr. Copenhaver and John got a cloth to use as a

background for painting figures. John had been to the Baptist Sunday School. Discussion of Joseph and his brothers, brotherhood, etc. John was amusing. We began asking each other trick questions about the Bible but I was not good at it.

Mrs. Copenhaver had got the *European Caravan.*[1] Talk of that.

John and I went to the woods for mushrooms but found none. We went back to his house where we talked to the Italian Frank Lieto—talk of a possible revolution, Mussolini, etc.[2] We went to Frank Copenhaver where we drank beer. I missed Eleanor all day. Began to read a book on zoology. Not many thoughts—or dreams.

1. Samuel Putnam *et al.,* eds., *The European Caravan: An Anthology of the New Spirit in European Literature* (New York, 1931).

2. Frank Lieto, Marion citizen who worked at the Marion Dry Cleaners and Dyers; Benito Mussolini, Italian leader who in 1932 remained honored in his own country and respected abroad.

Wednesday, June 15, Johnson City, Tennessee

I came to Johnson City, Tennessee, yesterday, in the afternoon because—as a result of my head cold—my sinuses became infected and for several days I have been having a dull headache that every day got worse. I am staying here, at the above hotel and going to Doctor Jones—at the Jones Eye, Ear, Nose and Throat Hospital.[1]

My room is on a top floor of the hotel. All the way down yesterday I drove in pain but at Abingdon stopped in a drug store and got aspirin.

Mr. Neff—the controlling owner of the hardware stores at Abingdon, Glade Spring and Marion—was in there. He is in the state house of deputies and has been the sponsor of a bill to tax the chain stores out of the state. His own stores are being hurt by the big chains and he has become a radical—on just that one point—being entirely a conservative apparently on all other points.[2]

We talked for a time and I said to him that some sort of state socialism was apparently inevitable. I don't think he liked the idea much. He is one who thinks of conditions a few years back when he controlled his own field and made a good deal of money.

He would like to return to that. Just the same he is a pretty shrewd and able man in managing affairs and when the revolution comes we should find, in America, some way of using such men.

I am however entirely with the communists in thinking that power must rest with labor. They must dictate. Such men as Neff would immediately begin to scheme. It is in the blood. The one chance is with the very poor and the defeated who have been beaten in life.

After the doctor had opened my closed nose it was as though I had been taken with a severe cold or a hay fever. I sat in a chair by my window in the hotel, my eyes watering, nose running, sneezing constantly.

The town is ugly but, from far up, you can see over the town to the hills. Dusk came on and birds kept flying past my window. They came in flocks—going with great determination and directness—like an army hurrying to an attack. A summer rain ran over the hills but did not last long. Solitary birds came, fly catchers apparently, dodging and darting. I brought Meier-Graefe's big and lovely *Vincent Van Gogh* and read it.[3] I could not sleep well and kept reading it at intervals during the night.

1. The hotel was the John Sevier in Johnson City, Tenn.; Dr. U. G. Jones, who had practiced in Marion, Va., occasionally treated Anderson for sinus problems in Johnson City, Tenn.

2. William Newton Neff, of Abingdon, Va., was secretary of the Vance Company, a chain of small hardware and farm-supply businesses; he had in 1932 just been elected as a Democrat to represent Washington County, Va., in the House of Delegates.

3. Julius Meier-Graefe, *Vincent Van Gogh: A Biographical Study,* trans. John Holroyd Reece (London, 1922).

Thursday, June 16, Johnson City, Tennessee

A day in a hotel room. I spent three hours of the day in a hotel room. Went to an absurd childish western movie. I have never seen a movie yet with good synchronization between the voices and the sound machine. The voices—strange, tinny and unnatural—seem coming out of the men's pants pockets.

There was a rather dramatic thing going on in the clouds all day and I sat looking at that and thinking of Van Gogh, my son

John and my sweetheart Eleanor. I was lonesome. The doctor had given me dope to ease my pain and I was dopey.

In the evening I went to a prize fight and rather liked the spirit of it—a rather amateurish show but the attitude of the fighters, toward each other, alert, determined, striking out and yet, at the end, nice toward each other.

Was pleased at the re-election of Gord Snaveley—as marshall in Marion.[1] He is corrupt, a bit crazy, really humble—with some feeling for law breakers. He is infinitely better than the reformers running against him.

1. Gordon Snaveley, who had served as town sergeant in Marion since 1927.

Friday, June 17, Marion, Virginia

I was returning to Marion from a trip over to Johnson City It was a warm summer day with occasional showers. I ran in and out of showers. On the road I saw many people trying to catch a ride. There were old men and young men, some of them quite respectably dressed and others in rags. I saw two different families—father, mother, and children—with little packs on their backs tramping the roads. I had goods in the back of my car and had room for but one passenger at a time. I picked up two men, carrying one of them a part of the way, dropping him at his destination, then picking up another. The first was an old man, respectably dressed, like a well-to-do working man of ten years ago and with a little grey mustache. He told me that five years ago he was a big wheat farmer in the West. He had a good deal of land but wanted more so he went into debt at the bank and bought more. He owed money at the bank and could not pay it. The price of wheat fell and fell. The bank examiner came to his town and told the bank they had to get rid of their frozen assets. The man was sold out. "In my section," he said, "at least seventy-five percent of the farmers will be sold out unless things change and change quickly." The man never had any children but he and his wife adopted some. His wife is dead. He has had to throw his children back upon their own people who are, he told me, very poor. "I have become a common workman," he said, "but who wants me?" The man was strong and alert at sixty-five but who nowdays wants a workman at sixty-five?

There is a little trick you soon learn if you are a man, as I am, who drives the roads a good deal and likes company. There is a way of making people talk. At once, when you pick a man up in the road, begin asking him friendly questions about his life. It is an old trick—"Tell me the story of your life." Of course, you don't put it as bluntly as that but every man and in particular every American is anxious to tell you his life history. He wants to explain himself. He wants you to respect and like him. There he is tramping the roads, out of work, out of money. He would like to explain to you how he got that way.

You pick the man up in the road. At once you ask, smiling, "Well, how do you happen to be walking the road? Where are you going?" In America every man who is broke, down on his luck, is half ashamed of the fact. Everywhere in America now you see people who are not yet broke. They have possessions. They have not lost their farms or their stores or their houses. In spite of the Depression they may still have some money left. Perhaps they are ashamed, too. It may be that nowdays all of us who are not entirely broke and see people everywhere in destitution are a little ashamed of our own safety. We have an inclination to say, "The fellow could get a job if he wanted to work." It makes us feel better. Or we say, "Look at these fellows. Nearly all of them own an automobile." We forget how it was here in America a few years ago, in times of prosperity. Then every man who had a job and any kind of an income and who didn't own an automobile was driven almost crazy by high-pressure salesmen. Radio salesmen were after him, automobile salesmen, refrigerator salesmen. He was made to feel that he wasn't any man at all unless he went in debt for a car or a radio. All the big men in American life cried out constantly, "Spend. Spend." Well, the poor fellow did it. Now he has the car and owes money for it. He can't run it and he can't sell it. The position of the American in times like this is somewhat different from the position of any other man in the world. That should be borne in mind.

For example let us compare him with the European man. In Europe the common man does not expect ever to rise in the world. The man is born into a certain position in life and in ninety-five cases out of a hundred he stays there. Let us say the man's father owns a little wine shop or a grocery store or is a small farmer, land owner. The son expects to follow in his father's footsteps. He doesn't expect to rise in the world and others do not expect him to rise. To be sure there are exceptions. Men of extraordinary energy or genius do arise and push themselves forward. But such men are rare, they are more exceptional. The man whose father owns a little wine shop inherits the wine shop when his father dies but he doesn't at once begin thinking, "How can I make my wine shop bigger?" He doesn't begin scheming to own a dozen wine shops. His father lived in a certain way and he in turn fully expects to live in the same way too, is quite content usually to live that way. For example, I myself have been going to Europe every five or six years now for perhaps twenty-five years. I always go to Paris.[1] In the Rue Jacob in Paris there is a certain little wine shop about the size of the Community Shoppe in Marion. The little shop is very neat. There are rows of wine bottles upon shelves running from the floor to the ceiling. The man now running that shop is about my own age. His father ran it and his grandfather. It was never smaller than it is now and perhaps never will become any larger. The man knows personally every customer that comes into his shop. He even remembers me. If, after five years, I go into his shop again, as I always do when I go to Paris, he looks up and smiles. "Hello," he says. "You are back here. You are looking very well. You haven't been here for a long time."

He has a son who will in turn someday run the shop but no one is telling him that when his time comes he should hustle to make the shop bigger. That he should live in a larger house than the one his father lived in or that he should be in any way anything bigger and grander than his father and his grandfather. You can see of course that this fact gives the son a certain solid feeling about life. He is a man who has his roots in the place where he was born. The fact gives him a kind of strength that is good to see. The man will not always have to be explaining himself to everyone. "I am the keeper of a wine shop," he says. Or, "I drive this dust cart." I have seen men going along the road in European countries driving carts that it was good to see. There the man went along the road. He had his whip under his arm. His hat was cocked on the side of his head. There was even a strut. "Well, look at me if you want to. I am here driving this cart. I am a cart driver. What of it?" Even the very beggars in some of the European countries have this air.

On the other hand there is the American. He can't, of course, be like that. He feels he has to explain himself. It is a very queer thing but the truth is that we Americans, who talk so proudly of our individuality and of our independence, are always going about explaining ourselves. It is easy to see how it came about.

We Americans have all been taught, from childhood, that it is a sort of moral obligation for each one of us to rise, to get up in the world. I am sure there must be thousands, perhaps millions, of Americans whose experience in this respect has been like my own. Progress. Progress. That was the cry. I was myself born of a very poor family. I mean really poor. Often we had nothing to eat and we boys in our family (there was a big family of boys) all had to go out at an early age looking for work. We were little more than children when it began. I do not believe it ever hurt any of us.

But there was something else. We were all taught that there was a certain kind of disgrace in being poor. How sharply I remember how the men of my own town spoke to me when I was a small lad. The mayor of the town did it, the merchants did it, the judge spoke to me, a preacher spoke to me. I was a rather energetic, hustling boy. I was strong, cheerful and willing. I wasn't afraid of work. I have become lazier since.

"Good boy. Be a hustler. Go after it. That's right. Make money. Money makes the mare go," they said.

There it was, right from the beginning. You had to have money, to rise in the world, to be a bigger, showier man than others in order to respect yourself. Of course, every man wants to respect himself. Money was the outward sign of inner merit. Men were still judged in that way in America. I must suppose that some of the men that spoke to me thus at that time, for example the preacher, the judge, and others, did not exactly mean what they were saying. It was easier, more simple to put it that way and then I must suppose too that in an earlier day in America, when the country was being built up, when it was being pioneered, etc. (but I myself am not so old that I can put myself in among the American pioneers. I do not mean that). . . .

(Just the same there has been a lot of pioneering done in my day, too. I mean pioneering in science, in mechanics, in building up the modern machine age.)

It was a kind of merit in being always active, always on the go. If you had got money men could judge you easier. "He has accumulated money. He must be all right." It was the easier [way] of passing judgment.

It is always, of course, easier to judge the merits of any man's work by physical facts. Here is a man who has built the highest building in the world, made the most automobiles, has driven an airplane or an automobile faster than any other man, is the richest man in the world. By the American standard that man looks, is almost automatically, [a] man of merit. It is an easy way of judging. It is obvious. It is simple.

But now we Americans have been caught up with. The newspapers, the politicians who want to get into office and others are telling us that the Depression we are now in is only a temporary thing. The chances are, however, that it is something more than temporary, that it may become permanent. There are a good many signs nowdays that we are at the end of one stage of civilization and must pass into another. A good man may think that what must pass is the age of capitalism, that some of these days soon now all of the great trusts, the chain stores, the big mills and factories and even the land must be taken over by the state. The age of individual opportunity to accumulate may be passing and if this is true it is going to be hard for the American to adjust himself.

If you do not think this is true the next time you are on the road pick up one of the Americans now down and out. Talk to him in a friendly way. Ask him friendly questions. See how quickly he begins to explain himself, to apologize. It may be that he has nothing to do with the circumstances that have put him where he is but just the same he feels guilty. He feels that in some way he is not a good American because he is not safe, because he has not risen above his fellows. I had two examples of this only yesterday. As I have suggested I was driving from Johnson City to Marion. I picked up the wheat farmer who for a few years was a prosperous farmer. Now he is down and out. He is old and knows he cannot get work. He was going to live with some of his dead wife's relatives and was ashamed. He needed a little encouragement from me to begin explaining himself. Although he had worked hard all his life, raising food for people to eat, he was in no way indignant about what his civilization had done to him. He should have been smarter, shrewder, should have taken more advantage of other men. He told me his life story. "It's my own fault," he said. "I was not smart enough." It is the average American's point of view yet and it is a little hard to contemplate. You would think in times like these men would be actively thinking and planning for the future. If it is true, as half of us now think, that we are coming to the end of one age and going into another, everyone here would be planning for the future. Our big men would be submitting plans. We would all be thinking and working to make all life here better for all of us. But as a matter of fact, nothing of the sort is being done yet by Americans. Only a few people —and they are not Americans, are as yet considered crazy and dangerous people—the communists and socialists, seem to be making any plans at all for the future.

However, yesterday, when I was driving the road and after I had picked up my first man and taken him to his destination I picked up a second man who did have a plan. He was a rather young man and looked as though he had been ill. He was rather shabbily dressed. I picked him up at the edge of a town and he told me that he had been going through the town trying to sell to someone a pocket knife he still had in his possession for twenty-five cents. He wanted to get the money to buy himself something to eat and I tried to talk to him to see if he had any plan for the future in America. He did have.

He said he had been thinking it over. He said he thought that the rich in America and the well-to-do people here ought to pass a law. He said he expected it would be done, that he looked forward to seeing it done. He said he thought that the poor and the unemployed in America ought to be killed. It was he thought the only way out. He said he had thought about it a good deal. He was a rather sensitive-looking man.

"But you would be one of the first to be killed," I said.

"I know. But," he said, "you see, I haven't succeeded. I don't believe I ever will succeed," he said. "I might as well be put out of the way." It is, as yet, I suspect, about the average American point of view. It is more simple. It is easier than tackling the terrific problem of what we are to do with America and Americans in the new age that is apparently coming.

1. Anderson had been in Europe in 1921 with Tennessee Mitchell Anderson as a guest of Paul Rosenfeld; in the winter of 1926–27, Sherwood and Elizabeth Prall Anderson were briefly in Europe.

Saturday, June 18, Marion, Virginia

I tried dictating just from my rough notes, at once. Usually I sit for an hour gathering myself together. I dictated an article for the newspaper that this morning seemed clear and O.K.[1]

In the evening at [a] party at Bob's house. Bob got drunk and there weren't any others drunk. Pat Collins cooked spaghetti. Funk and John and Robert Williams were there.[2] Collins held forth for a long time, after several steins of beer, as to why any form of socialism of the economic world wouldn't work. His point of view was the conventional one that the impulse toward greediness in humans was stronger and would defeat any altruistic impulses . . . man is evil, etc. These men are always quoting history incorrectly. Napoleon was the maker of the French Revolution, Lincoln was so and so. One doubts that any of them have done any reading at all since they left college. There is a confusion of terms. They use words as having a sense you never heard of before.

I was very lonely for Eleanor all day. Went to see her mother and took her a part of the book to read. Went in the afternoon to see a ball game between local business men. It was amusing for a few innings and then pitiful to see. Felt badly about the worse side of Bob coming out when we were with the men in the evening. There was a feeling of something coarse there determined to express itself.

1. Anderson dictated the prior letter-essay, that of May 17, 1932; the piece appeared as "A Plan," *Smyth County News*, June 23, 1932, p. 2.
2. Robert Williams, graduate of nearby Roanoke College who worked at Anderson's printshop for several months and who then began working in public education in Smyth County.

Sunday, June 19, Marion, Virginia

The day ended with a terrific thunder shower, that came after I had got into bed. I washed my car as I wanted to get out of town.

In the evening went, after dining, to sit on the court house steps. Dined with Bob but it was not pleasant. He had rather half kept up the drunkenness of the night before and it was unpleasant to see a sort of loosening and coarsening of all his features.

I was on the court house steps—drawn back into a hidden place where I could look out when darkness came. The town was like an absorbing book and I wanted to make a book called "Saturday Night." It was one of the times when a whole volume writes itself swiftly within you.

There was, as it happened, a sort of band concert given by an organization called the Moose—in the court house auditorium. Very humble people for the most part must belong to it. They came quite close to me, passing in, light falling on them, workers and farmers with their families.

Lovers. Girls in little thin dresses. Families marked by disease, what a procession. I was so excited that I trembled. It was one of the times when I, very lonely for Eleanor, upset about Bob, a bit tired perhaps—when I was most open to impressions. It was one of the moments that will be remembered all my life. What I most hate about this idea of death is that I shall perhaps never be able to distill into work the essence of all such moments.

Monday, June 20, Marion, Virginia

The afternoon, after work, with the Funks—man and wife and child—took them to Ripshin.

Mrs. Funk silent. She worships her man. She is very pretty and works hard but has no social faculty. I was to stop for a cold snack when we came back but it was really a big Sunday dinner. We went at once afterwards—into the garden—Funk and I, and she did not join us. Surely she is the old-fashioned sort of wife. I dare say, when they are alone together, they talk. She has had three children—with great pain . . . she is a frail thing and, to their great disappointment, they have all been girls.

Mrs. Copenhaver and I tried to name each five great Americans—the greatest—and hit it off pretty well. I named Jefferson, Lincoln, Henry Adams, Whitman, Emerson. She, being Southern, eliminated Lincoln. By agreement we later put in Melville and Jane Addams.[1]

I am trying to get a kind of counterpoint of thoughts and actions into the last chapter of the novel.

1. Henry Adams (1838–1918), American historian; Jane Addams (1860–1935), sociologist and reformer in Chicago.

Tuesday, June 21, Marion, Virginia

The enclosed book Eleanor picked up—on her last visit—when we were at Ripshin. It is book of notes kept—accounts, etc.—when Ripshin was being built.[1]

All day I counted on hearing from Eleanor—her mother and I waited all evening for a phone call but it did not come.

I took Mary and we went for mushrooms but it rained hard and there were none. We only got wet feet.

I wrote to Bob about drunkenness—trying again to make him realize the effect on him. Funk said, "I never saw a man change so under the influence of drink." I asked him to make the remark to Bob. I hope he will.

Bob is so nice in some ways. I handed him what I had written. It was pretty severe, although I did try to get some love into it. He never resents.

1. A ledger for Ripshin contained bills, lists, pamphlets, etc., relating to the building of Anderson's home in the Virginia mountains.

Wednesday, June 22, Marion, Virginia (I)

I saw a very black, straight-backed, strong-jawed Negro woman leading by the hand a white child. The white child had silken yellow hair and blue eyes. It was odd to see the delicate little hand of the child in that of the woman—a big, strong, black working hand.

They were walking under trees—the Old South.

Later a yellow woman, very pretty. Her hair had been straightened—it was parted in the middle and lay flat—framing her face. Nice eyes in both these women.

I remember once being on a steamer on the Mobile River. A beautiful brown woman stood on shore with a brown child in her arms. I remember yet her beautiful proportions . . . the way the sun fell on her shoulders. Her dress was ragged and I could see the brown beauty of her skin through holes. I wanted to jump on her. I wanted to paint her.

If I were a Negro artist I would write or paint or sculpt only the beauty of my own people. I would try to get the marvelous skin colors. There are roses on my desk—red with yellow hearts.

I would put such colors in the background of a painting . . . the Negro skin color contrasted.

At heart I have no faith at all in the social possibilities of any people other than workers—not scholars, lawyers, merchants, scientists. The communists are eternally right. Everything must rest in the end on the sturdy shoulders of the workers.

Wednesday, June 22, Marion, Virginia (II)

Yesterday a bad day with me. I have been upset again about Eleanor's apparent inability to write me letters that will give me any sort of picture of her life. When she is gone like this I would like to know little things about her, being in love with her—the dress she wears, who does she walk with, talk with. All of her letters are like telegrams that must be crowded in ten words.

Perhaps after all she is one who lives in the immediate present much more than I do. When she is with you she is so very sweet and considerate. It is strange that, in writing to her lover, she does not take time enough to tell him the little things any woman should know her lover wants to know. Often she ruins the day for me.

Yesterday I was furious and wrote her a long, scolding letter.

I went to Mrs. Copenhaver. She is punishing her husband by not dining with him.

Mrs. Copenhaver has got a kind of contempt for all men. There is a slight sense at least in which she would like to set up all her daughters against their men, retaining a hold on them herself no one else can quite have.

I am in the last chapter of my book and, as yet, it has not gone well. I have been, for two days, on edge, irritable, ready to fight someone. There is something about Eleanor that always takes this away. I shall be better and easier and work better when I see her again.

Thursday, June 23, Marion, Virginia

I have made up my mind to try to write less voluptuously to Eleanor. After all, these notes are for her. I began thinking in the night how much more natural writing had become to me and also how much more important. To me it is a cord between herself and me—like a boat that crossed a river to where she is. Not getting a letter is like missing a boat or if too brief and uninformative a one comes it is a boat too frail to cross on.

Writing is a kind of ceremonial with me. I have found no other religion. Do I write well, or badly? I can imagine a man in a church—devout but awkward. He tries to pick up the little forms of worship but can never perform them so gracefully as the man born with grace.

I went to a ball game with Jay and Jack—very beautifully played. Damascus and Marion—score two to zero. On the Marion side there wasn't an error or a false move. It was a day of little showers and the game was played between showers in the bowl-like place up by the state hospital and the figures, doing the job so well, against the green, the great white clouds up above. . . .

In contrast, to the Lutheran Church in the evening. There was an installation of officers of a young people's order called Luther League. Went to hear a man from Japan, what he would say. He said nothing—an earnest, dull man.

Kept thinking of the ball game, its comparative beauty—greater service to any God I could understand.

In the church lack of any sense of beauty, the building ugly. They had a half-attempt at form—candidates for office marching and carrying lighted candles—no training, awkwardness. The church should have been darkened for it.

Jay—too—falls into a false voice when in church. He says the word "God" in a way that would kill God.

Friday, June 24, Marion, Virginia

It doesn't pay to scold Eleanor. I have scolded her about her letters—that they are so brief and tell me so little of herself—and now I am ashamed.

Worked early yesterday and then ran up to breakfast with Jay Scherer. Afterward returned and worked three hours more.

Got into the car with Pat Collins and we went over Walker Mountain to Chatham Hill. We stopped to explore every wood, looking for mushrooms and finally found some magnificent *Cantharellus* and also *Coprinus*. I found two *Agaricus*. Magnificent—the first I've found here. There should be plenty within a week.

I went and sat with Miss May for an hour and was going home when I saw Funk who also wanted to talk. We sat on the bench under the tree in the court house yard and he began asking me about homosexuality, about which he seemed to know nothing. Came home and read Emerson's journal and dreamed all night of Eleanor.[1]

1. Bliss Perry, ed., *The Heart of Emerson's Journals* (Boston, 1926).

Saturday, June 25, Marion, Virginia

I have been rereading Molly Seabright's story—in *Beyond Desire*—just written, and think it good. The book wants just one strong forward impulse now. I must catch mood, my own nerves, everything for the boy's death.

Most of the day yesterday with Fallon—the florist from Roanoke—a giant, alive man—with a lot of shrewd wisdom. There is a lot of love of man coming out of him when you are with him.

Sunday, June 26, Marion, Virginia

I am waiting for a wire from Eleanor, telling me when I shall meet her and as I am very restless, sitting here, I hope I shall be on the way today. Thus also escaping the Sunday here.

I drove Fallon to Ripshin and it was very hot. He was most interesting when we got out of the car and walked in the woods. He knows a great deal about growing things. As it was so very hot I went to get my linen clothes out of a trunk I keep in Frank's attic. All my possessions are pretty much scattered now. I can think of little but Eleanor's return.

Monday, June 27, Marion, Virginia

Got notice that *Dark Laughter* had been sold to be published in Italy—with about $115 advance.[1] The day wasted. I was so on edge—waiting all day for some word from Eleanor about her return. There was a letter to her mother saying she might be home Sunday night and then one to me—mailed evidently at the same time—saying she would wire me Sunday or Monday.

Also a letter came saying, "I will tell you time and place in a postscript." No postscript. I was afraid all day you thought you had added it.

So I [had] this sense of dealing with a flea—but at the same time knew it wasn't her fault.

Just the same I was upset—driving restlessly about the country, unable to settle my mind into my work.

1. *Riso Nero*, trans. Cesare Pavese (Turin, 1932).

Tuesday, June 28, Marion, Virginia

A hot dry day. I let myself get worked up into a stew because I didn't hear from Eleanor. I went up and scolded at Mrs. Copenhaver who laughed at me. I imagined all sorts of preposterous things, being all day like a petulant child.

Then at 4:00 a phone call came and there she was, at Bristol—as lovely as ever.

Ham Basso—come to look into the matter of the paper at Abingdon.[1] Sold the Italian rights to *Dark Laughter*. Not much of a day but had a gorgeous ending.

1. Hamilton Basso (1904–64), newspaper reporter and copywriter, recently of New Orleans, who was thinking of buying a newspaper in nearby Washington County, Va.

Wednesday, June 29, Marion, Virginia

The day and myself alive because Eleanor has got here. In the evening she wore a long red gown—and looked very beautiful.

The black mass of her hair, above her round, rather Slavic face, the shining eyes and, beneath, the firm, beautiful little figure.

We drove in the rain, taking her mother to Crockett, and gathered mushrooms in the wood. I had worked earlier in the day. Hamilton Basso arrived. A queer, eager man came from Chicago and we talked of fine printing. I am reading a rather dull and conventional history of France.

Thursday, June 30, Marion, Virginia

Eleanor was very ill all day. She had eaten something that poisoned her and all day she was in pain.

In the evening she grew better. Mrs. Copenhaver and I had planned a birthday party for her and she came to the table. In spite of her illness she was very beautiful all day.

I dictated the account of the Sawyer family—background for Ned Sawyer, in *Beyond Desire*—dictating from rapid notes put down on the day before, and have an idea it came off all right.

Warm, still and very fragrant. Summer has come.

July

Friday, July 1, Marion, Virginia

I got down the last of *Beyond Desire*. I felt like celebrating. Went to see Eleanor and she was better. She seemed better than she was. Chicago—the Democratic convention—still it roared through the house.[1] I was in a gay, joyous mood inside and wanted to get away from all that so I took Eleanor for a ride but the day was very hot and the ride and the heat made her ill again.

We had planned to picnic at the farm of Eleanor's father and did in a lovely spot—her father ranging about and then, as soon as we had eaten, whooping us off home—on the grounds of Eleanor's illness.

The radio and the Democratic convention really calling him. He cannot do any such thing without doing it rudely—boorishly.

In the evening I insisted on having the doctor in for Eleanor and went off alone, very uncomfortable because of my own thoughtlessness in having her out thus in the sun.

She never will complain.

1. At the Democratic national convention in Chicago, Franklin D. Roosevelt and John Nance Garner were nominated to run in November against Republicans Herbert Hoover and Charles Curtis.

Saturday, July 2, Marion, Virginia

Was compelled to spend money to get new tires for my car.

Eleanor still ill, but better. I hope today her fever will pass. It seems like a violation of something in nature to have her ill.

I have dictated—from my rough draft—all but the last of *Beyond Desire*. Expect to finish it today.

Burt Emmett has offered me his Washington Mews apartment in New York and I will go there in July.

Sunday, July 3, Marion, Virginia

It turned suddenly cold yesterday. I dictated—the last of *Beyond Desire*—it is all in type now—and then went with Miss May Scherer to hunt mushrooms.

We went out the Gault Road and back by Adwolfe—got some.

Eleanor still had a low fever. She and her mother slept during the afternoon. In the evening I sat with them and embarrassed them by lying on a couch with Eleanor. Eleanor is to leave—on Monday.

Monday, July 4, Marion, Virginia

There is no pretense of celebrating this day here in the South. This one is a grey, warm, rainy day.

Went yesterday—with Eleanor—to her father's upper place where we met her mother, father and aunt. Mr. Copenhaver and I beat our way through underbrush and found some beautiful mushrooms.

There is a sort of very hot red *Russula* that is said by some authorities to be poison—and is recommended by others. I cooked up some and ate them. They were O.K. for me.

I wrote, for *Golden Book*, an article—"Why I Live Where I Live."[1]

1. "Why I Live Where I Live," *Golden Book*, XVI (November, 1932), 398–400.

Tuesday, July 5, Marion, Virginia

It rained nearly all day yesterday—a steady, warm rain. Bob and I bought Mary a silver fox fur. Eleanor went to New York. I am afraid about her throat. Ham Basso moved into this house.

In the morning Mrs. Copenhaver and I had a long discussion on communism. Times are growing even harder.

After Eleanor went I went with Mary to walk in the wet woods. It kept on raining. In the evening I went to lie on the court house steps watching the people in the street below. I shall send *Beyond Desire* to the printer now.

Wednesday, July 6, Marion, Virginia

I did a new travel note.[1] It rained hard all yesterday morning and is raining now, as I write. In the afternoon yesterday it was clear and cold. Took Ham for mushrooms. We got many new kinds.

We got into a creek bed that ran far up a mountain hollow. No sunlight came through. We went up it for perhaps a mile, very dark and hot, and it was strange to come out again into the light. We found *Aminita cæsarea*, I had never seen before—magnificently beautiful.

In the evening I held a mushroom school on Mrs. Copenhaver's front porch.

1. No travel note appeared in the next issues of the two Marion newspapers.

Thursday, July 7, Marion, Virginia

Mazie Copenhaver came and I took her for a lesson driving a car. For some reason her husband does not teach her the art. We got mushrooms.

Went and lunched with Frank and Ruth Copenhaver.

After we dropped Mazie, Ham and I kept on walking in the wet woods all afternoon.

Wrote a travel note.[1]

Tested out *Aminita rubescens*—had never eaten it. No damage. A busy day of people and many thoughts—a grey, rainy day.

1. No travel note appeared in the next issues of the two Marion newspapers.

Friday, July 8, Marion, Virginia

A long discussion with Mazie and her mother on one side, Hamilton Basso on the other. Mazie stirred it up by some intolerant thing she said.

With Mazie in a wood, looking for mushrooms. It happened to be a very open wood—too open—and suddenly my bowel began to have to be evacuated. I sent her off to a distant part of the wood, telling her there were roselles there, and got behind a big tree. I had to use my handkerchief.

I have written at such high speed since coming home from the West that now I must quit work altogether for a few days and go play.

Saturday, July 9, Marion, Virginia

I am vacationing for a few days. It was a gorgeously beautiful day yesterday. I took Mazie for a drive and we almost ran over a cat. We went to the upper Copenhaver farm.

I took my Parisian checker board to the Copenhavers and will have a table made for it. Ham taught us to play backgammon. It was a day pretty much without thought—had burned up my energy in work and was very happy just to loaf.

Sunday, July 10, Marion, Virginia

I took Mazie Copenhaver for a long ride yesterday. She, her mother, Miss May and I had a long talk on the porch in the early morning. It was about the lesbian scene in *Beyond Desire*. Mrs. Copenhaver was criticizing it, and this led to talk on lesbians. It was interesting to watch good Miss May's face.

Mrs. Copenhaver liked very much the later part of the book.

Let Mazie drive the car for fifty miles.

Went in the afternoon to see the boys play tennis.

I am very restless with Eleanor away and am anxious to go

where she is. Expect will drive to Norfolk tomorrow and then by boat to New York.

Monday, July 11, Marion, Virginia

I am expecting Louis Jaffé, of the *Virginian-Pilot*.[1] Will drive back with him to Norfolk. I have not been working—am trying to give myself a week of vacation.

It would be nice if, as you get older, you could keep all of your nerve and bodily strength till the last, going off finally with a bang. Bob played seventy-five games of tennis Saturday. What could I not do with that nerve force and physical energy!

Spent almost the whole of Sunday in the woods. It takes off the unpleasant feeling I so often have about the town on Sunday.

1. Louis Jaffé (1888–1950), executive with Norfolk Newspapers and editor of the *Virginian-Pilot*.

Tuesday, July 12, Marion, Virginia

I am still waiting for some word from that Jaffé. It is annoying—to announce he was coming, not to come and to send no word.

Annoying if he is not ill somewhere.

I am giving the later part of *Beyond Desire* its last reading and sending it off. Mr. Copenhaver is ill. Mazie and I went to Max Snider's woods and got mushrooms for three households. We found a whole log blooming with oyster mushrooms.

Thursday, July 14, At Sea

I am in a little ornate room, down in the bowels of a ship—a coastwise ship—on the Atlantic, going from Norfolk to New York, a very calm sea.

The room all heavily and ornately wainscotted, with overpaneled wood.

Yesterday I drove from Richmond to Norfolk in a terrific heat. Saw Jaffé's wife.

She flaps about more than any woman I have ever seen—all soft, too much yielding ass, hips, soft legs. I think she is probably a PEN Woman. There is something nasty, not enough mental, not enough physical. She smokes cigarettes all the time.

Jaffé is as nice as ever. He is limited but straight. He will play safe and succeed. There is tremendous vitality. When he walks across a room you think of a bear. He is stuck with this woman O.K.

Friday, July 15, New York City

I am again in New York, staying in the empty apartment of a rich friend.[1] He has gone away to the country to his country home and generously offered me his luxurious apartment in town.

Yesterday I was with another friend—the editor of a big daily newspaper. I had read something in his newspaper, an Associated Press story from New York. The item concerned Libby Reynolds, the wife of Smith Reynolds, one of the heirs of the great Reynolds Tobacco fortune.[2] The item from New York, concerning the woman Libby, wanted to give the impression that she was a woman of class. As everyone who reads newspapers knows, young Smith Reynolds was recently shot—or he shot himself—in the Reynolds house at Winston-Salem, North Carolina. The item in the newspaper said: "Libby Reynolds also came from people of class. Her people were not poor."

There it is—practically every newspaper in America carrying that item . . . the implications . . . if you are not poor but rich you are, automatically, a person of class. If you are poor you are of a low class.

The editor: "The man who wrote the article didn't intend to say that, exactly. It is a sort of American way of looking at things."

"Yes, I know, but why not delete it?"

Editor: "We aren't playing favorites. We are carrying the Reynolds story."

"In spite of cigarette advertising, eh?"

Editor: "Yes—in spite of that."

"Maybe you are, maybe not. I don't see why you couldn't cut out that suggestion that riches make people genteel. You publish your newspaper in the South. The South didn't always believe that."

Editor: "You don't understand. This stuff comes into a big newspaper office hurriedly. We can't have a philosopher in that hole."

"I don't see why not. They should be cheap enough now."

Myself, in this apartment, surrounded by many works of art. The man who owns the house collects rare works of art.

Men keep ringing the doorbell. I sit writing by a window in an upper room. It is a very quiet street. At night the property holders along here hire special policemen to go up and down. Men ring the doorbell and I lean out of the window. "Hello."

"Have you any work for a carpenter—for a house painter?" An anxious, tense look in the face. Hope—a little work. "Give me work for these hands to do."

A cry from millions of throats. Last night I walked in a little park. Every bench was occupied by a homeless man, out of work. Men were lying about on the ground.

How stupid everything is. They keep saying there is over-production.

Of what?

Too many shoes, too much cloth, leather, steel, wheat, corn?

Not if all were fed as they should be fed. How about the housing of people? Nine out of ten Americans are as yet miserably housed, in the cities in crowded tenements—in the country in poor shacks.

Building could go on here yet for three hundred years—with no stop—marvelous things could be done—cities rebuilt, towns rebuilt—every man, woman and child in America made comfortable. The materials are here, the country is beautiful, nature is good.

It wants only intelligence, a rebirth of intelligence running down through all the people.

The economists should be the teachers now. I've an idea. It concerns the writers of the future in America. For the time being, at least now, perhaps for many generations now, the significant young writers who will come will all write about the new economic slant life must take now. They will dramatize the life in mills and factories. They will catch and dramatize the new power of the machine in human life—making us all see how dramatically and strangely and suddenly the machine has changed life—so that at last we all realize.

A world coming into a time where history doesn't count any more. History having to be discarded too, for the time.

The strange drama of the giant—Industrialism.

Young artists and poets should go into the mills now. The old problems in literature—the man and two women, the woman and two men, how dead that problem is now.

The problem shifts now from the individual to the mass. If I were to look into the life of even a few men I will see today, here in the city, out of work, tramping the streets, I would have material for a lifetime of writing.

Love—as between a man and a woman. How can I think of love if I am hungry and out of work?

Is there a man over there—in that big apartment house—whose wife is unfaithful? What do I care?

Food. Food.

A chance to work.

A chance to work.

The individual problem—the soul of the individual—it is a dead thing now.

There is this big mass thing to be done, thought about, worked at, dramatized.

I went out early this morning and into a little corner drug store. There was also a lunch counter. Most drug stores are also restaurants.

There was a little Jewish man and his son running this place. The son was at the lunch counter and his father at the cashier's desk and as I came in an old man got up from a chair at the lunch counter. The son handed him a ticket for what he had eaten but, ignoring the father, the old man, shabbily dressed, walked out.

"Papa. Papa," cried the son. "He has no ticket. He has walked out."

The father rushed out to the sidewalk to confront the shabbily dressed man.

"The ticket! The ticket! You have not paid the ticket."

"Well!"

"You have not paid it."

"Well I have no money."

"But you did not say so. You did not ask, 'Can I eat?'"

"No, I do not intend to ask any more. I have asked enough. I am tired of asking.

"Call the police. Have me thrown in jail. I will not ask any more."

The Jewish man stood with his hands raised as the shabbily dressed man walked off. "Well," he said, turning to me. I smiled. "Well?"

"Well, he is telling the truth. He has no money."

"But! He did not ask."

"No," I said. "Well, I'll tell you, you take it. . . .

"Take it as an adventure," I said.

The Jewish man looked perplexed and then rushed into the store. The son was waiting. "Well, Papa?"

"It is an adventure," said Papa. "Ha. Ha." He tried to laugh.

"You see, son. You do not understand. It was not a customer.

"It was an adventure.

"Ha! Ha!"

1. The apartment of Burton and Mary Emmett, at 54 Washington Mews in New York City; the Emmetts' country home was at Valley Cottage, N.Y.

2. The death at age twenty of Zachary Smith Reynolds, heir to the founder of Reynolds Tobacco, created great scandal, as Reynolds had only recently married torch singer Libby Holman. Despite claims that the death had been by suicide, the widow and a friend were suspected of murder.

Saturday, July 16, New York City

Awoke early. There is a young couple across two streets. As I lie in my bed I look through between two buildings, as through a telescope and directly into a bedroom. It is perhaps also a living room. Although I am living here, for the moment, surrounded by expensive things, I am near a poor neighborhood. It is amusing to lie in bed and watch the young couple over there. There is a curtain that hides me and, anyway, my room is dark. The curtain, blowing back and forth, gives me glimpses.

They lie abed late. I have begun to build a fanciful life for them. There they are, in bed. He awakens. He rolls over and lies for a long time thinking of her. I shall never see this man and woman except in bed. When they step out of bed they step out of my line of sight. The bed is close to a window.

The man—a young man (I have, for some reason, fancied him a sculptor or painter. It may be his hair, a great mass of tangled black hair). . . . He is dark. The woman is blond. I can see her figure. She is slender.

She sleeps. He lies awake thinking. He is lost in thought.

"Why did I happen to marry this woman?" That thought would come to any man, any woman.

"I am now bound to her."

"I am now bound to him."

There were other women he might [have] taken. He notes her eyes, closed now, the lashes. Her face is a trifle broad for such a tall woman. I can see her figure. She must be tall.

Her nose, her hair in disarray.

He watches, looks intently, lies still.

Other women. For some reason a woman, quite forgotten for a long time, her figure now comes back into his mind.

She was a little dark thing. She was rich and had a sick mother. Formerly the young man I see lying there in the bed was a house painter. He worked at that during the day and studied painting at night.

He went to the rich man's house to do some painting. He saw the daughter of the rich woman there. Her father was dead.

It happened. He was young and handsome. She came into a room, where he was at work, to give some directions. She was very small.

She was a little, intense thing.

Suddenly . . . such things happen. She began talking to him.

He told her of his dream of being a painter. He stopped working. They stood talking. He was in overalls, spattered with paint.

Afterwards, she started it. She asked him, blushing, if she could see his work some time.

He had no studio. He had a room. He painted there.

However, he met her. She arranged it. She had been tied to a sick mother. She was lonely, wanting a lover.

It is amazing how bold such shy women can sometimes become.

The man in the bed is remembering her this morning. He is looking at another woman asleep. He might have had that one, with her money. But for her money he might have taken her. He almost did.

Once. It was Sunday evening and he went to her house. She let him in, by a rear door.

He could have gone up into her bedroom with her. She was

romantically in love with him, quite helpless. He did hold her and kiss her for a long time. He let his hand run over her body. She was helpless. She was willing. She trembled violently when he touched her.

Thinking of that woman, now, in bed with his wife, the man I am watching begins to touch his wife. He touches her lips, her shoulders. Suddenly he puts out his hands, draws her to him. She awakens.

He says something to her. "Get up. Get my breakfast." She protests. They begin to struggle. He puts his feet against her back and kicks her out into the room.

He laughs. "Get my breakfast, you lazy hussy." She jumps back at him. They wrestle. It is the beginning of a day. It goes on for a long time, amid laughter. He throws her out of the bed again and again.

She goes to start the breakfast and he comes and leans out of the window. My looking into his thoughts has disturbed him. He looks up and down a street. He cannot see me.

He calls his wife back to him. She is partially dressed now. He is gentle with her, caressing her. Their lips meet and cling together.

They lie still, close together, for a long time and then again he is disturbed. He gets out of bed and I see his arms go down to her. He is a strong young man. He lifts her gently out of the bed. But for my own thoughts, going along between the two buildings and into the room, he might have stayed in the bed close to her for a long time.

It is as though he were pulling her away out of my sight. "She is mine. Do not begin thinking of her." Their day has begun. I also get out of bed.

Sunday, July 17, New York City

Very hot and murky. Had breakfast with Eleanor at her apartment and rode up to Dyckman Street, going to the Emmetts'. Eleanor still and far away, half asleep. Thinking as I walked over here of days with C. and K. near here.[1]

Of Eleanor. I would be only too glad to go on as we are. We can't—on account of others. I must put it plainly.

I'm willing to try that. It will be too difficult for her.

Her people would be upset.

If she can cut loose and wants to, I will.

It would leave me altogether lonely.

Thinking of yesterday—the hot long walk in Bronx Park, going to the museum in the Botanical Gardens.

The wild horses—the strange behavior—the eyes of men standing about, wanting to see the love-making if it came.

The old man at the second-hand book store—half-rascal, half-man. The mushroom book, the heavy sleep at Eleanor's house.

1. Possibly the painter Charles Bockler and his wife Katharine.

Monday, July 18, Valley Cottage, New York

At Burt Emmett's place. Bill, Phil, the station, the old man under the trees, shelling peas.

The walk up through the old fields. Bill, in relation to land ownership.

Telling Burt and Mary about Eleanor. The attitude of Burt and Mary toward life—its niceness, nicest of all rich people I have known.

Talk with Burt about communism—under the trees. The winds.

The big car. The three workmen in the road who fixed the tire. Their thoughts.

Burt shaving in the early morning, fixing up arguments in his mind about communism.

Liverights seem to like *Beyond Desire*. I am to have $1000.00 advance. Day of thoughts of Eleanor.

Tuesday, July 19, New York City

The whole day drawing itself into the evening. I awoke at five with a violent headache, I believe from drinking some of Burt Emmett's homemade wine. I had to sit up in bed, my head reeling. I took a headache pill and it passed. Went to walk about the place and breakfasted. They are nice rich people. Burt has bought himself an annuity to be safe. Now he spends his money freely on art and people. There are all sorts of people about his place and also horses, donkeys, etc. There was an old man, I found under a tree, shelling peas, an Italian working in the garden, a young man dusting poison [onto] potato bugs.

The young man an interesting figure—tall and lean like my son John. He is a skillful player of contract bridge, a top-notch man, and could make his living at that, did for a time.

He suddenly gave it up and began farming the Emmett land. It was land just lying there, untouched, owned by a rich man.

However, there is the framework existing—ownership, capitalism. Burt will not want the land, or any rent it will bring in, but if the young man goes on farming it, without paying, something not so nice will grow up between himself and Burt.

The evening very happy with Eleanor. She gave me the little book to read. I've a notion we came closer [to] each other than we ever did.

Wednesday, July 20, New York City

My son John came in—hitch-hiking from Boston and Martha's Vineyard. We went to dine at one of the few sidewalk cafés in New York—Café Royal on Second Avenue—and later walked in the crowded street. It was very hot and I was tired.

The man in the phone booth phoning to his girl's friend, trying to be strong. "She's been drinking. Well, she's had a drink or two." "Who has she been with?" Jealousy, fear—trying to be the strong male. His bluff called.

Fat man in the street, addressing a crowd.

"You take now . . . a day like this now . . . a glass of beer. You take."

Ecstasy. "You take. You take."

The difficulty of talking with John. Robbery at the Lafayette—orange juice for $2.00, coffee for $1.00, toast for two $1.25—robbery.

They cut off all the best part of the toast.

The way people make you self-conscious in a restaurant. Imagine being a really prominent man, always being recognized everywhere you go, a Lindbergh—an impossible life.

Thursday, July 21, New York City

With John to see a Russian movie, *The Diary of a Revolutionist*. It was gorgeous picture-taking. The titles were in English but the people talked Russian. It was communist propaganda—very fine. The place was packed with working people.

In the evening to Tom Smith where I got nicely drunk—perfectly able to walk. Tom wanted me to. There were things to be said to each other. It came out O.K.

After it I felt I had to see Eleanor so called her. She had just come home. I went to her apartment and talked for an hour. I do not remember much I said but think that, on the whole, I was nice. At least I had very, very nice feelings inside me. John left for Bel Air this a.m.[1]

1. John Anderson was to visit the painter Charles Bockler and his family near Bel Air, Md.

Friday, July 22, New York City

I have started the writing of a story—"Man Talking."[1] It may not come off.

Dinner last night with Burt Emmett and the rich doctor. The boy in the police station who stole and pawned the objects of art.

The story should be built about that.

At noon to the Shelton with Eleanor to swim and lunch. Ben Hecht and the woman. The ugly mouth of the successful man. Drank too much again. The woman in the restaurant who worked fifteen hours a day.

1. "Man Talking," a story apparently not completed or surviving.

Saturday, July 23, New York City

I walked uptown to Forty-seventh Street, where I was going to make the final revisions of *Beyond Desire* with Commins—the editor there, Emma Goldman's nephew.[1] There was a crowd of employees gathered about a restaurant on the avenue. It had closed suddenly and they were not paid.

I worked with Commins in the morning and in the afternoon and we cut out about ten pages, places where I had been rather didactic—fancying myself as an economist, etc. Commins and Milt Grass were both enthusiastic.[2] They both said it was the first real American proletarian novel. Went to lunch with Commins and he told me stories of Goldman and about an Italian boy, playing the piano in a house of ill fame, who read *Winesburg*. I got a bottle of whiskey and inscribed a copy of *Perhaps Women* for the head of the United Cigar Store.

Ran out to see Eleanor about the letters from home—concerning Jack Cronk who is trying to settle down on Eleanor's mother and father.[3]

The parks are full of men—some of them well enough dressed, sleeping out at night on benches, all looking tired, and in the meantime the street in which I am living temporarily is filled with empty rooms, the people having gone off for the summer—expensive and comfortable beds, not used.

The energy of a whole people meanwhile being used just to keep themselves alive—not a really constructive thing going on in the whole country.

Eleanor and I walked down Madison Avenue from Fifty-seventh and were panhandled in almost every block.

1. Saxe Commins, editor for Horace Liveright; Emma Goldman (1869–1940), Lithuanian-born political activist imprisoned during World War I for anti-draft activities, whose autobiography *Living My Life* (New York, 1931) Anderson had read.

2. Milton Grass, an official with Horace Liveright's publishing company.

3. Anderson always disliked John "Jack" Cronk, a maternal first cousin of Eleanor Copenhaver, who was hoping to live advantageously on Copenhaver property or in Anderson's home Ripshin.

Sunday, July 24, New York City

It was a day when I did not think much. I went to the pool with Eleanor where we swam, then lunched, then worked. I was very happy but lazy as I am now. We went to her place to lie on our backs. I read aloud. Hours passed so—as pleasant as I ever knew in my life. We ate simply, then read again. I went home early and to bed where I slept quietly.

Monday, July 25, New York City

In the spiritual flat. It may be due to too many emotional reactions to life—taken too fast, while here. Eleanor is still undecided or pretends she is. I watch her closely. At the least sign from her that I am a handicap in life to her I shall get out.

Confusion regarding what is fair and right to her. I went with her yesterday to the Public Library, sitting near her and reading while she worked.

There was a man came in, librarian of the Russell Sage Industrial Relations Library, Eleanor said. His wife was sitting in there.

What Eleanor did not see was a little thing she did, how her hand touched her man.

Something complete and very real.

Myself wondering if Eleanor can ever quite feel that toward me, taking into account my past, etc.

I am half sick trying to think my way through all this.

Tuesday, July 26, New York City

I would like to put down here, every day, if it were possible, something—a sentence or phrase picked out of the day just gone—that would make that day remembered.

There are no two days alike—thoughts, feelings, happenings that induce thoughts and feelings.

There are too few days at best. I'd like to hold onto some one little thing out of every day I live, something marking it off from all other days.

It might be something seen in Eleanor's eyes—a silent moment with her.

The way clouds hang over a building.

An old man asleep in the park, thoughts of him.

Trying to go into him, be him, just for a moment.

In order that my life not be limited to my life—this effort to enrich it always forever going on.

Wednesday, July 27, New York City

Last night with Eleanor to Café Royal and then to hear the communist kids on a street corner. Fine sincerity. It touched me.

The afternoon in publishing houses. Gloom like a Pittsburgh fog.

No hope, no courage.

The middle-class American world in distress isn't a nice thing to see.

Thursday, July 28, New York City

Trying to help Eleanor a little in the San Francisco matter. It is rather fun digging into statistics.

Went to see a movie with Eleanor—*The Russian Soil*—very slow tempo, lovely picture-taking.

Waldo Frank's complaint about the attitude of the Communist Revolution toward the writers. Bunk. If artists cannot go through a revolution and survive let them die.

Very happy all day thinking of Eleanor's fineness, the fun of being with her. The best human I have ever been close to.

And a superb lover.

Friday, July 29, On the Train

I am on a train, going from New York to visit my daughter at North Amherst, Massachusetts. The morning papers are filled with the story of the Bonus Army being driven out of Washington. Although there is nothing very noble in the idea of these ex-soldiers always clamoring for pay for their fighting, so much having been made of patriotism, giving all for country, etc., at the time of the World War, it should be remembered that the government itself studiously put up the notion of financial reward, job assured, etc. Also the soldiers know how the bankers cleaned up in the war and how they are now being taken care of by government.[1]

The whole thing but another evidence of the breaking up of a social structure.

I went in the early morning to sign a communist manifesto at Seventh Street and Avenue A. I like the fighting boys and young men. They are the best we have. I am convinced the future will be in the hands of the proletariat.

In the afternoon to a ball game—Giants and Pirates, the Pirates team very fine. They won two games.

In the evening to see a special exhibition of a new Soviet picture with Eleanor, where I saw Dreiser.

1. In the summer of 1932, as many as twelve thousand veterans of World War I gathered in Washington, D.C., to demand during the Depression early payment of the "bonus" money promised them for their war service and payable in 1945. When many of the camping soldiers refused to leave the city under orders of President Hoover, they were dispersed by the United States Army with the use of tanks and tear gas.

Saturday, July 30, On the Train

Arrived at my daughter's house at noon and in the afternoon we went into the woods, where we walked and collected mushrooms. During the walk she told me of her pregnancy, which alarms her because her husband is out of work.

Her husband's father came, a little old working-man type but with pretty much middle-class ideas. He clings to the belief that men like Hoover and Cal Coolidge are the outstanding American men. Cal Coolidge has his law office in the town—or rather small city—where I got off the train.[1]

The whole New England country has always an odd effect upon me, the little fields, the closeness, the lack of richness. . . .

Something cold and a little withdrawn in the people. I was, as I always am, glad to get out of the atmosphere of it.

1. Calvin Coolidge (1872–1933), conservative Republican president of the United States (1923–29).

Sunday, July 31, New York City

I am up early, as Eleanor and I are going to the country. I spent the morning with Mimi and Russell and rode down to New York in the afternoon, rather dead.

Later I felt more alive. Then Eleanor and I had a misunderstanding. It came about through her telling me of what she thought my attitude toward our being seen together in her apartment and in this rich man's house where I am staying now. In this case she was wrong. She isn't, usually.

August

Monday, August 1, New York City

The day—yesterday—with Eleanor at the Emmetts'—at their country place—and very happy feeling their liking for her. Everything brought out her charm and theirs.

Again the odd feeling of being separated from life.

A happy, happy day. The separation from life—being inevitable with the possession of money.

Tuesday, August 2, New York City

To see *Ukraine*, one of the best movies I ever saw—the best really.[1] Fine use made of stills—the story not told too simply and yet everything clear and very exciting.

Afterward I went to the office of *New Masses* where a man told me the inside story of how the Bonus marchers at Washington were sold out. The old game of "get the leaders."

Went to see a great demonstration—30,000 Reds—very young and fine, marching to protest against war.

1. Anderson saw *Arsenal: The Ukrainian Revolution*, showing at the Workers Acme Theatre, Union Square and Fourteenth Street.

Wednesday, August 3, New York City

A hot murky day with occasional showers. I went to the place where the young communists are trying to make movies—no money, no studio, very little outlet for the movies when made. They can only be used in a few theaters in the big cities and locally before groups of workers gathered in rooms.

A man named Tom Brandon—a fine-looking, red-haired young man—took me to where some young painters, writers and musicians are trying to solve this problem.[1]

Mimi had come to town with her husband and I took her to Café Royal, where Eleanor came to meet us.

These notes are written to Eleanor to remind her of these tangled days.

Mimi's husband nice and likable but hard to talk to. It may be the New Englander in him. He does not go out—"put out," we say in Virginia. Perhaps he can't.

A walk back to Eleanor's apartment where we had a drink—both Eleanor and I busy telling about the city—history of buildings passed, etc.—both trying valiantly to make conversation, working upstream.

1. Tom Brandon, vice president of the Film Forum, who talked with Anderson about the possibility of making films treating workers honestly.

Thursday, August 4, New York City

I spent the evening not being too nice to Eleanor. I went there after dinner. When she came in it was with something of her father's manner, a bit rudely. She did not smile but walked past me and went upstairs. She went to the bathroom and later changed her clothes. I sat in the darkness in the little front room. She came and threw herself down. I appealed to her. "How about a little show of affection if you have any?"

She had none. I do not tire like that and when I am tired cannot sleep. She slept. I am more sensitive than she is. Many little things hurt me that she does not notice.

On the other hand I am more silly and foolish.

If a man were not a profound egoist he would never be a writer. He would not think his thoughts and feelings of enough importance to set down.

Friday, August 5, New York City

Went with Mary Emmett to the offices of Liveright and got final page proofs of *Beyond Desire*. Another novel is already stirring in me. I would like to tell more fully the story of the working man who goes the other way. Perhaps I can. With Mary Emmett to drive through the park and got her interested in telling the story of her own early life.

Have agreed to go to Washington next week to protest against the treatment of the Bonus marchers there, their being driven out of Washington like hungry dogs.

Eleanor, Mary, Burt and I to Café Royal where the notable thing was the almost unbelievable innocence of Burt as to life in the world now.

Saturday, August 6, New York City

Very hot. Eleanor and I very happy last night, reading proofs for the new novel. Worked all day at that.

Amazed at Burton Emmett's naive outlook. A talk with him at lunch. He believes everything apparently he sees in the *New York Times*.

Saw Maurice Hanline in the afternoon—the dissatisfied middle-class man—formerly with a big salary, working for the movies, now broke.

The futile struggle to save himself by bluffing, borrowing money, keeping up a front.

The horrid picture he drew of Horace Liveright now.[1]

Satisfied my new book is correct.

1. Horace Liveright, Anderson's publisher, was very ill, and his company was facing financial problems.

Sunday, August 7, New York City

Burt accuses me of hating business men. It is not true. What I hate is immaturity. So many business men can go on year after year never thinking or feeling the way down into the roots of things. If they are nice they are nice as boys are nice. These great trusts, organizations become playthings. They quarrel and fight over their playthings.

So often the man who controls a great railroad or a great industry did nothing to build it. For example, the cigarette industry. They have not let me go into their cigarette factories but once, in Chicago, in a show window, I saw a cigarette-making machine. It was as beautiful to me as a fine painting.

It is because of these marvelous machines that the cigarette industry has become what it is but who made these machines? The chances are that they were built up slowly by workmen, mechanics, unknown men. They were built as the cathedrals were built.

And one has to think too of the workers who attend these machines. There are these thousands of young men and women, older men and women bound down now to this new slavery.

Suppose I make a lot of money by buying shrewdly, at the right moment, the stock of one of these companies—a cigarette manufacturing company or a shoe company, textile plant, what you will. The stock advances in price.

If I am an American business man I can go ahead, get rich without ever thinking of where my money comes from. Money is like blood—it is energy made fluid. This money I have got. I think I have got it by my own shrewdness and smartness. It's true.

But this money I have got is blood. I am a man who goes about, flies about alighting on the shoulders of these obscure people, taking blood from them.

We are living in a certain kind of society. I do not blame the person who benefits by all this obvious unfairness. It is not the person to blame but the structure itself. But what I do blame in business men is this not knowing, this terrible economic ignorance, often this pride in having money that came, like blood, up out of the social roots of life.

I ask only of business men that they be aware. I myself took money from Burt. I never gave him value received. I stole the money from him.[1]

I am not ashamed of that. It happened. I had something he thought he wanted. I should have been able to give it to him as a gift. What he wanted was of no value to me. I think it has no true value.

If I am impatient about business men, often bitter, it is not because they are good men or bad men. It is because they will not tell themselves the truth, will not face life. It is because they seem so often to prefer to remain children.

1. This refers to Emmett's long-term subsidy of Anderson's writing in exchange for literary manuscripts.

Monday, August 8, New York City

I am leaving, on an early train, for Washington—with several other writers.

To Tom Smith to talk of new books.

To see a Mrs. Cram who offered to pay my way to Brussels, to the World's Congress for Peace. Suddenly decided to go. Will sail a week from tonight.[1]

To see Horace Liveright—looking very ill and thin, broken and drinking hard. His place full of crazy people.

With Eleanor in the evening reading proofs—more and more happy being with her.

1. Probably Mrs. Edith Cram, liberal political activist whose support of this congress was described as coming from only "a friend."

Tuesday, August 9, New York City

I am still in New York but will be leaving tomorrow morning with a group of other writers for Washington—there to protest, to the President, for the brutal treatment of the Bonus Army.

To the office of the Committee for the Defense of Political Prisoners where I talked informally—and nicely—to a room full of young college men and women.

I finished final reading of the novel and am already thinking of a new one.

With Eleanor to see *'Tis of Thee,* a sharp, funny satire on government now—more full of meaning than two-thirds the serious criticism put out. Eleanor very lovely. A happy, busy day.

Wednesday, August 10, New York City

To the Emmetts, at Valley Cottage, where Eleanor and I read proofs, rode horses, pitched horseshoes and walked. In the morning, while she worked upstairs, I talked to Leo Katz the painter downstairs.[1]

Later in the evening to Katz' house with Mary and Burt, where we saw Katz' painting. It was night and I got out of it several times by complaining of the light. There were some marvelous technical performances with water color—the lot of painting on the whole very unhealthy in tone as is the painter. He has an inclination, when showing his big canvasses, to go off into all sort of absurd, mystic talk regarding their significance. I was glad to get away with Eleanor in the bus at nine—the night very hot, the bus crowded, me holding a Negro child on my knees. Eleanor in grey, she looking extraordinarily lovely.

I call her attention to the object of art in her bed.

1. Leo Katz (1887–19?), European-trained American portrait and mural painter.

Thursday, August 11, Washington, D.C.

To Washington, by the early morning train—four writers and a Negro editor—to protest using the Army against the Bonus soldiers, etc.[1] Hoover had wired he wouldn't see us but we went to the White House and after an hour were admitted to one of his secretaries.

The man is a writer. He read us a written statement. I understand he laid off for a year to write a novel. Hoover had pushed him out to stand before us and speak to us as a fellow writer.[2]

The whole incident was rather pathetically gaudy and I think I shall write a public letter about it tomorrow. I am now running to the boat to go to Norfolk.

1. Anderson accompanied Waldo Frank, Elliot Cohen, and James Rorty from New York to Washington, D.C., where they were joined before visiting the White House by William Jones of the Baltimore *Afro-American*.
2. Theodore Joslin, secretary to the president (1931–33), provided his own explanation of the Bonus Army episode in *Hoover Off the Record* (Garden City, N.Y., 1934), 262–80.

Friday, August 12, Virginia Beach, Virginia

With Jaffé at Norfolk. Wrote letter to Hoover, enclosed.[1] Went with Hugh Davis to get Englishman Tommy Tucker out of jail.[2] Went fishing with young Maurice Long, caught some big fish.

This at Hugh Davis's house at Lynnhaven Sound. Jaffé came. Letter from Eleanor upsetting plans. Talked to Eleanor about plans.

A grey lovely evening with a moon.

1. "Listen, Mr. President," *Nation*, CXXXV (August 31, 1932), 191–93.
2. Hugh Davis (1887–1946), brother-in-law of Louis Jaffé and a corporate lawyer in Norfolk and Virginia Beach; Tommy Tucker, unidentified.

Saturday, August 13, Norfolk, Virginia

It is perhaps absurd to try to keep up these daily notes. I spent yesterday out of doors here, at Hugh Davis's house, and in the evening went to Louis Jaffé.

There was a wire from New York *Daily Mirror*, trying to dig up something on my divorce from Elizabeth. This is probably due to my making President Hoover uncomfortable.

Sunday, August 14, Marion, Virginia

A curiously vital day. After the long drive I slept twelve hours. John—moved by the book—hit me a terrible wallop with his fist. We hugged each other and cried.

Eleanor's head came.[1]

I went to see Bob's new home site and loved it. Bob was very sweet about helping me get my mail cleared up. Eleanor's head came and we are to have an unveiling at 5:00.

1. Artwork sculpted in San Francisco by Valenti Michael Angelo.

Monday, August 15, Marion, Virginia

A busy day. We unveiled Eleanor's head. The shape of the head and all the features, except the mouth, finely caught.

John in his joy over the book hit me so hard I could not breathe freely for an hour.

To Bob's for lunch where we had buffalo steak.

To see John and Gerry's new house—plain rooms with white walls, very nice. John['s new painting] is a fine thing.[1]

1. Gerry Gordon and John Anderson were companions in 1932, but they never shared a house.

Tuesday, August 16, New York City

Back in New York. I have come in secretly and am hiding out today to do the last work on the novel before sailing.

Eleanor looks tired. She has been overworking. I brought with me the "Book of Days"—to work on on the boat.[1] My nerves are unstrung with weariness.

As I left town Funk rushed up to tell me I was being watched by the government secret service men. That anyway is amusing.

Wassum, Angell, and Annabel's guest on train. Wassum on food.[2]

1. "The Book of Days," a large anthology of his previously published writings that Anderson worked on intermittently for years but never completed.
2. Charles S. Wassum, owner of Royal Oak Boxwood Farms in Smyth County, who had an office in New York City; Angell remains unidentified; Annabel was the wife of John P. Buchanan, the local attorney; her departing guest remains unidentified.

Wednesday, August 17, New York City

I spent the day in hiding, yesterday, and got final revision of the novel. Went to lunch with Eleanor at the St. James and to dinner at the Shelton. The hotels are empty. On all sides you see something that appears to be gone. Eleanor looked tired. I wrote her a letter, enclosed, which I didn't send.

Legally free today.

Darling,

I have been thinking about the conversation tonight. It is quite true I am sad and lonely—the days away after being so near you before, the chances to see each other, all these gone. I really do not like being the center of things and hunger for quiet with you.

I am thinking of what you said and think I understand that, for a time, at Virginia Beach (if I understood) you loved me, as you put it, "the way any man would want a woman to love him." I presume you meant as a young girl would love her man, thinking him great, or infallible—something of that sort.

I think I am a bit like Tom Riddle in that I do not expect that.[1]

Today, at lunch, when I spoke of the new position of your father you also said something. You indicated, or said, that I thought, or had said, that Frank Copenhaver and Emmett Thomas were all right, etc.[2]

I let it pass but it wasn't true. What I have felt and do feel is that they are what they are, not expecting from them anything but what happened. Therefore I do not believe I would have been caught off base by them, as your father was. Your mother told me that she influenced your father to throw up his hands.

Dear, if you marry me, our relationship will not be like that. I shall probably never love you in the simple, naive, worshipful way your father loves your mother.

I am after all an artist. When I said tonight that our relationship had produced work I think you were a bit hurt, or shocked. It is true, dear—you nor any other woman will ever be all and all to me. I am not the typical American man in that. I shall probably live always, first of all, to write beautifully and clearly.

I am telling you this because I want you to understand that I understand why you cannot love me now—knowing me better, as you began to love.

This I do want. You have not married me. Now it is all right for you to have long times of doubt but when we marry, if you do marry me, I will want you to enter into it accepting me, with all my limitations, as absolutely your man.

And I will do that for you as woman.

If, dear, there is the chance that you can get some man you can love always as you thought you loved me once and you believe in that do not marry me. Wait for it.

As for myself that phase of life is gone for me. I think I know something more real and sweeter. I'm after that.

Oh Eleanor, my dear one.

1. Tom Riddle, a character in *Beyond Desire*, a prominent southern attorney who simply waits confidently and shrewdly for the librarian heroine to accept a socially and financially desirable marriage with him.

2. An unexplained reference to Frank Copenhaver and Emmett Thomas, two of Anderson's friends in Marion, Va., men who were not as socially prominent as the Bascom Copenhaver family.

Thursday, August 18, At Sea

I just did make the boat last night—rushing up the gang plank at the last moment, Burt and Mary and Miss Zugsmith waving me off.[1]

Was so tired I fell into bed without knowing how to open the window and so slept badly. The sea is very quiet.

Yesterday a mad day. Delivered the novel. Lunch with Mrs. Cram. Saw reporters, spent an hour with [a] photographer. Saw Eleanor, only for a few minutes. There will be a letdown in me now—the book off my hands. I'll write some notes home. I need Eleanor.

1. Leane Zugsmith (1903–69), Kentucky-born author of proletarian novels and a publicity agent for Horace Liveright; Anderson had read her *Goodbye and Tomorrow* (New York, 1931).

Friday, August 19, At Sea

It is good to be aboard ship with this kind of people. The group I am with are all radicals. They are charming people, nearly all representatives of groups of workers. There is but one rather stupid-seeming man, a socialist of the politician type.

I am particularly attracted to a young red-haired sailor from Alexandria, Louisiana, and by a young man from the Students' League, University of Brooklyn. There are two women, a Jewess— the secretary of the organization back of this peace move—and a Lithuanian woman, who has been a cotton mill worker for years.[1]

It is amazing to think that this sort of people—so charming and alive—are looked upon by the great class of middle-class Americans as dangerous.

There is a Mr. Dana of the old New England Dana family— *Two Years Before the Mast, New York Sun,* etc.[2] We sit at table in a group and walk about the decks. It is absorbing to get this look into these lives.

1. The sailor, James "Sandy" McFarland, represented the Marine Workers' Industrial Union; the student, Joseph Cohen, represented the National Students' League; the Jewess, Belle G. Taub, represented the National Committee for the Defense of Political Prisoners; the Lithuanian, Sonia Kaross, represented the Lithuanian Working Women's Alliance.

2. Henry Wadsworth Longfellow Dana (1881–1950), grandson of the poet, a well-known pacifist and editor; Richard Henry Dana, Jr., who had in 1840 published *Two Years Before the Mast,* an autobiographical sailing narrative intended to halt mistreatment of sailors; Charles Anderson Dana (1819–97), admired editor of the New York *Sun.*

Saturday, August 20, At Sea

It became cold and cloudy. Some of the crew put on a boxing match. There was an American movie, really a filthy thing. I didn't stay.

The Jewish woman, named Belle, told me of her childhood and young womanhood in Russia, in a village, the constant fear of pogroms, etc.

Sonia—the Lithuanian woman—is reading my book. She is just the Doris of the book.[1] She is excited by it. She is very beautiful. She went to work in a cotton mill and married at seventeen.

She began telling me the story of her child. The child was twelve, weak and sickly. She took it into the waiting room of the best hospital in the city. She instructed the child, "Tell them you do not know who you are."

Then she went out and phoned the best surgeon in the city. "The child is there. If I keep her she will die. Cure her or kill her."

The newspapers of the city got hold of the story. The child was sent away to a sanitarium. She grew well and strong.

1. Anderson was comparing Sonia Kaross with the fictional Doris Hoffman of the novel *Beyond Desire.*

Sunday, August 21, At Sea

We had a meeting of our peace delegation in a smoking room and each one spoke. I was struck by the entire sincerity of everyone in the party. No one person is trying to push forward and be important. Each one comes from some body of men or women for whom he is anxious to speak.

Our Negro is a fine young fellow and very intelligent and shrewd. He has had a varied and strange life. He is to me a quite new kind of Negro man.[1]

The Lithuanian mill girl is very intelligent, in a way my own mother was intelligent. She has had a hard, bitter life but is not embittered. What has happened to her is that she has never had a chance to learn to play. When we walk singing up and down the deck or dance she finds it difficult to join in. She feels this and regrets it. She tries to be gay but can't make it.

I like Brodsky—a big noisy man but with a quick, intelligent mind. Under his noise there is something fine.[2]

1. The Negro, Joseph Gardner, a workman from Chicago.
2. Joseph Brodsky, New York attorney, representing at the conference the International Labor Defense.

Monday, August 22, At Sea

It is odd how the notion of peace frightens certain people. We decided to have a peace meeting on Sunday afternoon aboard ship and, after giving permission, the ship's officers became alarmed. They had Brodsky, Dana and myself upstairs and tried to commit us to not saying certain things, etc. We refused. Already notice had been sent about the ship and a crowd came, people from all classes, down into our third-class dining room. Brodsky handled the meeting and did a good job. Dana spoke and then myself and then the meeting was thrown open to all. A number of our delegates spoke—the best being Gardner the Negro ex-serviceman. He is a real speaker and fast thinker. Everyone has grown fond of him. He has a fine head and a captivating smile. He talks simply and forcefully, telling boldly the Negro soldiers' story.

At the meeting there was a well-fed Britisher, an English

manufacturer, who got terribly excited. He tried to convince the audience that all we delegates were Bolsheviks, etc. Later he came to me and apologized, saying he didn't mean me. It was the workers, daring to speak out, and the Negro that alarmed him. I said, "You are wrong. I am the more dangerous." The strike as a weapon against war had been advocated. "You are wrong to think me harmless," I said. "To have war you have to build up hatred. You need the writers for that. If we writers begin to strike each one of us can be as powerful as a thousand workers. You are wrong and silly to underestimate us."

Tuesday, August 23, At Sea

The sun has come out after two grey days, during which I was very sad. I think it is largely through hunger for Eleanor's presence, as I want her now to share every experience with me.

I must manage now to push forward the workers of our party, as there is too much inclination to push me forward, because I am a little known to people.

We have meetings every day which are educational. It is very interesting to me that our best speaker is the Negro Gardner. He has real intelligence with the Negro eloquence, his speeches full of vigor, rhythm and Negro life. He and the sailor from Alexandria, Louisiana, are great friends. Yesterday the sailor went off to the forecastle of this ship and talked to the sailors. I have no doubt he told them the story of our mission. They were not allowed to come to our public meeting.

Dana, the American, New England aristocrat, is well informed on European tangles and is our source of information.

I am getting sharp impressions, educational to me, and must fight to be allowed to stand aside and take it all in.

Wednesday, August 24, On the Train

Going up from Cherbourg to Paris—through Normandy, the day cloudy and then bright and warm. There are several in the party to whom the country is all new and strange. Again the feeling of a land lived on a long time. Land—it arouses love in me.

The country is very green, a lovely soft rolling country of orchards, meadows and pasture lands. Women are washing clothes in the stream and other women binding wheat in fields. In the compartment with me big, nice, noisy Joe Brodsky, McFarland the sailor, and the little pair of scholars going to school at Geneva.

Thursday, August 25, Paris

We arrived in Paris at noon and I spent the afternoon and evening racing about with this group of workers from America—Sonia, Joe, Belle, Little Joe—showing them the sights of Paris.[1] There is a rumor we shall not be allowed to go into Holland but I doubt if they will stop us. How many actual communists there are in the crowd I do not know.

This is the last stage of our journey as a party as, after we arrive in Amsterdam, the party will break up. Big noisy Joe and I go to London and home by Liverpool.

It is interesting but tiring to travel with such a delegation. Afterward I shall get many funny reactions from it.

I must write a piece, say for Scribner's, called "The Delegation."[2]

We are told that the Russians, headed by Gorki, are stopped at the Russian border.[3]

I am writing in the early morning. Now I must stop to rush to the train.

1. Little Joe, Joseph G. Roth, Socialist machinist from Ithaca, N.Y.
2. Eventually published as "Delegation," New Yorker, IX (December 9, 1933), 36–38, this essay discusses the Bonus Army episode; Anderson's essay on the European peace conference remained unfinished.
3. Maxim Gorki (1868–1936), Russian author of stories and novels, leader of the Writers' Union of the U.S.S.R.

Friday, August 26, Amsterdam

I have been up and about the city. I rather depended on finding my Dutch translator, Waldie Van Eck, to show me about here, but she has gone off to England on her vacation.[1] I shall go this afternoon to see the Rembrandts at the Rijksmuseum.

Oh my dear, this is the most lovely city. Something here very quiet, clean and orderly that touches me deeply. There are charming sidewalk cafés. Everyone is on a bicycle. The canals are everywhere. I hope, I dream that I may be here with you.

I am so bound to you, my dear, that when I am away from you for ten days something in me goes a bit jangled and out of tune. I want you in so many ways, my love.

1. Although Waldie Van Eck was interested in translating Anderson's writings into Dutch, her major Anderson translation was *Kit Brandon* (Amsterdam, 1947).

Saturday, August 27, Amsterdam

A busy day, running about to meetings, meeting scholars, intellectuals, artists, writers and workers from all the world. When I should be writing here in my journal I have instead to go off and to try to prepare a speech for this World's Conference Against War.

It is an odd place for me to be.

Sunday, August 28, Amsterdam

The day yesterday spent at the World's Conference. The crowds tired me. The opening was not good. The intellectuals were too intellectual, the French—Barbusse and Rolland—were too flowery.[1]

It was impossible to hear the speakers. The crowd milled about in the great hall. When the crowds sang everything became clear and fine.

The Russians were not allowed into Holland.

Congress

I am writing from the rostrum of the International Congress Against War at Amsterdam. There are thirty American delegates here, representing many thousands of war-hating Americans. We Americans sit with the English. The great body of the delegates are French and German, who sit close together. They occupy a good section of the huge hall. The Congress is drawing to an end. There are speakers and delegates here from almost every nation on earth. There is a tenseness broken by the wave of song, by cries, by thousands of fists raised.

The Red Front!

The Red Front!

The Red Front!

The "Internationale" is sung in many languages. The very building shakes with it.

We are in a huge automobile exposition building. Yesterday, Sunday, was the great day. Outside the halls, through the quiet Sunday streets of Amsterdam, along canal banks, under the shade trees marched thousands of youths, singing and shouting. In the evening there was a vast mass meeting in another hall a thousand feet long and some three hundred feet across. It was packed with standing thousands. Speakers arose and spoke, from Germany, from France, from India, from China—veterans in the struggle against war. Again the building shook with shouts and song.

It is a real international meeting, the largest, the most determined ever held.

There is one cry rings out. It is on every man's and woman's lips. It is that the old pacifism, comfortable middle-class women meeting in clubs and signing peace petitions, the workers standing still, wearily praying for peace, hoping for peace, voting for politicians who talk peace with soft eloquence while all the time the munition factories run night and day, new poison gasses are invented and the money wrung from the people in taxes is spent on always more and longer ships. "An end to the old meaningless pacifism" is the universal cry here. It is the central cry of the whole Congress. The best speakers are the workers. They speak briefly, with raised fists. What a contrast to the eloquence of the intellectuals. Here are ragged words, hard fighting words. War words against War. To strike in munition plants, to refuse to transport arms, to fire guns, to pay taxes. The workers trying desperately here to get at understanding, to know each other, to make comradeship between workers of all countries a fact, a fighting fact against war.

The Congress is a success. It will stir up real war against war in many countries.

1. Henri Barbusse (1873–1935), French author of World War I materials, who moved from pacifism to communism and who died in the U.S.S.R.; Romain Rolland (1866–1944), French winner of the Nobel Prize for literature (1917) and a pacifist who became a Communist and activist for world peace.

Monday, August 29, Amsterdam

It was the big day in the Congress. There were many speakers and hands wishing to speak. They had me on the list but I went to the chairman and surrendered my place.

The hall was filled with a vast herd, mostly men in shirt sleeves. They were mostly French and German peasants and workers. When some favorite speaker arose to speak the crowd also arose. The "Internationale" was sung in many languages, the rafters shaking. Fists were clenched and upraised. There was something stirring and exciting. The excitement grew all day, the crowd getting larger and larger. The air in the hall was bad. It was unbearably hot. I could not understand most of the speakers. In trying to make themselves heard they screamed.

I went outside into the streets. Everywhere marching columns of youths, also singing. By 3:00 I was exhausted with emotions and went to my hotel where I slept for three hours.

When I got back to the place of the Congress there were even more thousands of people. New columns of marching youths coming. There was a vastly larger hall—300 feet across, 1000 feet long. Everyone stood. More singing and speaking.

Tuesday, August 30, Amsterdam

The Peace Conference here is over. The dramatic thing of the whole evening happened—a sailor from an Italian warship brought suddenly to the floor in his uniform, a fine-looking Italian boy, taking his life in his hands. If he were photographed. . . . Men walked about with clenched fists. He spoke against Mussolini and the war fever in Italy, cursing it. There is evidently disintegration going on in the fleet of Italy. He was hurried away.

I spoke for one minute on the problem of the writer in America.[1]

1. For Anderson's summary of his revolutionary experiences in Amsterdam, see Jones and Rideout, eds., *Letters of Sherwood Anderson*, 271–72.

Wednesday, August 31, On the Train

In the morning to American Express—a fine letter from Eleanor. Then with Das and Dana to the newspaper office, one of the great dailies of Holland, where we were shown about by the managing director.[1] It is a very beautiful example of modern-style building for use, every inch used, everything wonderfully arranged. Form not forgotten in the design. Perhaps it springs in this simple fine purity out of pure economy of space as it should. There is beautifully effective use of color also, bright red, a darker red, two shades of blue, with grey and white. I hope later to write of this building. They have promised to send me photographs.

In the afternoon to the Rijksmuseum to see a special Rembrandt show where I got a fine book of reproductions for my son John. Cost me $8.00 American. Afterward some Holland literary people called at my hotel and later I went out for the evening with them.

1. "Das" or "Dos" was not the writer John Dos Passos but instead a citizen of the Netherlands who showed Anderson about the city of Amsterdam.

September

Thursday, September 1, London

A bright clear morning. Joe Brodsky and I came up from Harwich last night and got here at 9:30. We went to stand in a crowded pub—to eat and drink ale.

In Europe more than in America you feel the sense of strain—God knows what will happen in Germany. France has built up tremendous hatred of them.

The speech of the old communist woman yesterday must have been something rather terrifically fine.

In England there is a great cotton strike at Lancaster—150,000 out—and a bus strike is threatened in London.[1] It is a terrific time. It is odd to walk about, feeling always that what is now going on in the world may crumble away.

1. As many as two hundred thousand English cotton-industry workers began striking on August 28, 1932, over management's dismissal of two thousand union "organizers."

Friday, September 2, London

I have been in bed with a bad cold. It seems always to happen to me when I come to London.

I bought a fine Harris tweed suit at Burberry's for $32.00.

I was ill all day but walked about, seeing the sights of London until evening when I had to go off to bed.

The criticism of the Soviet Union I find in the English papers seems all to be centered about the idea that the Russian is not machine-minded, cannot use the machines without too great waste, and that therefore the idea itself is wrong.

It seems a poor enough argument. It might well fail for a long time in Russia and yet succeed in England and America.

A night of fantastic dreams.

Saturday, September 3, At Sea

We sailed from Liverpool at 1:00, a very cold, bleak day. As we left the dock a storm swept down the harbor, a high wind with rain and hail. It is good I had on my new tweed suit—very heavy and very warm. At sea the sun came out. I am in with two attractive and not too attractive women from Ohio—rather of the cultivated sort. They should be good enough company and not too good, to take my mind off some work I should be doing on the way home. I will sit at table with these women. My roommate for the voyage is a rather stolid-looking Englishman named Jones.

Now as I write we are outside Liverpool harbor with a heavy, cold wind but a bright sun has come out. I am happy to be going back toward Eleanor.

Sunday, September 4, At Sea

We are just leaving Queenstown in Ireland, the boat very heavily loaded on account of strikes on some other steamers.

I have got rested and have begun to think again, aside from Joe—World's Conference, the proletariat. I have been reading Lawrence and that awakens in me—as he always does—the individual that is Sherwood Anderson, aside from everything.

And then the sea doing something to me as it always does. A life thus—in nature, powerful, cruel, now quiet, vast, waiting like death. It makes me say to myself, "Are you afraid of death?"

Can I answer "No" cheerfully?

As long as I can I am free.

Nothing possesses me quite—not even life.

The poet lives in me.

Monday, September 5, At Sea

A stormy, grey, rainy morning with many people ill. At last we have struck out across the Atlantic. All day yesterday we ran along the Irish coast, going from Liverpool to Queenstown and then to Galway. All day there was no sun and the sea was rough. I stayed by myself—working all morning and in the afternoon staying on the deck and walking about alone, looking at the sea.

My mind was occupied all day with thoughts of Eleanor and with all my relations with all women. It seemed to me that, as I thought of it, I was not altogether to blame for my confusion. I think I am rather primitive. Between myself and nature there is, I'm sure, something always going on that is not a common experience. This I gather from what I hear from the lips of others. There were gulls flying all day yesterday at the back of the ship. They are very graceful in flight. I think all people see that.

But there is something else indescribable—a kind of intimacy between myself and the flying bird, not myself, in fancy going into the bird, being, in fancy, in the bird and part of it, as human, but a going in as wind might go in, a kind of sinking into nature and coming out as a part of some whole of which the bird happens to be a beautiful part.

If you keep away from people sometimes they become nice. They sit and walk about. Then their voices give them away.

I think we must all be in a dreadful, hurtful time. We are all mixed up in regard to our relations with nature, to each other.

Are we at the door of something or is it death?

Tuesday, September 6, At Sea

A high, clear, cool wind and the boat pitching and rocking. I had to quit work—on the "Book of American Days"—and go to bed, a violent headache. I awoke early to find my cabin mate—a Welsh preacher, journalist, and literary man—on his knees, his head in the lower berth, praying to his God. It gave me an odd feeling of embarrassment and I rolled over, my face to the wall, trying to think why the old direct appeal to God had become ridiculous to men of our age.

We have found nothing yet to take its place.

A ridiculous dream of myself and Eleanor as man and wife,

getting on a train—she in a long wedding gown, at a small station near Clyde, my native town. All the people of Clyde I knew as a boy were there.[1] We were getting on a slow train to Tiffin. I felt very ridiculous, like a young boy caught kissing a girl, and Eleanor also looked embarrassed—as though she had been caught doing something she should not do.

1. For information about Anderson's boyhood in Clyde, Ohio, see Sutton, *The Road to Winesburg,* 17–49.

Wednesday, September 7, At Sea

It is between worlds. A steady wind blew all day—bright sunshine, then a flow of rain, then grey, then the sun again. An odd feeling of apartness from all life. The broken waves, near the boat, make the most delicate lace.

I kept hearing talk of America, England, Ireland, Wales, Scotland. The Americans talked like fools. I grew proud. I began to sing to myself. I proclaimed to myself my own knowledge of America.

Mines, forests, rivers, cornfields, wheatfields, factories, cities, towns, mountains.

Far West. Far South.

Deserts, waste places, unused lands, working men's houses, insides of working men's minds.

Tall office buildings, business men, their minds.

I recited. I sang to myself, trying to make some song of my own life roll in me like the long roll of the sea.

Women, working women, factory women, stenographers, mothers.

Pine forests in the South—all America has given me.

My own struggles, my disappointments, my loves.

My attempts at love.

Little mountain streams running through mountain forests, men plowing, planting, putting in farms.

Towns asleep, cities asleep. Myself awake.

The unknown woman in the field. The still, still, clean pine forests.

The ruggedness, the dirt, the factories. The waste of energy. It in me. Me in it.

The hurt, the pain, the shallowness. A life lived, still being lived. Let someone else sing of death.

Life not death is the adventure.

Boats on rivers, railroad trains. Men in jail.

Fairs held in fields, in fairgrounds.

Horses. Negroes.

Travel, going far, wide and swift.

Restlessness. The feeling always of beginnings.

The stupidity. The kindness.

Drink, food. Lying in bed with a woman. A child crying in a house in a dark street.

Terror. Light. Fear. Bravery.

One and all.

One and all.

'Tis of Thee.

'Tis of Thee.

Thursday, September 8, At Sea

Reading Wells—a stupid man—the old stupid belief in the big, beautiful business man. I read Lawrence's *St. Mawr*—the prose warm and full of flesh. Also a book of short things—*England, My England.*[1]

I had the bad night, wanting Eleanor, and it resulted in a day of headache. Finally it happened in a dream but I wanted still her warm actuality.

Now that I have been away from her these weeks she seems more beautiful than ever to me.

1. H. G. Wells, *The Science of Life* (Garden City, N.Y., 1931); D. H. Lawrence, *St. Mawr* (New York, 1925); D. H. Lawrence, *England, My England, and Other Stories* (New York, 1922). Anderson's reactions to these works and books by and about Lawrence are in "A Man's Song of Life," *Virginia Quarterly Review*, IX (January, 1933), 108–14.

Friday, September 9, At Sea

In the afternoon yesterday we came into a heavy fog off the Banks of Newfoundland and we are still in it, at 10:00 this morning. The fog horn kept calling, like a lost cow, all night.

I have met an Englishman named Moore—formerly in the British Army—now a newspaper man, who has told me of the British way of imperialism—much, I am sure, like our own.

At the borders of India there was a territory not yet occupied by the British. It was a mountainous country. A good many years before Lord Roberts had been in there.[1] There were a few post stations set up.

Some robbers robbed one of these post stations, taking five pounds, so it was decided to teach the whole section a lesson. No doubt it was practice also for the troops, getting them used to real warfare, etc. It was a rough country of small mud villages and little upland fields. Artillery was taken in and several airplanes. They got into the country over the mountain roads with much difficulty but met no resistance. However they were there for business. It was good practice for bombing planes. All of this sounds childishly cruel but army men get like that. They have these terrifically dangerous toys to play with and must play. They must play.

And they find phrases for it right enough—"empire," "progress," "the white man's burden," etc.

So they started to destroy. They burned the crops, they pushed over the mud huts in the towns, they bombed many little mud towns from the air. All the people of that faraway border country able to flee had fled except the old men and women who could not flee.

But, you see, when you are bombing a defenseless town from above you do not need to bother about the people who happen to be left in the town. You are far up above and even if you swoop down you are moving at speed.

Of course I don't know, never having been a bomber, but I imagine that, when the bomb strikes, you can look down. You see a cloud of dust, buildings crumble. It is all, I dare say, a bit unreal—you do not have to see the mangled bodies. "Ah—a hit."

Anyway the man on the boat said they did that country up—destroyed the crops, the towns, all the huts. And afterwards they collected the whole cost of the performance from the natives. The natives who could flee had fled but they let them come back, under British rule now of course. They could impose taxes, retribution, for that five pounds stolen from a post office, some hundreds of thousands of pounds with interest, I dare say. You know, the English are not the only ones who do it. We Americans do it too. We also have become imperial, conquerors.

I understand that of course the British newspapers said little of the affair mentioned above. It was a small affair. There was an uprising—in territory not yet occupied by the British. It was put down, a small affair. The man on the boat told me of the natives coming back into their country, a ragtag lot, he said— poor people, little hill farmers, coming back to destroyed villages, crops destroyed.

Driving a few poor cattle, poor saw-backed camels, etc., mothers with children, heads of families.

Weeping perhaps—a little frightened.

After all very much as workers of an American factory go back into the factory after they have lost a strike.

As our American farmers go back to their fields in the spring after the machinery of modern life has robbed them of the last year's crop.

An old story. Peace. Empire. Imperialism. Thump. Thump. Onward civilization.

Don't too much blame the British. We Americans do it. Ask the natives of our possessions. The French do it. It is the modern imperialistic way of peace.

While I am at it the same man—the British ex-soldier—told me another—a massacre this time. It was in India proper.

There had been riots incited in India. Crowds of rioters were gathered in the street. I presume they wanted their own Indian way of life.

It had to be put down. Of course, that sort of thing has to be put down, as you must put down workers, strikers, etc., in our own modern imperialistic state.

In this case [just] what they did. There were some 15,000 Indians gathered in an Indian city, having a meeting, as an antiwar meeting might be held say in Union Square in New York.

They decided to teach that crowd a lesson too.

In that case they didn't do it themselves. They surrounded the city with their armies.

In India, I dare say, as in America, there is always plenty of hatred that can be stirred up. Suppose you've surrounded in this way, in America, 15,000 Negroes asserting their rights. You wouldn't have to send the soldiers in. You could arm the civilian whites and send them in. They would do the job.

So they did it in India that time, the ex-soldier told me. They sent in one tribe that had been taught, encouraged to hate another. They did it. The ex-soldier described what happened, the gore, the horror of it. He said the British newspapers made a note of that. There was a riot at B, natives were killing natives.[2] There were a few people killed, the papers said, but afterward quiet was restored.

1. Frederick Sleigh Roberts, Baron Kandahar (1832–1914), commander of British forces in India after 1885.
2. Anderson identified the city by only its initial.

Saturday, September 10, At Sea

It was such a day as seemed to justify the whole trip—a sharp wind, a sea, clouds floating, the sun glorious on the sea.

I went in the evening and got the woman Mildred, thinking I would experiment to see if it was a woman I wanted, or a person loved that was also a woman.

There wasn't much doubt. The woman Mildred, a slender blonde, aroused my passions and I could have had her. I asked her if she wanted me and she said she did but just the same I didn't want her. "Come, we'll walk that off," I said and presently came away.

Sunday, September 11, At Sea

A great storm blew all day with a wind that some of the seamen said was a seventy-five or eighty-mile blow and with waves that looked like the hills at home. On the third-class deck forward the water washed across the deck rail-high.

Joe Brodsky and the little New England school teacher, Miss Prentice, stayed forward, on the B deck, watching the magnificence of it until the officers ordered us away to the back of the ship. The storm raged all day and is still going this morning although not so severe. I was so excited by it I could hardly sit down but hung over the rail of the ship all day fascinated by the power of the waves and wind and at night was exhausted.

Monday, September 12, At Sea

Of interest.

Miss Prentice, the little New England school teacher, her attitude toward the storm, her delight in it.

Reminder of Harriet Monroe, of *Poetry* magazine, wild and virginal also, her delight in rank strong profanity, on the lips of another.[1]

The nuns on board, like walking coffins going about.

Two Jewish-American girls from New York, always trying to be cute.

Mildred, from St. Louis, woman whose flesh is, no longer, sweet. She keeps trying to make her body seem sweet with clothes and cosmetics. Her eyes are hungry. She keeps going hungrily about, seeking a man who will make her body sweet to her.

Moore, the English newspaper man who wants to be a poet. Talk with him over the rail at night in the storm. His talk of battlefields, what the war did to him.

Germany must not come down to the Channel.

His failure to grasp the real poet's outlook, or the artist's outlook.

His wife who has an obscure nervous disease that will kill her. His knowing. Her not knowing. His satisfaction in the knowledge. He doesn't want her.

The two fairies at table. The nastiness of the pervert, going always toward death.

Priests, death also, their coarseness.

The old Welsh literary man in the cabin, kneeling on the floor praying. His going toward death.

The life in fat Joe. His rough, downright fineness.

The Irishman being kept by his wife, his trying to be jolly. The unconscious brutality in the treatment of third-class passengers. The steward, good-natured coarse vulgarity mixed with shrewdness . . . how he fascinates the women.

If the ship should go down these people, most of them, should be received by death with open arms. Most of them already belong to him.

The sea was very soft, quiet and lovely after the storm. The woman Mildred got ginned up and came for me on Saturday night but I told her abruptly I was sleepy and going off to bed.

She has made up her mind to have me in bed with her but it won't work. She does arouse me, perhaps the male in me flattered. After being with her for a time, that look of hunger in her eyes, I have an erection. I think all women must know how to call you to them.

These American women—demi-vièrges—go abroad hoping thus to find courage to have a man. Men have been pawing this one over all her trip. They have kissed her, felt her breasts. There is no center to her life. Besides pure sensuality, of which she hasn't too much after all, she is hoping to find, in the rod of some man, the savior.

As I retreated she advanced. Perhaps, before the boat lands, she will have one of her business men. If I were not in love I might go to bed with her. She has exposed every part of her body to me eagerly.

She grows determined and then puzzled.

I can conceive of a woman whose whole passion is to give the body, making men happy, but she is not like that. "Give me. Give me."

She is full of death. She feels it. She is frightened. The woman getting toward middle age, hanging onto her conception of physical beauty, fighting to retain it. She feels it slipping away. Perhaps a man can make it live on.

You are like a farmer. She is the land but she is poor, thin, worked-out land. Too many rank weeds have grown. You would wear yourself out trying to find and make live and grow any real beauty in her.

As we sat together I looked at her intently a long time. A queer thing happened. It was as though this blonde American woman began to live her whole life before me. Her face kept changing. She was a child of twelve, a young woman of eighteen, then twenty-three. A puzzled, childish look in her eyes.

Then suddenly she got old—an old worn-out, pale, meaningless thing like those women who travel aimlessly and helplessly about the world, wives of well-to-do American business men.

I came away from her so, gladly thinking of the rich fertility of Eleanor and loving her.

1. Harriet Monroe (1860–1936), Chicago poet and editor, founder of *Poetry: A Magazine of Verse* (1912–).

Tuesday, September 13, At Sea

We are within sight of land. These whole last two days, af ter the half-hurricane, have been like a dream—or rather the storm was like some fascinating and half terrible dream passed through. Yesterday—bright and clear with a gentle wind. We saw the spouting of whales. Porpoises came and played alongside the boat. Joe and I with Moore the Englishman will get off the boat at Boston and go down to New York by train.

To Mildred

I suppose I owe you a kind of honesty after the semi-experi- ence we have had. Perhaps you have, after all, only touched to life in me the writer, always curious about people—but perhaps there is also something more human.

I see you as one of our Americans. We American men have done frightfully unclean things to our women. I see them here in this room where I am writing, old women, middle-aged women, wives of well-to-do business men. The cabin lounge is rank with them and their men.

Death of the mind, of the body, the spirit. What a farce upon love.

As though a man could devote himself to getting, close his mind, close all the windows of himself for years and then have something to give.

I am sorry for you hungry American women—your minds also become poison, slow death, lips always saying old dead common- places. There are too many of you. I admit it is not your fault.

You will have to fight, I presume, for your own thing.

Some of you do survive, cut paths of your own, carry real beauty on into old age. I know some such American women.

There is, alas, no definite road. So many of you have too much mind and spirit—half educated—to just lie and wriggle your legs and backs, making some man come—a meaningless shot into what should be life's tender center—you want too much for just that.

Business men—insurance agents, etc., away from home, in dress clothes—trying to be something.

You do not want just that and yet you have not been bold enough, daring enough to find your own road.

Education life can give, even in America.

Well, there is too much to say. It can't be said.

Isn't it hell? You may become for me a minor character in a story—to frighten others.

(Letter to an American Woman—met on a boat—who tried to give herself to me but I didn't want her. Not sent.)

Wednesday, September 14, New York City

Off the ship *Scythia* at Boston and lost Joe and the others. Also lost a group of newspaper men come to see me.

Also lost the blonde Mildred who had been pursuing me. Went by bus to South Station where I was taken for Sandy McFarland.

Found the Englishman, Moore, at the station and rode with him and Joe to New York. Dined with Moore and went riding on the bus, enjoying his first American impressions. Got Eleanor on the phone and very happy to hear her voice.

Thursday, September 15, On the Train

On the train, in the early morning, going to Roanoke to meet Eleanor. A beautiful, soft early fall morning—going into the country. I love to meet the woman I love.

Yesterday an amusing, fast day—Tom Smith, groups of newspaper men interviewing me, more photographs, Heywood Broun proposal, Pearson of the *Sun*, Moore the Englishman, the crowded train, glad to be alive, going, going. . . .[1]

The new book. It's full. The nice feeling of solidity.

1. Heywood Broun (1888–1939), New York journalist and critic and sympathizer with leftist causes whose proposal to Anderson is unexplained; Pearson, probably a writer for the New York *Sun*, although no Anderson material appeared in the next several issues of that newspaper; Moore, the Englishman who had on board ship told Anderson the story of cruel British imperialism.

Friday, September 16, Marion, Virginia

The open letter to Hoover has obviously struck deep in the country. I am flooded with letters.

Eleanor met me at Christiansburg—more lovely than ever. How I love her. We had a wonderful drive and a sweet evening. The country here is very lovely now, with the hills covered by the first soft fall haze. There is much, much to do. I am more and more convinced that I need Eleanor. My love of her grows, grows. . . .

Saturday, September 17, Marion, Virginia

The queer feeling that comes in reading a new book—by yourself—when it is first in book form. Questionings. "Have you done it?"

Beyond Desire.

I feel I have done it. The book anyway was written in love. It may cause a storm of protest. I don't know. To me it seems to flow along like a river—going on and on—tributaries coming in. It seems to me the most important novel I have done—up to now.

The day with Eleanor and the night—very warm and real. The picnic in the quiet valley. Mr. Copenhaver—Eleanor's strange attitude toward him. The day was a glory out of doors.

Sunday, September 18, Marion, Virginia

Notes for Eleanor—

People do not seem real. They seem like figures of a dream.

I was exhausted from the emotions playing through me—my whole life, its blunders, evils, the good in it—after you left. I slept like a babe.

Anyway, dear, it must mean something to you, your womanhood, to have been able to stir a man so deeply. What I said goes—if you decide against being my woman you will owe me nothing. You have more than paid as you went.

I would like to have you get clear the point made about taking you to the train. It wasn't that your father took you. We had to part. It was the assumption that he had the right to say whether or not I could take you—you not yet the woman with her own man but the child. It isn't what happens. I expect to be, perhaps always, somewhat an outsider to them. I can't be to you—and have you—you know. I think marriage will put an end to that assumption—you must know it, dear—rather extra baggage, carried patiently because of love for you.

Thank God it will be one way or the other soon. I shall be on edge.

Monday, September 19, Marion, Virginia

I am a bit flustered inside—needing to get quiet, to work. There was the emotional experience of seeing Eleanor again, after a month away, the excitement of that.

Then her leaving. I seem unable to get over her loss.

There is a stack of mail.

There is the uncertainty as to how the new book will be received.

I feel myself in a queer waiting mood. I must get outdoors, quiet myself.

Tuesday, September 20, Marion, Virginia

I am wasting the days in futile uncertainty, Eleanor gone off to New York. There is the uncertainty as to what may yet happen between us.

Uncertainty as to reception the new novel may have.

I have been reading Bowers—*Beveridge*—and it saddens me.[1] He seems such a fine thing to have burned himself out—for so many rotten things. The goodness, energy, fineness—burned up for such futilities. He is a true symbol. It is a terrible book.

I went to Funk to help make wine but [he] was not there. Wherever I go these days—since Eleanor left—I am queerly separated from everyone. So much of my life seems hanging in uncertainty these days.

It rains—slowly, sadly.

1. Claude G. Bowers, *Beveridge and the Progressive Era* (Boston, 1932); Anderson preferred Bowers' *The Tragic Era* (New York, 1929).

Wednesday, September 21, Marion, Virginia

Eleanor has written me, saying that Harry Hansen—in the New York *Telegraph*—has attacked *Beyond Desire* venomously.[1]

This may not be the answer. Some time ago some personal letters of mine were sold or stolen. They got into the hands of a dealer who sent out a catalog. He quoted, in the catalog, from one of the letters, my saying, of Hansen's book, *Midwest Portraits,* that it was inexpressibly dull.[2] It was but I would not have said so publicly.

I have been half ill because of Eleanor's being away from me just now and have been silly. It is a hard time. I feel the new book a really important one—a book marking a new departure in American writing. I am like a woman who has just borne a child.

The days pass slowly. I am glad I am here, rather than in New York. If Eleanor were here I would be happy. The hills here are lovely now.

1. Harry Hansen, "The First Reader," New York *World-Telegram*, September 19, 1932, p. 23; Hansen wrote that in *Beyond Desire* Anderson was too much influenced by Gertrude Stein and too indecisive and naive in his attitude toward sexuality.

2. Harry Hansen, *Midwest Portraits* (New York, 1923).

Friday, September 23, Marion, Virginia

I felt a cold coming on and I spent most of the day out of doors.
I have the limited edition of *Beyond Desire* to sign.
I worked on the book—"The Book of Days."
Eleanor writes she is seeing Lucy. So much is on the fire.[1]

The out of doors is saving me these days. No one not a prose artist can understand what the writer goes through just after his book is published.

There are all these people—out of his imaginative world. They are taking on a new reality, in the minds of others. He is as anxious for them, that they be understood, as though they were living people.

1. Eleanor Copenhaver was discussing with her supervisor Lucy Carner whether she might continue to work with the Young Women's Christian Association if she married Anderson.

Saturday, September 24, Marion, Virginia

A curious, interesting picture of the life of domestic animals. I had gone for mushrooms and had found none. I drove on to the house of Cecil Wolfe. There was a neighboring farmer in the yard and Cecil was taking a bath. He shouted, wanting me to wait. When he came out he told me he and his old woman were going to a funeral. He had been cutting corn for several days and hadn't shaved. He said his old woman shaved him.

Cecil owns a jack and the farmer neighbor had brought a mare to be served. We went up back of the barn to attend to that. The mare was a big black work mare—rather handsome, with rather fine dignity. She was on it but was dignified about it. I used to see race stallions brought out to serve racing mares when I was a boy following the races.

How splendid they were! What gusto! The stallion came out of the barn. Gene Aldridge would cry, "Look at him."[1] There was the black pacing stallion—Solarian—what a fellow. He was huge but as he went toward the mare his step was so light and jaunty that it seemed he might have walked on eggs without breaking the shells.

And the mare. There was the usual teasing. The stallion approaches the mare. He bites her along the neck and back, then approaches her womb. She squeals a little and kicks out but, if she wants it, gradually becomes quiet. A soft look comes into her eyes and she squats a trifle, her limbs trembling with anticipation.

Cecil's jack is an absurd little beast with its thin shanks and great ears.

In order that he may mount a big mare a slight pit has been dug in which the mare stands with the little jack behind and above on raised ground. He did not appear to want the mare and teased her in an indifferent way while she refused to look at him.

The whole thing was rather tragic to me. Animals also have dignity. It seemed undignified.

The whang of the jack is as large and as long as that of a stallion. The jack was being handled by a pale, sickly-looking farm hand. There was a grey, dirty-looking sky overhead. The object was to get a mule.

Mules are both male and female but they cannot reproduce.
Evidently however they like their own kind.

It was necessary to bring out a female mule to arouse the jack. The handsome black farm mare seemed by now lost in blind sex desire of which she was ashamed. Aroused by the female mule the jack's great prick stood stiff and directed by the sick-looking farm hand he mounted the broad back of the mare. She closed her eyes and trembled. The farm hand took his great cock in his hand and directed it into the mare's womb.

He seemed to fuck half heartedly. Soon he spilled his shot and crawled down.

There was talk. "Do you think she has enough, that she will catch?"

The pale farm hand was encouraging. "I can make him do it again. I'll take him into the barn beside the female mule. She always arouses him. He'll soon be excited again.

"You leave the mare standing here. We'll give her another shot."

"No," the farmer said. He began putting the saddle on the mare. "A little seed is as good as a lot."

I had a thought, a hope, that he did not want to see his fine handsome mare put again to that indignity with the ugly little male. The pale farm hand acquiesced. "You take now a cow. She is alone in the field with a bull. He is after her and after her. She will never have a calf."

The farmer with his mare rode away and after a visit with Cecil and his wife I also left. I felt I had seen something not nice and as I rode along in the car I met the farmer with his mare going home. We spoke. I looked at the mare. It seemed to me there was a queer look of shame in her fine mare's eyes.

1. Gene Aldridge, probably one of Anderson's boyhood companions at the racetracks that he loved to visit.

Sunday, September 25, Marion, Virginia

It will be a tense day for me. I have written a letter today to Eleanor, putting it up to her to say, now and definitely, whether she will marry me or not.

I have decided. If she is not going to do it I will begin, at any cost, another life.

It has been terrifically hard to be compelled to push her thus to the very wall but it has become necessary.

Monday, September 26, Marion, Virginia

It would be an odd thing if I could really put down here the real history of these days. I am trying to get up courage to give up the idea of marriage with Eleanor.

Neither one of us really wants marriage.

Because of circumstances it has come to this—that giving up the idea of marriage will have to mean now the giving up of each other.

The hours and days I have had with her have been the only warm happy days I have had in my life. In every way she is superior to every other woman I have ever known or loved . . . or thought I loved.

I have to put down here the prediction that my new novel *Beyond Desire* will not be a success with the public. There are precarious hours and perhaps even years ahead. If I can find courage to give her up—not take her into all this—I should.

Tuesday, September 27, Marion, Virginia

The nerve strain of these days has begun to tell on me. I slept, an exhausted sleep. The night was rainy, with the streets of the town deserted.

I have made up my mind I might as well go on to Russia. It will be too deadly, being here.

There are no indications that I get that my book will succeed. The tone of letters from a publishing house always tells the story.

There was not a word from Eleanor yesterday. It is strange that, in a crisis like this, she should be altogether silent. Since she has left here, leaving me all uncertain about the future, tense and nervous, there hasn't been a word of tenderness.

I cannot blame her. It isn't that she doesn't feel. It is just impossible for her to write the sort of tender things that might carry me through.

Wednesday, September 28, Marion, Virginia

There is a kind of return to sanity. Eleanor wrote me a sharp, accusing letter which I deserved. It will be rather a shame for her if she marries me and, this morning, I am not at all sure she will.

I live too intensely inside, think too much.

Just the same the storm I have been passing through now is going away.

It is a day of frequent hard rains.

If I could only see her, touch her. I have to live in someone outside myself. I have never known another person I love as I do her but I am not nice to her either.

Thursday, September 29, Marion, Virginia

This is the first day I have actually known that Eleanor is going to marry me. I am singing inside.

I went and got great quantities of mushrooms. The day got bright and fine. I was happy with Mrs. Copenhaver.

I have written to urge on Eleanor that she let me go and be near her at Kansas City this winter, while she works there. Then, when the job there is done, that we marry and run off together South—for some months' actual rest.

Then me to do my lectures in the spring and take Eleanor with me for the summer in Russia.

Friday, September 30, Marion, Virginia

Two wonderful letters from Eleanor. She loves me. She wants to marry me. It is the first time she has told me so—out and out.

It was a gorgeous fall day and this is another. John and I spent the afternoon playing, gathering mushrooms, pickling them, making a big au gratin. We had Dave, Bob and Mary for dinner.

There was something singing in me all day.

More than any other person I have ever known Eleanor lives in the Now. The Present. It is a marvelous quality. I have written her to ask that she work it out some way that I may be in Kansas City while she is there. I have never loved as I love her.

She sent me a strong pocket magnifying glass to carry in the woods.

October

Saturday, October 1, Marion, Virginia

A gorgeous day. I went with Grundy Vernon to gather mushrooms. He is a workman hurt in a modern big industrial plant. He cannot work any more. Lawyers have beat him out of most of his compensation.

I was full of Eleanor all day—thinking how much I wanted to be a real lover to her. I am afraid of my own stability of character. I shall try to be honest and fine with her.

I thought, when I went in there, the Copenhaver house was very sad.

I gathered many mushrooms and took them about to people's houses.

Sunday, October 2, Marion, Virginia

Thinking all yesterday of marriage with Eleanor—not as marriage but as a chance to dignify both our lives. If we can but do that.

It was one of the days when I could not work—the excitement, outside my rooms and off the surface of my paper, being so great.

I went to Chilhowie to see the neighborhood fair and the football game and in the evening to a little shabby circus with a high-sounding name, The Mighty Haag Shows.

There were two magnificent elephants, both females and both made to do horribly undignified things. I was ashamed for the human beings who liked to sit and see these great beasts made into rather silly and meaningless things like themselves.

Monday, October 3, Marion, Virginia

I am putting some of Eleanor's dear letters with these sealed envelopes to keep there.[1]

Went to the country with Frank and Ruth. It was glorious at the farm, a soft, warm fall day.

Today I feel like going back to the notebook—"Book of Days." It is a good thing to work on these days.

I may run down to the meeting of Southern writers, at Charleston. I might be able to say something of importance there.

It is for me one of the exciting days when there are too many thoughts and ideas in my head. I cannot work consistently on one because others keep intruding. I will not get much done.

1. None of Eleanor Copenhaver Anderson's letters to Anderson have survived.

Tuesday, October 4, Marion, Virginia

I should not write when I am as I am now, at this moment. I have been at work and am tired. I left all the windows of my room open and became chilled.

The day is cool. There are heavy clouds floating in patches of blue.

I am pretty intense—wanting Eleanor all the time.

The hills change constantly. Every day now new color comes into the trees. There is a new moon.

I am like a man on a voyage at sea. Eleanor has told me positively she loves me but she is in one place [and] I am in another.

I am reading the life of Pasteur.[1] I read a little and then work. The days pass with infinite slowness.

1. Piers Compton, *The Genius of Louis Pasteur* (New York, 1932).

Wednesday, October 5, Marion, Virginia

I got and stayed tense all day yesterday. Couldn't shake it off and when night came had to dope myself to sleep.

I got a pack of Lawrence books—his letters among them.[1] I got into them a little and they show what I've known all the time.

Health and strength.

It's a beastly word—"soul"—but I know no other. I feel Lawrence with health there. He gets bigger and bigger when you put him against the men of his day—Bennett, Wells, Shaw, etc.[2]

There is a kind of kingship. I believe I can work out the article I want about him.

1. *The Letters of D. H. Lawrence*, ed. Aldous Huxley (New York, 1932); D. H. Lawrence, *Apocalypse* (New York, 1932); Catherine Carswell, *The Savage Pilgrimage* (New York, 1932); Mabel Dodge Luhan, *Lorenzo in Taos* (New York, 1932); J. M. Murray, *Son of Woman* (New York, 1931).

2. Arnold Bennett (1867–1931), English realist novelist.

Thursday, October 6, Marion, Virginia

The letter enclosed from a woman who was once my secretary. I think she got rather into love with me. There was a day, just before she left me, I think I might have taken her.

She came down, to the office, dressed like a bride. All day—we were alone in there—she was all ripe to be taken. I had to go out of the office several times not to do it.

I felt it would be too damn casual to me and too important to her.

Later, after several years, I saw her one day. She suddenly told me. She went off to New York and got herself a man, slept with him, etc. It didn't last but she said she was nonetheless glad she had done it. She said it all to me as though it were a kind of reproach that I hadn't.

Now, by this letter, she seems to have become oddly mature. There must be any number of such women, going about, to the end, unfed and unfeeding.[1]

They so want to.

1. This woman wrote from the Midwest to ask for the friendship that Anderson had once promised her and for any one of his paintings to decorate her home.

Friday, October 7, Marion, Virginia

Eleanor says she will work to leave New York the nineteenth. Twelve more days and two Sundays to be got through. There was the first heavy frost of the year last night.

In the evening Funk and I started for a walk, going out the Scratch Gravel road and climbing the hill at the back of the cemetery.

He started that strange Republican talk but I asked him to quit and he did. The moon was out and the clouds lovely. Too fine a night for Hoover and Roosevelt.

We began speaking of Emmett Thomas, the queer political man, and he began telling me little stories of the pulling and hauling, the distrust and meanness of county politics.

Afterwards we got on T——— G——— and he told me things I didn't know but might have suspected—about his following women around town. He goes for young girls. Sam Dillard found one crying in the court house office. G——— had tried to put his hands on her. He stopped the girl going to her father.[1]

Naturally such a man is very strong on public virtue.

It was odd to spend such a night, under such a moon, thinking of such men.

Afterward we spoke of children that must be raised in such a place and Funk was nice in his attitude. I liked him.

---

1. T——— G———, name here omitted to avoid possible family embarrassment; Sam Dillard, sheriff of Smyth County, Va., since 1920.

Saturday, October 8, Marion, Virginia

An exciting morning, after a very dead day yesterday. I was stale and could not sleep. I wanted Eleanor all day and all night, in my sleep. My sleep was filled with sex dreams of her.

I awoke this morning tired but began writing to her. What I was writing ran off into something, not addressed to her as a letter.

Perhaps it was the beginning of a novel. I shall put it aside and take it up later.

Monday, October 10, Marion, Virginia

The incident of Frank Lemmon and wife, what happens to him when drunk.[1]

Ruth, the tall school teacher, with the love in her eyes.

The little rich woman whose husband has lost his money. Her confusion. Her helplessness.

Frank in the hotel room. Drunks who hide in hotels.

The gorgeous day. The two children with Dave's mother.

The new kind of novel.

Dave's head of Lincoln.[2]

Bob with his house.

The strange, locked-up thing in Bob's wife Mary. The gorgeous coloring in the hills.

The dream of Eleanor crawling over the barrels in the warehouse. The valley in the soft evening light.

The camp fire. The sparks going up. Country ham.

These people, in a kind of ecstasy of gossip.

The town. The town. The town.

1. Frank Lemmon, Marion, Va., oil distributor and member of the chamber of commerce.

2. David Greear, local Virginia youth whose artistic ambitions Anderson encouraged.

Tuesday, October 11, Marion, Virginia

It is again a day when I cannot do much. I pressed too hard yesterday.

In dreams—I was in a kind of loft, the whole front of the building gone. Huge black clouds raced across the sky. I could see the shore of a sea and the lights of a city. John and Ernest Hemingway were somewhere about. There must have been a stairway. In the midst of the storm, Eleanor arrived with two other women. She was beautifully clad.

Today I could be happy and could rest if I had Eleanor to play with.

Wednesday, October 12, Marion, Virginia

Another day with not much work done. I went and sat with Mrs. Copenhaver, taking Lawrence's *Apocalypse*, and we read and talked for two hours.

The best time of the day was just before dark when I went alone into the country to get mushrooms. It was a cold fall night. The sky was much alive. I kept thinking of Lawrence. There was a kind of life seemed to come up out of the cold ground, out of animals met in the road and out of the flaming sky. The farm houses all seemed very still in the evening light—as though the very houses, like the fields, were at prayers.

Thursday, October 13, Marion, Virginia

An exciting morning. Yesterday spent largely out of doors, walking in fields and later going with Mrs. Copenhaver and Miss Lind to get ferns for Mrs. Copenhaver.[1]

Mr. Copenhaver, in the evening, got very ungracious, it seemed to me, and I left the house depressed and blue.

I walked again and that partially cured me.

This morning, in my room, I got the conception of the book "The Family" and put down at least a few paragraphs. If I could do it and not make it too close to the Copenhaver family, bringing in other figures, etc. . . . It is a thing I would love to do now.[2]

1. Etha A. Lind, a teacher at Marion College, which was next door to the Copenhaver home in Marion.
2. None of this project survives, and it was probably soon abandoned.

Friday, October 14, Marion, Virginia

To remember the day at Pembertons' place, south of Abingdon, Col. Grey, Ida O'Keeffe, the walk to the old slave burying place, the children, the walk through Lick Hollow, papaws, mushrooms, the view from the hill.[1]

Old men and young women, Ida in the moonlight, in the garden, the great tree.

The tale of the Prussian sculptor.

The apple and the crow's feather.
The house, with the sense of old people about, the fat cook.

1. Abingdon, seat of nearby Washington County, Va.; Idah O'Keeffe Ten Eyck (sister of the painter Georgia O'Keeffe), who was visiting at the Holston Valley, Tenn., home of Mrs. J. Pemberton, where Anderson had visited her in the company of a Colonel Grey, unidentified.

Saturday, October 15, Marion, Virginia

I have to put down a queer day for yesterday. I was upset and worried about Eleanor but a letter came in the late morning mail.

Also a letter from two people I love dearly—Ruth and Roger. I could not bear the thought of their separation and wrote a letter to them both that took all morning.

I went from that to the new novel and by noon was in a state. I went off with Bob to a football game and there, in a moment of inattention, got run over and roughly handled by three players. I was thrown, some three yards, and three players fell over me.

For some reason I was all day terribly depressed by the thought of Mary's sister and could not get her out of my mind.[1]

Then, because of my depression, I drank too much wine.

It was a bad day.

The magazine *Time* had a nasty review of *Beyond Desire*.[2] I began again reading *Fathers and Sons*, Turgenev.[3] I doped myself to sleep as I was afraid of my thoughts—the wrong I might do Eleanor by marrying her, etc.

1. Mary Chryst Anderson's sister Janet.
2. "Beyond Control," *Time*, XX (October 17, 1932), 52, that begins: "Sherwood Anderson used to call himself a story-teller, but that was long ago."
3. Ivan Turgenev published *Fathers and Sons* in 1862; Anderson owned the edition published in 1917 by Boni and Liveright.

Sunday, October 16, Marion, Virginia

A steady drizzle of rain. I have been writing a piece about the old workman, Gil Stephenson, who died yesterday.[1]

In Eleanor's letters there is, recently, a note of discouragement about Russia, as though the leaders there had lost touch.

I wrote Eleanor about the days—always coming—when you walk in streets and feel no love going out of people, into people. I went on two days to Rich Valley, the first day to a football game and the next to a horse fair.

There were crowds of people but I could not connect myself with one of them. I went away and sat down on a hill. The people all seemed little isolated particles and I seemed one too.

By night I was a wreck. Funk saw me on the street in town and said, "You look as though you had been ill."

A letter came from Eleanor. It was full of love. It cured me.

There are days when I feel something in the air, trying to flow—between people. I try to get in the way of it—to have it flow through me.

1. Gil Stephenson, who had worked in the printshop of the Marion, Va., newspapers for more than forty years.

Monday, October 17, Marion, Virginia

It rained all day—a steady drizzle. I went to the print shop and wrote about old Gil.[1] The town was deserted and ugly. I came home and presently succeeded in getting into work.

There was something both very ugly and rather sweet and fine about old Gil's funeral and burial. People are in a forgiving mood. They like being.

Went to see Little Dave cast his head of Lincoln.

Frank Copenhaver has been very ill again. He suffers horribly—asthma—fighting for breath. I have got into the new novel but will have to set it aside now and give attention to the book of short stories.[2]

1. "Death in Harness," Marion *Democrat*, October 18, 1932, pp. 1, 8.
2. *Death in the Woods and Other Stories* (New York, 1933).

Tuesday, October 18, Marion, Virginia

This is really a letter to Eleanor. She will be leaving New York tomorrow night so I can't write her there any more.

Darling—A bad night . . . well not so bad. It was this way. A little sense of nearness to you came, thinking of you starting home, so my imagination got the better of me. All night in dreams asleep—and when awake I dreamed of you and then—in a half-dream. . . .

Seeds of new life all over me in the bed.

This all mixed up all day with thoughts of the new novel, me being alive with that.

Funk sick in bed and also Frank. I fixed Frank's wine and took whisky to Funk. I got mushrooms. It is raining again today.

You will be tired when you get home.

I wrote a letter to Idah Ten Eyck.

I wrote to Roger. I sent off the outline to the new short story book.

Wednesday, October 19, Marion, Virginia

The day Eleanor will be leaving New York.

The night passed in a rather dazzling aliveness, had been reading *The Savage Pilgrimage* and Lawrence and his wife Frieda slipped into my dreams.

They were fighting, on a country road, and Frieda (this in the dream) in order to annoy Lorenzo—knowing his feeling about such things—tore off all her clothes and danced naked in the road, compelling him to come and beg her to dress before someone came.

The trees seem more alive with color this year than ever—a more delicate aliveness.

I had, in the morning yesterday—when I sat down at my desk to work—suddenly a clear fine conception of a new short story, to be called "Old People In the House." I wrote quite a lot of it.[1]

I am tense, waiting for the coming of Eleanor. Waiting for her coming is like waiting to get well after an illness. Absence from her is an illness.

1. "Old People in the House," a story told to Anderson by Idah Ten Eyck, was not completed and does not survive.

Thursday, October 20, Marion, Virginia

On this morning I was to have set out for Radford to meet Eleanor but she has wired she cannot leave New York yet. I am uncertain and upset.

Then came the thing about Mr. Copenhaver's childish attitude about the matter of expense for the school board, etc. . . . and Bob's not exactly nice attitude toward me.

I shall have to clear that up.

In the meantime many impressions flowing in on me and my trying to work. I could put in here the letters—received to-day—explaining much, but will put them into another day's envelopes.

The idea of the story "Old People in the House" grows in me.

I have been to see Bob. We have fought out our fight. It may help.

Friday, October 21, Marion, Virginia

The whole day spent in anxiety about Eleanor. Then, this morning, her letter.

A great sweeping sense of her absolute preciousness to me.

Fear eating at me that it is [the] uterus and that I have, in some way, hurt her.

I want nothing but to be near her.

Yesterday tense and there will be this day to go through. Before the day is out perhaps I shall know where she is and can go to be near her.

Saturday, October 22, New York City

When I tried to talk to Eleanor over the phone from home my voice went to pieces.

It is a tumor on the uterus and her brother says that eighty percent of women have them. In many cases they remain small and comparatively harmless. Her brother says it has been there for a year. I did not know.

I was terribly afraid I might have done something to her.

She is in the operating room having it taken away. The place is unbearable to me. I spent the afternoon and night on the train coming here in a kind of daze. Every turn of the wheels of the train took me nearer her. I just got to the hospital as it happened. I had a moment with her.

She was very beautiful, very strong and lovely. All my blood called out against anything being done to her. I was helpless.

I feel helpless now. I feel her in the hands of others.

I hate the very tone of the voices of the people in this place. I hate any kind of disease touching her.

I am trying so hard to get at something—a slow anger burns in me. It isn't against any human. I guess life just twists, this one one way, another another way.

I feel your mother, rather hurt, like a little girl, because she isn't with you. I feel your father angry, not wanting to be as he is just now, insisting that she shall not go to you. I feel that he feels I want her to go and that, if she goes now, it will be, in some way, an assertion of my wish.

So I feel shut out there.

I half don't care whether or not I have you ever—if Lois, or your father, or your mother, or Randolph, or Mazie or Abe or the doctor or anyone will guarantee to me nothing will happen to you.[1]

It isn't so much now, to me, a personal love—in the sense of your ever giving yourself to me. To hell with that now—me and all I stand for. You exist as a thing in life so close, dear, to me, outside my having you—that all I want is [a] guarantee.

The anger isn't against anyone but just that there isn't any-thing—the little stinking money I have, or any will of mine—that can do anything if you dare, for one minute, to take chances with Eleanor.

The new story depends on your getting well. More than need-ing you, for myself, dearest, I need your living figure in life. Your illness has brought this home to me.

They all nowadays, dear, make fun of me because of what they call my striving. Well, it is, always has been, a striving toward life—never illness, never death, never denial of life.

I have always, all my life, needed a figure—a woman because I am male—outside myself, to make real to me something I terribly need to go on being alive, wanting to the end to be alive. I have found it in you and that's that.

It isn't now whether you want me or not but I can say this—if you have any belief at all in me, as a living force in my time and place, then it is up to you to see Eleanor for the time, until you are quite well, as a person you must be very very careful with—that she be quiet, get well, not to take any chances with her.

I command it. Damn your eyes if you don't do it now, dear.

The very anger in me makes me work. It has to have an outlet, I presume.

Perhaps it will bring into my story something hard it needs. Life itself has this hard quality. It may be my only way of reaching toward you now.

You look at a tree and it is hard and erect enough, reaching, I presume, toward a sky and light it cannot touch.

1. Abe, otherwise unidentified but referred to elsewhere by Anderson as a handsome New York City taxi driver with literary ambitions, about whose attentions Anderson occasionally chided Eleanor Copenhaver.

Sunday, October 23, New York City

A terribly restless night—a nightmare of frightened dreams about Eleanor. I walked about my room and read, trying to get quiet. With daylight the fear passed.

In the evening I took Randolph to see *Of Thee I Sing*. It seemed utterly silly and meaningless to me. When I saw it with Eleanor, it was great fun.

I took Randolph to dine at Lubin's, on Fourteenth Street. The whole evening was a kind of daze to me.

There is in him a curious thing. We talked of Pasteur and he said he had read Pasteur's life several times, it being a part of his studies, but when I began to speak of things in Pasteur's life he seemed to know nothing of them.

They are all curiously blind to a whole side of Eleanor, by far the most sensitive and alive one in the family. She is so positive in putting away from her any marks of attention that seem to put upon anyone else and they have all jumped to the conclusion that she doesn't want attention, just as her mother once said to me that Eleanor did not care much for clothes and nice things about her.

I wanted Randolph to tell her that I would be sitting near, in the hospital, every day until she is better and can see me and he began to say it would only worry her—which it wouldn't at all.

Randolph has a certain heavy stolidity. He is determined to live well and get through life with the least possible disturbance to himself.

I wanted him to stay on here, for another day or two, and he said, "Oh, I've got to get back to get at my exams." He is leaving at 2:30 today, Sunday, scarcely thirty hours after Eleanor's operation, and he, being a doctor, can go in and sit with her. I have a feeling, down in me, that he has a date in Washington with some girl, for Sunday night, and that is what he has in mind.

Even the play *Of Thee I Sing* seemed a bit too subtle for him as he kept saying, "I don't get that," over the most obvious points, but just the same, there is in him, down deep, something rather solid.

What gets me is where Eleanor gets all she has. She is so obviously a combination of all the good in both sides of her people.

I shall be glad, glad when the next few days have passed.

There are certain times when, if someone could say, "It is Sherwood Anderson, the writer, who is so interested in this patient. . . . " There is always the chance the doctor, or someone, in such a place might have respect for me. It is the only time I want to use it but cannot do it myself. I wish Eleanor could tell the nurse, for example. Something might be gained in assurance that I would get every possible word out from her.

Among these people, doctors, nurses, etc., you get such a feeling of being shut out, as though they had found all laymen silly in the presence of sickness. I suppose most of them are.

Monday, October 24, New York City

Instead of the nightmare night, as on Saturday night, I fell into the deepest, most restful sleep I'd had in months. There were no dreams, just a heavy, restful sleep.

On the night before I was beside myself on account of Eleanor. Every time I fell asleep horrid dreams, of her suffering and clinging to life, came. Randolph was over sleeping in the house with Lois and I wanted to call him, at 2:00, at 3:00, at 4:00, but didn't. I kept awake and walked about the room, smoking cigarettes.

I had planned to stay right out at the hospital but when Randolph told Eleanor she was upset. She was afraid Lois and I might meet out there and that Lois might make some kind of scene and, Randolph said, seemed upset, so I said I would go up to my brother Karl's and then, as soon as she was out of all danger, that I would go on home.

I didn't go to Karl's but came here, where I could be in touch all the time by phone. The nurse is a corking one. Eleanor is better this morning, although she had a restless night.

Randolph and I talked a little of Lois and he despises her as I do. There is no doubt of Randolph's fine maleness and I think that any male man would dislike the woman. I believe she is the enemy, not of me, nor does she really love Eleanor. I believe such people bloodsuck the souls of others. They are simple facts in nature.

What she hates is a third thing—marriage, the fact of marriage between Eleanor and myself.

I have thought all along that Eleanor would not really free herself from this woman until she did it, on the bold, announced grounds that she was coming to me. I believe this has been done. Perhaps Lois made a scene. It is perhaps partly what made Eleanor tense. Anyway she is my woman and I can go away or be here knowing she is fine and I love her.

Tuesday, October 25, New York City

As you, dear Eleanor, will not see this for a long time I will be frank in it. I met Mazie at the train—to take her to you. She had written a card to her mother in which there was the sentence "Neither of the two friends [meaning me and poor Lois] will be glad to see me." It hurt me horribly because I was loving Mazie so much, at the moment, and was so grateful to her for coming—so I asked her not to send it.

Later, after she had seen you and you slept, I took her to dine and was very male and not nice, accusing Lois of playing on your sympathies and upsetting you.

Also of draining you and refusing to let you go and live your life. You will know how I went on, dear, as you have heard me and will hear me.

But afterward, alone, I was very sorry. I began to think how horrid it would be if I had to give up living with you and was suddenly just terribly sorry for Lois and full of shame for my own inadequacy.

These are being dreadful, dreadful days, dear. I try to write and keep telling Mazie and others that I am working, etc., but I'm not.

I want nothing but to sit beside you and be near until you are well again.

Wednesday, October 26, New York City

This day I began on the story of "Thanksgiving"—a dedication to the gods for Eleanor getting safe through.[1] I saw her at the hospital. She was entirely lovely.

1. Several versions of this unfinished work survive in manuscript.

Thursday, October 27, New York City

It is early morning and raining. I am waiting for a call from Mazy—at the hospital with Eleanor.

I have been reading Leane Zugsmith's book *Never Enough*, a stout book, amazing observation.[1] Where did she get it all?

Wrote to Sergel, about a trip out there, to be in his house, a chance to get on a real footing with a man.

Believe I am getting on a real footing with Mazie. She let me pour out on her all my feeling about Lois—getting it out of my system, without bringing Eleanor in. She stood up to me, was fierce and fine.

Walked alone in the city streets at night and was all alive to it.

1. Leane Zugsmith, *Never Enough* (New York, 1932).

Friday, October 28, New York City

The enclosed are the distracted little notes from Eleanor, on the day before she was operated [on].[1]

There is something in the air, the city, the books I read, in most people I see.

Where has the lack of faith in life come from? Why not just living, breathing, going along?

You get at last an old wisdom. It comes up out of the ground, out of the few people you meet who have it.

It's so damned hard to hold it in the face of something.

Really lack of love of life is the true second-rateness, the true whoredom.

To get my hair cut, hating the ordeal, a tall slender young Jewish man, not clean, who hated me because I hated having his hands touch me.

An evening, last evening, with my brother Karl—he fifty-eight but, for the evening, extraordinarily young, like a young man of thirty—alive, amusing. We dining and walking, about liking each other.

1. Notes not surviving.

Saturday, October 29, New York City

This letter represents an attempt to get at a man as friend. I couldn't afford to go to him. I wanted to go. He wanted me to. He sent me this money to come.[1]

It gave me a queer feeling taking it. I'll go on out anyway and talk to him of it when I get out.

It will be a relief to be out there, not in Marion—until Eleanor comes.

At any rate I am writing on the book "Thanksgiving." It is absorbing all my energy now.

1. Roger Sergel, at Anderson's request, had sent money with which the writer could travel to visit the Sergel home in Chicago.

Sunday, October 30, New York City

Randolph, Mazie and Channing are all in New York. I am trying to place them in relation to the thing I am doing.

I wrote very hard on "Thanksgiving" and was exhausted. I went to see Eleanor and rode down on the bus but the whole ride down was a sort of half-dream.

Her face was very beautiful against the pillow. I dreamed of [the] doctor, running away and away with her, myself running, unable to catch them.

Monday, October 31, New York City

Tommy, an old man about town, telling about his experience in sleeping with a virgin. By his story she had come to him. He knows many famous people who come to see him. She wanted to get into the big world. She offered herself to him.[1]

He took her but says it gave him no pleasure. She had no skill, was twenty-eight, frightened. The whole thing makes an ugly picture. He did not want her.

I changed the subject quickly. We were standing and talking in the bedroom where it happened.

We began talking of John and Nita and it suddenly came to me that, when I have finished this novel, on which I am now at work, I'd like to do one on John's life.[2]

"American Money."

In the evening, in the hospital. I did not expect to see her—Eleanor very, very lovely. I could sit with her for an hour. She was very beautiful.

1. Thomas R. Smith, of Horace Liveright's publishing company.
2. Anderson did not complete or save his planned work on John Emerson.

November

Tuesday, November 1, On the Train

A grey, cold day. In Pittsburgh, where I had breakfast in the station, a damp cold that chilled the blood.

A talk with Leane Zugsmith, at lunch, trying to find the basis for a quiet nice thing she has, she trying to give me the impression it was due to a system of philosophy she has.

Melissa in the afternoon, feeling something rather terribly loose and unformed in her. It was a bore being with her.

My brother Karl, her father, has, in the last few years, hardened, matured, got firmer and finer.

At Eleanor's bedside in the evening and, for a few minutes, she put her arms about my neck and held me and I was happy.

The trip to Chicago is an experiment in friendship . . . with Roger Sergel.

Wednesday, November 2, Chicago, Illinois

It has been a little hard, getting back into the novel "Thanksgiving" today, after coming here, a queer impulsive move on my part, having some idea of finding here—in Roger or Ruth—a thing wanted and needed.

Hating to go back to Marion just now, Eleanor not there, the queer loneliness of waiting there. I think I will go back there, however, early next week.

Thursday, November 3, Chicago, Illinois

In the park the trees are almost bare and dead yellow and brown leaves are driven about by the wind. The city is very dirty and unswept.

Tales at table of hunger marchers and of children going to school unfed.

Roger's business goes on growing. He and Ruth are both brainy and capable.

At table I told about the letter from Embree, enclosed, and we spoke of peonage in the South.[1] The children became excited. They hadn't heard of any such thing.

I worked on "Thanksgiving" until I was tired through and through.

1. Edwin Rogers Embree (1883–1950), student of racialism, head of the Julius Rosenwald Foundation of Chicago and author of *Brown American: The Story of a New Race* (New York, 1931). Anderson had asked Embree to confirm the treatment of southern blacks described by John L. Spivak in *Georgia Nigger* (New York, 1932)—mistreatment that Embree confirmed with his own additional examples.

Friday, November 4, Chicago, Illinois

I am obsessed these days to have my own house, if it isn't more than two rooms, to have a few sticks of my own furniture and my woman.

I move restlessly about, from place to place.

I am in Chicago now, in this house. Next week I will be in my rooms in the Sprinkle house. I work but, after working, I want Eleanor.

Will I get her? It seems to me everything centers in that now.

It is a queer time to work. Everything you do seems thrown into a muddy pond. There is nothing comes back. You freeze wanting warm affection from someone.

Saturday, November 5, Chicago, Illinois

Again the day absorbed in Mary in "Thanksgiving." In the afternoon, yesterday, after a struggle with Ruth, clearing the air, I could not work.

Then to Ferdinand, whom I found alive and busy and real. We walked until it rained.

Monday, November 7, Chicago, Illinois

After the walk in the woods yesterday, a sleep and then out with a group of eight to dine in a Hungarian restaurant and to sit talking and drinking until midnight.

Roger seems to me to be surrounded by rather stupid men here. There was the deadly strong business man and his wife of the night before. Last night also John Frederick.[1] Something too prissy. Later Roger told me the story of his relations with his mother, her grip on him.

The woman, his wife, who has never succeeded in getting him away from his mother.

Then the newspaper man, with the communist wife. A good deal of sex in her. He is one of the most utterly naive men I've seen. He tried, I think, to compliment me but got off into telling me about the Canadian writer Morley Callaghan and Callaghan's being sorry for me because the public did not accept me more.[2]

1. John T. Frederick, professor of modern literature at Northwestern University and founder of the journal *Midland* (1915–33).
2. Morley Callaghan (1903–), Canadian author of novels and short stories.

Tuesday, November 8, Chicago, Illinois

Presidential election day. I finished the first [draft] of the first book of "Thanksgiving" and, when I had finished it, a great feeling of depression and fear took hold of me. I was in this house so went and took a drink of Roger's gin, which was hot and strong and did me no good.

I went to walk and, in the grey light, all the streets seemed shabby and dirty and I thought all the people passed must be half desperate about life as I was.

I walked a long time and, coming back to this house, threw myself on the bed, wanting to pray, but I couldn't.

I slept and went to dine with Ferdinand and Clara and managed to keep up the conversation and be cheerful. Ferdinand has lost the savings of a lifetime. He is however cheerful and works hard. He is more social than Clara who likes very few people.

Back at the Sergels' Ruth was in pajamas and very handsome. She went off to bed presently and Roger and I talked on until after 1:00, trying to think of some kind of management of the world, money and supplies, that would make living more bearable.

Wednesday, November 9, Chicago, Illinois

To mark the failure of what was back of my coming here—the surrender to an impulse, good in itself, it not working out. I doubt if it has been understood.

To check it as an experience and as connected with the passing of money, between man and man.

Thursday, November 10, Marion, Virginia

Darling woman. I am putting this note into my daily envelope because I feel restricted about writing to you just now.

I got home from Chicago—having, I'm sure, missed the last of your letters there, and none has come here. I feel terribly restricted about writing you because you are back with Lois and, I'm afraid, a letter brought up to you, by her, my scrawl on it, might start again a tenseness.

I want your mother to go there and your father objects—on account of cost. I had to sit listening to that. I got up and came away. The idea of thinking of cost now—with you. I was never more baffled in my life. I, it seems, in a time like this, when the one dearest in all the world to me is ill—I cannot come to you, sit with you, read to you, do little things for you.

I am frightened that you have left the hospital too soon. Lordy God, when this time is over! Dear one.

Friday, November 11, Marion, Virginia

Walked a little with Mr. Funk, and he kept going on, in an old tired way, about the election and I finally said to him, "Do you not think it would be better, if we walk at all, not to talk so, going over this mess? If we must talk so you go walk alone and so will I." So he quit and became nice, telling of the prisoner he was defending who has paresis.

The man, a business man, got it into his head he was a slick criminal. He must have been reading detective stories. So he tried to do a slick crime and got caught at once.

Now he doesn't want his lawyer to let the court know he has a diseased mind.

It is very difficult for me to go to Mrs. Copenhaver here—she being my only companion in the town now—because her husband is jealous, thinking I influence her mind. He himself wants to be the dominant thing in her life but has let his mind decay. So he tries to impose himself by constantly opposing everything. Just now he is [in] opposition to her going to be with Eleanor while she is ill.

Saturday, November 12, Marion, Virginia

A distracted day. I had gathered together all the short stories for my new story book and now have left them all somewhere, in a leather portfolio. It is annoying.

It is a bitter, cold day with snow. Little white patches of snow begin to appear.

Went to a showing of fox hounds and was selected as one of the judges in the horn-blowing contest. Went with two other men to a distant hill where we stood, in the darkness, to listen. Some of the horn blowers were quite marvelous, the sound running amazingly over the wintry hills.

Sunday, November 13, Marion, Virginia

I have spent the morning—in fancy—on the Grey farm in Kentucky, Mary's reaction to a story heard when she was a child—a question of authority, in the matter of cutting down two young oak trees, near a barn.[1]

Yesterday an odd, shut-in day, grey and cold.

I feel shut out from the Copenhaver house these days because of the enmity to me in the father.

A lovely gracious note from Eleanor. It made the day warm.

1. Anderson used this memory from Mary Emmett's youth as the basis for his story "Brother Death," *Death in the Woods*, 271–98.

Monday, November 14, Marion, Virginia

Reading in bed a novel by the Spaniard Zamacois—very blunt and cruel.[1] Eleanor wrote me about the thing in *Nation*—myself.[2] There is such delight in preaching funeral sermons.

Mrs. Copenhaver has to write of Jim White Sheffey. How nice it could be if she could write honestly about the difficulties of such a life.

The sun came out and I was in the woods, walking and getting mushrooms. There were two trees such as I had been writing about during the morning, trees standing very red and alive, with all the leaves clinging in an open field.

1. Eduardo Zamacois (1873–1971), writer of erotic psychological novels; Anderson was probably reading *Roots*, trans. E. Vivas (New York, 1930).

2. Anderson probably was not the author of "Desperate Need," *Nation*, CXXXV (November, 1932), 506. See his letter for November 20.

Tuesday, November 15, Marion, Virginia

The notable thing of yesterday was the drive, just before dark, out Scratch Gravel, on the Gault Road to the chinquapin patch, for mushrooms.

I found them, the bricktops, in masses—lovely colors, from straw yellow to deep orange, on the edge of red.

Then there was the drive home, thinking of Roger Sergel and of Eleanor, the sky having the same gorgeous drift, from straw yellow to red, as the mushrooms—wanting a companion, male or female, wanting both, to share such things with me.

Wednesday, November 16, Marion, Virginia

I wonder what will be Eleanor's thoughts if she ever revisits with me through these notes these times.

In the night I was kissing her body—in dreams—and suddenly had fulfillment which left me empty as I awoke to an empty bed.

The figure of Lois, all through Eleanor's illness, has stood like a ghost between me and real contact with my loved one but Eleanor also has it all wrong in thinking I hate Lois—or distrust Eleanor.

I have been terribly defeated and baffled. I am now.

Thursday, November 17, Marion, Virginia

This is one of those days when I am sunk in a gloom so thick that there is no light at all.

It seems my letters have offended, or hurt, Eleanor and the last letters from her were harsh, at least for her.

Then there was the matter of Lois discovering my subterfuge of using Eleanor's mother's envelopes—so now I am afraid to write at all.

From the beginning I have hated all this concealment but, in this case, I thought it would prevent the flaring up thus of Lois's hatred for me.

There is no quiet in me at all. I cannot get quiet and peaceful, night or day, when I am away from Eleanor, or when I think I have hurt her.

My position, all through her illness, has been terrible for me. I am not really recognized, by anyone, perhaps not by her, as her lover—with a recognized lover's rights.

This is due to my ridiculous position—a man who has so much failed in marriage.

On days like this I am pretty much recognizing myself as what I probably am—a ridiculous man. I am ashamed and humbled by life. It hurts to live at all.

I thought I would go hunting but today I cannot bear anyone's company although I know that if, later in the day, a letter comes from Eleanor, having in it any tenderness, I shall begin to live again.

The ground will seem good to me again and the skies. I am half afraid to go alone into the woods with a gun. There would be a constant temptation to put an end to it, the misery and hurt I bring to people, my inability to make life sweet for others.

More than once the only thing that has held me back, from clearing the slate, has been the thought that Eleanor would blame herself. That I couldn't bear.

It is however good that I have taken the resolution not to write to her any more until she comes home. In my present state I would only be saying something more to hurt her.

Friday, November 18, Marion, Virginia

It cannot possibly be many days now before Eleanor comes. She has amazingly the power to make my days bad or good. It is dreadful to be so dependent on another but, for me, it is true.

When she writes, as she did yesterday, her letters full of love, my whole world changes.

I am so stupid and do so need love.

Saturday, November 19, Marion, Virginia

The best moments come not in any relation at all to most people I know, but always now in relationship to Eleanor. Companionship becomes more and more necessary and, if I could find a man friend, someone with whom to share also such moments. . . .

The best moment yesterday, in Clagghorn Valley, Funk gone off with his dogs uphill.

I stood on a hillside, looking up and down the valley. It rained a little. There were many little poor farm houses.

There were great grey clouds of mist rolling down the sides of the mountains. It was all suddenly very majestic.

First, a warrior—half wild, with a strong man's body, going over such hills, singing war songs . . . feeling in himself ability to compete with life and nature. Second, a white boy—always present in me—who runs singing through green forests and tall grass in the moonlight.

Funk's remark as we later walked down the hill to the car—"What a heavy-featured man you are."

Sunday, November 20, Marion, Virginia

It will be for me a depressing day. The enclosed from poor Eleanor. I dare say I deserve it. What is gorgeous about her is her power to forgive.

I did not write the letter to the *Nation*. I have not seen it. I presume some [one] of the communist organizations that keep pestering me has got a hurried reply from me and has published it.

If you love and are loved you have also—terribly—the power to hurt the other. I must have hurt her terribly. How incompetent of me. What I want most to do—make her happy—I do so miserably. I am sorry I mailed the letter today. Now I shall manage to get through the day but tonight, Monday and Tuesday nights will be horrible to me.

I will be afraid again—horribly afraid that, by my own stupidity and lack of finesse, I will have killed the thing dearest to me.

Sunday evening.

The town and the whole country now, with nearly all the leaves gone from the trees, is very naked. The tops of hills in the distance are like old jagged paint brushes.

I wish I could be in the berth with you when you wake up, somewhere west of Lynchburg. I so love to see things with you.

There is a hill, up back of Bob's house, that old road, turning off the highway by the broken old stone chimney—where you used to ride. You get a marvelous look at the town from up there.

It is going to be great fun, when you get a little better, to take you out, afternoons. Perhaps we'll still get some mushrooms, brick-tops. They are like miniature sunsets.

I wish I were a painter now. I'd do a delicate, nice thing of you in bed.

Monday, November 21, Marion, Virginia

I wrote yesterday the foreword to the book of short stories. It was a miserable day for me but I kept busy, out of doors, and took a sleeping pill so I slept.

This morning is grey and cold. I shall stay in the field hunting birds. I am terribly in love with Eleanor but my case seems hope-less and perhaps should be.

Tuesday, November 22, Marion, Virginia

Oh, the blessing of your mother to me. I have come to feel with you and Mazy. I could not bear the thought of anything happening to her. She has been my mainstay.

I have dared talk to her of my love for you. It is the only one to whom I dare talk.

Thanksgiving.

Thanksgiving.

I shall not mind another day. There is something significant in your coming on Thanksgiving day.

Oh, sweet one. Oh, dear one.

Love me, dear.

Dare to love me.

No matter what anyone says, true or false, love the poor man—

Who has such queer strength and queer weakness.

I will sing songs to us.

Let's go back to the true thing.

Not you

or me

but something—a third thing that can come out of our poor struggle.

In our hearts we know that we both want the finest truest thing there is.

Oh my lover.

Notes to Eleanor

What we should have—
There should be in you, Eleanor, if you really want to marry me, a desire to make me a home.

Even if it is just a couple of rooms.

I guess I could help. I have a kind of talent for that but I want it in you too.

You shouldn't pay any attention to anything I have ever said. I say so many things. Anyone who says so much says a lot of nonsense.

I am no different from any man in wanting someone—a woman—to want me to be warmly clothed, decently fed . . . more than this, I think, Eleanor, dear—not so much to have as to want.

I am sitting in my room thinking. I have the feeling that, during your illness, I have been of no help at all.

A lot of thoughts come because I have the blues today. I guess I poured most of a kind of bitterness in me, not against anyone but rather against fate, into my daily journal.

The daily journal is funny too. I guess I am trying to make it half take the place of a man friend—a comrade. I have tried pretty hard to be worthy of a man friend too but I've failed a lot. Maurice came very near. We were getting at it, but he died. It seems almost unfair of him. He was pretty precious to me, as you are.

Thinking, regarding us . . . naturally dear, being as I am, I do think of the things surrounding you. This I always do. I can't help it.

For example I think of the sheer ugliness of the apartment in New York, where you lived so long with Lois. I never went into the place without thinking of it.

There is such a different point of view Lois and myself have. If there had ever been a chance I might have made her respect my point of view and I might have got respect for hers. . . .

That became impossible. You were partially to blame. Let's admit that. Perhaps if you had, from the beginning, been bold with her, had taken me into your mutual home, had said boldly to her,

"I am determined to look this man over. I am a woman in my own rights"—then she and I, some way, might have conceivably got at each other. She can't be quite as rotten toward me as she seems now. I have no real right to a conception of any other human being as distorted as I admit mine is now about her.

All right, admit that—your mistake. It should bring us closer. I have made enough of them.

You know, dear, several times, when it came to the question of marriage, you have said, "There are questions to be asked."

So it has come home to me now that I have to ask questions.

Being shut off from you, as I have been during your illness—made to feel, I admit by circumstances, a rank outsider, thrown back on myself, you there, away from me, suffering, in danger—I have thought a lot about your life.

So, I have thought, you can chuck me if I am wrong, how you were rather loved out when you were a child. I wonder if it hasn't rather gone on ever since with you, as it rather has with me. We are so queerly alike, in a certain experience of life.

I have always, dear, this picture of your life—hotel rooms, strange places, nothing much, in the way of little womanly possessions, really belonging to you.

I think of you as one who has chosen to play a certain role in life.

I can't quite make out whether it is quite honest or not.

If for example you lie, night after night, in an uncomfortable bed, or live in an ugly apartment, and build in your own mind the notion, which you came to believe, or at least half believe, that such things do not really matter to you. . . .

Your interest rather in starving coal miners, or economics, etc. . . .

At the same time you having revealed to me, your lover, in a thousand little ways, your quick warm response to the sensual.

Your real love of beauty when I do strike it in my prose.

Dear, you must know, in your soul, the beauty of your head, with its background of blue-black hair, your lips, your really wonderful eyes, to try to conceal so much.

I remember once you said to me, "Look out for me if I ever do surrender."

Then the drawing back from that—as though you hadn't a right, or didn't want it.

Fool woman.

I have to say that and also "Fool man"—that I am to ever, for one moment, let you get away with such nonsense with me.

I'm your man or I'm not and, if I am your man, that, at any rate, doesn't go.

Isn't it conceivable that Lois also . . . she must be somewhat woman, not having the thing I am talking of here—and you know I am talking sense now—not daring to go after it. . . .

There is more excuse for her than for you.

You have real physical beauty—IT—my dear—just plain, everyday sex appeal, and, you little cheat, you—you know it.

Conceivable that Lois, feeling she can't get what I am here talking about. . . .

Makes a virtue of despising it—love, conception, warm bodies together . . . tricking you a little into the same damn fool attitude.

I am fool particularly for you because you have IT—and know it.

The surrender you once spoke of and that you said I was to look out for.

I'm not afraid of it. I admit I was, having fooled with too many women who hadn't the IT you have.

Women selling out their own womanhood and getting rather sensitive men confused.

You could make any damn thing you wanted to make out of me yet, fool woman. I'm material. I've got rich possibilities in me no other woman has ever touched.

You could make a real writer of me—a rich flowering.

I ask you plainly, bluntly, now that you have given this other side of Eleanor, woman of the world, woman of affairs, so much scope.

You damn little cheat—because you wanted the other all the time, and didn't think you'd get it.

If you think you can outthink me you're a fool.

Oh, you want peace. Well, let go. If you are going to take a man tell everyone to go to hell.

"That's mine, for what I can do with it.

"I'll be woman to him anyway."

You see, dear—this is my real proposal of marriage to you.

I've been as muddled as you have been.
Marriage is marriage.
I've never yet married.
I'm willing to take the chances and the risks of it with you.

There is a peace you can get—if you want it, dear.
I guess—in spite of everything, I've a right to a kind of place among the Men of America.
I've got it to offer and do offer it. All I ask of you, Eleanor Copenhaver, is no fooling with me. Other women have done that to me, half stuff, too corroding. Come through and let us both have what peace and growth there is for us or—well, chuck me.
That's all the question.
You little female thing—to my male.
Damn anything else now.

Wednesday, November 23, Marion, Virginia

A very quiet, subdued day. The letters from Eleanor made me happy again. I have been tense now she has definitely promised to come home and I feel she will be here in the morning.

I went and rode a long time alone, very lonely, not wanting to be with anyone.

Thursday, November 24, Marion, Virginia

Thanksgiving.
Eleanor is at home.
Her eyes look very gentle.
She still loves me.
I love her more than ever.
It is a marvelous day.
To see and touch again her body—look into her clear eyes.

Friday, November 25, Marion, Virginia

It is a day of illness. There is let-down, now that Eleanor is here and I feel strength in her. She will get well.

I shall not try to work. It will be glorious out of doors.

Coda: December

Sunday, December 11, Marion, Virginia

I don't like it sometimes when you say, joking, "You've had a big emotional day," laughing at me. It makes me think, sometimes, "Have I shared it too much with her? Is she tired of it?"

Sometimes it makes me want to draw away. Here I am, a heavy-bodied man, and I want to be a slim boy. I want to run over the hills naked, through the mist, never tiring.

When we were driving home tonight, over the hill by the fairground, it came to me, a longing so sharp it hurt like it hurts you when you twist your wound.

Sometimes I think I'd rather have you, a woman, running with me in that otherness, that place that doesn't even exist quite, than all the rest.

In that world you wouldn't ever be afraid of loving me too much, kissing me, touching me with your hands a thousand times a day. I like to think that sometimes we can be together and just believe in love and the miracle, nothing else.

Like your father says about God.

I'd like to teach you more and more to be that way with me—letting go, all the pent-up warmth in you out playing.

Sometimes I think of how many years we've missed and how few we may have.

And I think of the partly pent-up side of you too and want so hard to be the one who sets the play-child, the little girl, the warm woman all loose in you.

The running poet's just as real as the heavy man.
I want you often to dare to let your tenderness loose.
Let it play.
Let it have its day.
Eleanor, dear.

Friday, December 16, Marion, Virginia

Morning.

It must have been from reading the pages of Mexican poems. In the night, I looked at my watch, 2:00, very still. My fancy began making a song to you.

Rather, for you.

Eleanor, most beautiful name.

It was a pleading song, a big song that got little, a little song that got big.

It seemed to me there wasn't life, only pieces of life.

The piece of life that was in the head.

The piece of life in the breast.

The piece of life down below.

I wanted to call the life, more and more, down out of your head and breast, down below.

As I was singing I was stroking you with my hands, always stroking down and down.

Calling something down, to live there for a time, down below.

To let it flow down.

To let it go down.

It was down sometimes too much in me—not enough in you.

Let it flow down.

Let it go down.

I was thinking of what people say. "We get married and then it's spoiled.

"We respect each other but it's spoiled."

Mazie said it once to me.

Then I thought as I sang, "Here's where the singer comes."

It can be sacred—live in itself

To let it flow down,
    go down.

Until it is all rich, full life there.

    Flowing down.

    Going down.

Nothing at all up above, in the breast, in the head.

The body is a house.

There is this room in the house.

To flow down to that,
    go down to that.

I wanted to sing to you of myself too—why I am so often afraid, apologetic.

Because, unlike you, I made it not nice down there.
You making it all again nice.

I wanted to sing it and in the night did sing it, all to the rhythm
  of
  Flow down.
  Go down.

Tuesday, December 27, Marion, Virginia

I want it very, very much, our year, out of doors, sucking up
the sun and wind, working, being lovers.
  Long afternoons, on beaches, in pine woods, on the road.
  We would come back from it, refreshed to the bone, ready to
tackle life again.
  Not that we aren't ready now but I want this year with
you—seeing, smelling, tasting.
  Sucking up the sun.

It gets sweeter every day, being with you and near you, dearest
woman.
  More and more you give me the sweet, strong feeling of someone, dearer than all the rest of the world, at my back, beside me,
believing.
  Eleanor, you are a peach.

Wednesday, December 28, Marion, Virginia

Poem to My Woman
After Love

Back of the grey fog there is a pine forest. Put your hands over
your head like a bird. Now draw in the breath.
  Blow hard.
  See, you have made a gateway through the fog. Run quickly
through.
  Make your running a dance. Do not mind old wounds.
  Now you are under tall, straight trees. There are birds singing

but you do not see them. The sky is still grey but it is warm and nice under the trees.

The trees are pines and there is a soft carpet of pine needles underfoot.

Push on.

Go singing.

Go dancing.

You came out into a great meadow. You went into the fog in a black dress but in the pine forest it became red. You thought you heard birds singing. There are a million little threads of song in you. Often your lover, lying close to you, hears the songs. He hears the low notes and the high notes—tender, far away.

When you came out into the great meadow your dress became golden yellow. How proudly and beautifully you walked. Now the grey of the sky is breaking up and streaks of golden light come down to fall upon you.

On the great plains there are proud horses—coal-black. They begin to march in battalions, escorting you. Proudly they march, the troops of proud horses, knees raised, hoofs striking the earth, heads held proudly.

Now amid them, escorted, you are dancing. You run.

Let the song in you break.

Let it roll.

And run.

It is water, dancing in a stream.

It is wind in little bushes.

Dance now over the hills, through far forests, upon the surface of the waters of rivers.

You are Queen.

Dance down to the sea.

Dance to islands in the sea.

Dance South.

Dance North.

Dance, woman.

You are Queen.

Afterword

SOCIAL EVENTS

Sherwood Anderson, of Marion and Grayson County, and Miss Eleanor Copenhaver, daughter of Mr. and Mrs. B. E. Copenhaver of Marion, were married Thursday evening, July 6th, in a quiet ceremony performed before a small group of relatives at the home of the bride's parents. The ceremony was performed by the Rev. Hugh J. Rhyne, pastor of the Marion Lutheran Church. After the ceremony, Mr. and Mrs. Anderson left on a motor trip to a Virginia resort. They will live at Mr. Anderson's home, Ripshin Farm, near Troutdale.

—*Smyth County News*, July 6, 1933

The assessments and resolutions of New Year's Eve of 1933 must have been for Sherwood Anderson quite different from those of the previous New Year's Eve, when he was in great doubt about his ability ever to win Eleanor Copenhaver in marriage. Anderson began 1933 with the sure knowledge that Eleanor and he would soon be married, that her family would have to accept him completely as a husband when they had not all been so generous to him as a lover, and that somehow his career as a writer and her career as a social worker would have to coexist.

For Eleanor Copenhaver had no intention of giving up her work in order to be a traditional wife to Sherwood Anderson, even if a traditional marriage were what the writer thought he wanted. Sherwood might, as husband, be able to travel openly now with Eleanor in her investigative studies of women industrial workers for the Young Women's Christian Association, as their relationship would finally be licit and public. And Eleanor would continue to test and develop her husband's commitment to social change—a commitment less strong than her own radical stance but basically sound enough for their bond. The two were apart often, for Eleanor's work required even more traveling without

Sherwood than was necessary during their courtship. During the years of their marriage, however, the couple would spend much time together in summers at Ripshin and in winters throughout the South and would have frequent visits together at Rosemont, although neither the writer nor the social worker could stop traveling for very long.

For in his later years, Sherwood Anderson was more a celebrity than he might earlier have liked: he was invited frequently to attend writers' conferences, he served as guest professor at college seminars, he faithfully kept diaries of his activities to please Eleanor, and he undertook a major project that she had encouraged him to begin—the writing of his memoirs. Anderson had much to tell in his memoirs, and the writing of his life story (he had twice before written autobiographies) would occupy him until the time of his death.

That death came when Sherwood and Eleanor were once again traveling, when she had taken leave from her YWCA work (in her twenty-first year of such work) in order to accompany her husband on a goodwill trip, arranged by the United States government, to South America—the most exotic travel that they would have shared. On board their ship they took the mass of manuscripts that Sherwood was going to organize and complete as his final memoirs, and they were optimistic that this ambitious book would do much to restore him to public attention as a still-vital and important writer. Unfortunately, Sherwood became ill on board the ship and died of peritonitis on Saturday, March 8, 1941. Eleanor brought his body home to Marion, Virginia, for burial on March 26, 1941, in a cemetery high atop a hill that overlooks the town of Marion and her family home Rosemont, the place where Sherwood had met and courted her many years earlier.

After Sherwood's death, when Eleanor was forty-four, she found the hidden letters from 1932 that the author had secretly left for her in a cupboard at Ripshin. These letters, meant to be a daily gift from the man who most loved her, must have comforted the widow in her loss and encouraged her to undertake bravely the management of a complicated literary estate that would require her close attention, even when she returned to full-time YWCA work.

In 1938 Eleanor had become chief of the Industrial Division of the YWCA, a position that she continued to hold for a decade and that gave her at times national and international prominence. From 1947 to 1949 Eleanor served the YWCA as representative of the International Division of the National Board in Italy, where she worked in organizing clothing workers and in advising on relief projects in Rome, Genoa, Milan, and other Italian cities. In 1951 she was assigned to work with the United Community Defense Services, an entity created to deploy trained professional staff members to various industrial areas to aid in transfer to economies based on the burgeoning national defense industries. Still Eleanor Anderson was traveling across her nation on her professional work, labor interrupted occasionally for study of labor conditions in Latin America.

Eleanor Anderson combined her work for the YWCA and her literary caretaking until her retirement from social work in 1961, after which she devoted her energies to managing Sherwood's literary estate and divided her time between an apartment in New York City and her family home in Marion, Virginia. Despite her own reluctance ever to write anything about Sherwood, Eleanor was to all inquiring scholars open and friendly; her one closed subject tended to be her own career, about which she could have spoken quite proudly but which, even decades after Sherwood's death, she subordinated to caring for his memory.

At her death in 1985, at age eighty-nine, Eleanor Copenhaver Anderson came to share with Sherwood the grave in Round Hill Cemetery in Marion, Virginia; and the epitaph that Sherwood had in the late 1930s written for his eventual gravestone would now apply equally well to both of these brave voyagers:

Life, Not Death, Is the Great Adventure

Selected Bibliography

BIBLIOGRAPHIES

Modlin, Charles E., Hilbert H. Campbell, and Kenichi Takada. "Sherwood Anderson: Additions to the Bibliography." *Studies in Bibliography,* XXXIX (1985), 166–68.

Rogers, Douglas G. *Sherwood Anderson: A Selective, Annotated Bibliography.* Metuchen, N.J., 1976.

Sheehy, Eugene P., and Kenneth A. Lohf. *Sherwood Anderson: A Bibliography.* Los Gatos, Calif., 1960.

White, Ray Lewis. "A Checklist of Sherwood Anderson Studies, 1959–1969." *Newberry Library Bulletin,* VI (July, 1971), 288–302.

———. *The Merrill Checklist of Sherwood Anderson.* Columbus, 1969.

———. *Sherwood Anderson: A Reference Guide.* Boston, 1977.

———. "Sherwood Anderson: Fugitive Pamphlets and Broadsides, 1918–1940." *Studies in Bibliography,* XXXI (1978), 257–63.

———. "*Winesburg* in Translation." *Ohioana Quarterly,* XIX (Summer, 1976), 58–60.

BY SHERWOOD ANDERSON
BOOKS

Windy McPherson's Son. New York, 1916; rev. ed., New York, 1922; London, 1923.

Marching Men. New York, 1917.

Mid-American Chants. New York, 1918.

Winesburg, Ohio. New York, 1919; London, 1922.

Poor White. New York, 1920; London, 1921.

The Triumph of the Egg. New York, 1921; London, 1922.

Horses and Men. New York, 1923; London, 1924.

Many Marriages. New York, 1923.
A Story Teller's Story. New York, 1924; London, 1925.
Dark Laughter. New York, 1925; London, 1926.
The Modern Writer. San Francisco, 1925.
Sherwood Anderson's Notebook. New York, 1926.
Tar: A Midwest Childhood. New York, 1926; London, 1927.
A New Testament. New York, 1927.
"Alice" and "The Lost Novel." London, 1929.
Hello Towns! New York, 1929.
"Nearer the Grass Roots" [and] *"Elizabethton."* San Francisco, 1929.
The American County Fair. New York, 1930.
Perhaps Women. New York, 1931.
Beyond Desire. New York, 1932.
Death in the Woods and Other Stories. New York, 1933.
No Swank. Philadelphia, 1934.
Puzzled America. New York, 1935.
Kit Brandon. New York, 1936; London, 1937.
Plays: Winesburg and Others. New York, 1937.
A Writer's Conception of Realism. Olivet, Mich., 1939.
Home Town. New York, 1940.
Sherwood Anderson's Memoirs. New York, 1942.

LETTERS AND DIARIES

Letters of Sherwood Anderson. Edited by Howard Mumford Jones in association with Walter B. Rideout. Boston, 1953.
Sherwood Anderson/Gertrude Stein: Correspondence and Personal Essays. Edited by Ray Lewis White. Chapel Hill, 1972.
Sherwood Anderson: Selected Letters. Edited by Charles E. Modlin. Knoxville, 1984.
Letters to Bab: Sherwood Anderson to Marietta D. Finley, 1916–33. Edited by William A. Sutton. Urbana, 1985.
The Sherwood Anderson Diaries, 1936–1941. Edited by Hilbert H. Campbell. Athens, Ga., 1987.

EDITIONS AND COLLECTIONS

The Sherwood Anderson Reader. Edited by Paul Rosenfeld. Boston, 1947.
The Portable Sherwood Anderson. Edited by Horace Gregory. New York, 1949.
Winesburg, Ohio. Edited by Malcolm Cowley. New York, 1960; New York, 1976.

Sherwood Anderson: Short Stories. Edited by Maxwell Geismar. New York, 1962.

Mid-American Chants: 6 Midwestern Chants by Sherwood Anderson/11 Midwest Photographs by Art Sinsabaugh. Note by Edward Dahlberg. Highlands, N.C., 1964.

Winesburg, Ohio: Text and Criticism. Edited by John H. Ferres. New York, 1966.

Return to Winesburg. Edited by Ray Lewis White. Chapel Hill, 1967.

Sherwood Anderson's Memoirs· A Critical Edition. Edited by Ray Lewis White. Chapel Hill, 1969.

A Story Teller's Story: A Critical Text. Edited by Ray Lewis White. Cleveland, 1968.

Tar: A Midwest Childhood—A Critical Text. Edited by Ray Lewis White. Cleveland, 1969.

The Buck Fever Papers. Edited by Welford Dunaway Taylor. Charlottesville, 1971.

Sherwood Anderson/Gertrude Stein: Correspondence and Personal Essays. Edited by Ray Lewis White. Chapel Hill, 1972.

Marching Men: A Critical Text. Edited by Ray Lewis White. Cleveland, 1972.

The "Writer's Book" by Sherwood Anderson: A Critical Edition. Edited by Martha Mulroy Curry. Metuchen, N.J., 1975.

France and Sherwood Anderson: Paris Notebook, 1921. Edited by Michael Fanning. Baton Rouge, 1976.

Sherwood Anderson: The Writer at His Craft. Edited by Jack Salzman, David D. Anderson, and Kichinosuke Ohashi. Mamaroneck, N.Y., 1979.

The Complete Works of Sherwood Anderson. 21 vols. Edited by Kichinosuke Ohashi. Kyoto, 1982.

The Teller's Tales. Edited by Frank Gado. Schenectady, N.Y., 1983.

Sherwood Anderson: Early Writings. Edited by Ray Lewis White. Kent, Ohio, 1989.

ABOUT SHERWOOD ANDERSON
BIOGRAPHIES

Carlson, G. Bert, Jr. "Sherwood Anderson's Political Mind: The Activist Years." Ph.D. dissertation, University of Maryland, 1966.

Dinsmoor, Mary Helen. "An Inquiry into the Life of Sherwood

Anderson as Reflected in His Literary Works." M.A. thesis, Ohio University, 1939.

Phillips, William Louis. "Sherwood Anderson's *Winesburg, Ohio: Its Origins, Composition, Technique, and Reception.*" Ph.D. dissertation, University of Chicago, 1949.

Schevill, James. *Sherwood Anderson: His Life and Work.* Denver, 1951.

Sutton, William A. *The Road to Winesburg: A Mosaic of the Imaginative Life of Sherwood Anderson.* Metuchen, N.J., 1972.

————. "Sherwood Anderson's Formative Years (1876–1913)." Ph.D. dissertation, Ohio State University, 1943.

Townsend, Kim. *Sherwood Anderson.* Boston, 1987.

Williams, Kenny J. *A Storyteller and a City: Sherwood Anderson's Chicago.* DeKalb, Ill., 1988.

CRITICAL STUDIES

Anderson, David D. *Sherwood Anderson: An Introduction and Interpretation.* New York, 1967.

Bruyère, Claire. *Sherwood Anderson: L'Impuissance créatrice.* Paris, 1985.

Burbank, Rex. *Sherwood Anderson.* New York, 1964.

Chase, Cleveland. *Sherwood Anderson.* New York, 1927.

Fagin, N. Bryllion. *The Phenomenon of Sherwood Anderson: A Study in American Life.* Baltimore, 1927.

Howe, Irving. *Sherwood Anderson.* New York, 1951.

Miller, William Vaughn. "The Technique of Sherwood Anderson's Short Stories." Ph.D. dissertation, University of Illinois, 1969.

Taylor, Welford Dunaway. *Sherwood Anderson.* New York, 1977.

Weber, Brom. *Sherwood Anderson.* Minneapolis, 1964.

COLLECTIONS OF ESSAYS

Anderson, David D., ed. *Critical Essays on Sherwood Anderson.* Boston, 1981.

————, ed. *Sherwood Anderson: Dimensions of His Literary Art.* East Lansing, 1976.

Appel, Paul P., ed. *Homage to Sherwood Anderson: 1876–1941.* Mamaroneck, N.Y., 1970.

Campbell, Hilbert H., and Charles E. Modlin, eds. *Sherwood Anderson: Centennial Studies.* Troy, N.Y., 1976.

Ohashi, Kichinosuke, ed. *Sherwood Anderson*. Guide to Twentieth Century English and American Literature, VIII. Tokyo, 1968.
Rideout, Walter B., ed. *Sherwood Anderson: A Collection of Critical Essays*. Englewood Cliffs, N.J., 1974.
White, Ray Lewis, comp. *The Merrill Studies in "Winesburg, Ohio."* Columbus, 1971.
———, ed. *Sherwood Anderson: Essays in Criticism*. Chapel Hill, 1966.

SPECIAL JOURNALS

American Notes & Queries, XV (September, 1976).
Midwestern Miscellany, XII (1984).
Newberry Library Bulletin, ser. 2, no. 2 (December, 1948).
Newberry Library Bulletin, VI (July, 1971).
Shenandoah, XIII (Spring, 1962).
Story, XIX (September–October, 1941).
Twentieth Century Literature, XXIII (February, 1977).
Winesburg Eagle: The Official Publication of the Sherwood Anderson Society, I (November, 1975–).

Index